D0933584

HERBERT HOOVER
THE GREAT WAR AND ITS AFTERMATH
1914–23

Papers Presented At The

HERBERT HOOVER CENTENNIAL SEMINARS

HERBERT HOOVER PRESIDENTIAL LIBRARY ASSOCIATION

WEST BRANCH, IOWA

FEBRUARY AND OCTOBER 1974

HERBERT HOOVER

THE GREAT WAR AND ITS AFTERMATH

1914–23

Edited with Introduction by

LAWRENCE E. GELFAND

University of Iowa Press Iowa City

Library of Congress Cataloging in Publication Data
Main entry under title:

(Herbert Hoover centennial seminars; 1)
Includes bibliographical references and index.

(Herbert Hoover centennial seminars ; 1)
Includes bibliographical references and index.
1.   European War, 1914–1918—United States—Con-
gresses.   2.   European War, 1914–1918—Diplomatic history
—Congresses.   3.   Reconstruction (1914–1918) Diplomatic
—Congresses.   4.   European War, 1914–1918—Food question
—Congresses.   5.   Hoover, Herbert Clarke, Pres. U. S.,
1874–1964—Congresses.   6.   United States—Foreign
relations—1913–1921—Congresses.   I.   Gelfand, Lawrence
Emerson, 1926–   II.   Hoover Presidential Library
Association.   III.   Series.
D570.1.H38   940.3'14   79–10139
ISBN 0–87745–095–1

University of Iowa Press, Iowa City 52242
© 1979 by The University of Iowa. All rights reserved
Printed in the United States of America

CONTENTS

Discussants at the First
Hoover Seminar-Conference

FREDERICK C. ADAMS
Department of History, Drake University

NICHOLAS BERRY
Department of Political Science, Cornell College (Iowa)

* CHARLES CAREY
Department of Political Science, University of Iowa

STANLEY ERICKSON
Department of Political Science, Augustana College (Illinois)

* LAWRENCE E. GELFAND
Department of History, University of Iowa

ELLIS W. HAWLEY
Department of History, University of Iowa

ARLIE HOOVER
Department of History, Pepperdine University

ALLAN JONES
Department of History, Grinnell College

* RICHARD KOTTMAN
Department of History, Iowa State University

JOHN NORTON
Department of Political Science, St. Ambrose College (Iowa)

RUSSELL ROSS
Department of Political Science, University of Iowa

ROBERT SEIDEL
Department of History, Cornell University (New York)

JAY W. STEIN
Department of Political Science, Western Illinois University

JOHN D. WENUM
Department of Political Science, Illinois Wesleyan College

ELLSWORTH WOODS
Department of Political Science, Drake University

* Discussants on Professor Rothbard's paper presented at the Fourth Seminar-Conference.

Preface

As part of its centennial commemoration of Herbert Hoover's birth, the Herbert Hoover Presidential Library Association, Inc., sponsored a series of four scholarly seminars, each treating an integral period of his public career. The first seminar, held in February 1974, focused on Hoover's activities relating to the first World War and its general peace settlement, 1917–23; the second held in April concerned his years in the Commerce Department, 1921–28; the third in June dealt with the presidency, 1929–33; and the fourth in October considered Hoover's years as "elder statesman," post-1933. Scholars in the United States and Canada, having a serious interest in the Hoover Era, were invited to participate. At each seminar there were approximately thirty persons in attendance, a group small enough to afford informal exchange of ideas and extensive discussion of each paper presented. All sessions were held in the Herbert Hoover Presidential Library at West Branch, Iowa, the University of Iowa at Iowa City, and some dinner sessions were conducted at the Highlander Supper Club in Iowa City.

Dr. Francis O'Brien, who then served as director of academic programs for the Hoover Presidential Library Association, arranged, managed, and moderated the four seminars, invited speakers and discussants. In some instances, he suggested topics for the papers. Neither he nor the Hoover Presidential Library Association imposed any constraints upon the participants. Interpretations and criticism expressed in the papers and commentaries ranged widely across a broad political spectrum.

With but a single exception, all papers included in this first volume were presented at the seminar held in February 1974. Professor Murray Rothbard's paper was delivered at the fourth seminar, which met in October 1974, but his paper seemed more appropriate to the theme of this volume, and it is therefore included here. Tapes of all the seminars, including shortened versions of each paper, remarks of commentators, and the general discussion that followed each paper, are available at the Herbert Hoover Presidential Library.

I want to acknowledge important contributions by the following persons to the seminars and ultimately to the realization of this volume: Dr. Francis O'Brien, professor of politics and constitutional law at Southwestern University, Georgetown, Texas; the staff of the Hoover Presidential Library and especially its director, Thomas T. Thalken and its assistant director, Robert S. Wood; John M. Henry, former executive secretary of the Hoover Presidential Library Association, and R. Lawrence Angove, the present executive director of the Association. All of these persons acted on convictions that these Hoover Centennial Seminar papers deserved to be published and made available to the scholarly community and to the public-at-large. I also want to express appreciation for the encouragement provided by the Board of Trustees, Hoover Presidential Library Association, whose members are anxious to stimulate active and continuous research while at the same time encouraging public interest in the life and career of Herbert Hoover, his political philosophy, and his contributions to the world of the twentieth century.

L.E.G.

Introduction

In November 1963, the Herbert Hoover Presidential Library at West Branch, Iowa, officially opened its doors to a curious and eager scholarly community. What had hitherto represented the darkest corner of American political historiography, namely, the era of the Harding-Coolidge-Hoover presidencies, 1921–33, at long last promised to undergo illumination with an anxious legion of historical researchers awaiting the opportunity to examine and interpret the fresh accumulation of manuscript documentation. As of 1963, it was widely believed that President Harding's papers had essentially been destroyed soon after his death. A meagre, hardly fruitful collection of Coolidge papers survived at the Library of Congress. Anticipated treasures to be found in the Andrew Mellon papers remain buried inasmuch as this collection, if indeed it exists, has not yet (1978) been made accessible to scholars. As historians in the early 1960s surveyed available collections at various echelons of the Executive Branch of national government, the story was pretty much the same: the papers of Republican officials during the 1920s had not been placed in repositories where interested scholars could undertake adequate basic research. To be sure, the papers of Secretaries of State Charles Evans Hughes, Frank Kellogg, and Henry Stimson were accessible at the Library of Congress, the Minnesota Historical Society, and the Yale University Library respectively, but no repository had endeavored to launch a systematic program for accessioning the papers of other officers in the State Department, American ambassadors and ministers. Evermore glaring were the failures of libraries to attract the documentation of cabinet officers (the Ogden Mills papers at the Library of Congress is the outstanding exception), principal military and naval officers, and members of the various independent agencies within the federal bureaucracy. It would not be an exaggeration to assert that political scholarship covering this important era had not proceeded much beyond the quasi-journalistic and polemical accounts of the 1920s that had appeared during the 1930s.

When in 1960, Professor John D. Hicks published *Republican Ascendancy 1921–1933* for the New American Nation Series, his bibliographical essay called attention to serious difficulties confronting scholars studying the period. Whereas assorted collections of individual congressional leaders (e.g., Borah, Norris, T. J. Walsh) were available, the absence of papers from officers in the Executive Branch was noteworthy. Hicks commented on the scattering of manuscript documentation around the country, but more strikingly he emphasized the fact that even those accessible collections were poorly processed, making their use by scholars exceedingly difficult. He observed:

> Despite the best efforts of dedicated librarians, most of the larger collections are almost impenetrable jungles. If one knows the right questions he can sometimes, without too great an investment of time, find the right answers, but in general it takes the work of many patient monographers to extract the secrets that the manuscript collections make it their business to conceal. . . .[1]

Hicks's synthesis of the 1920s, valuable as it was at the time of publication, has become a period piece within the last sixteen years. In part, this was due to the questions with which he and his liberal contemporaries of the 1950s were concerned; in part, the perishable quality derives from the sparse building blocks with which he was compelled to construct his political chapters.

At a time when scholars were moving forward with the historical reconstruction of the New Deal, World War II, and even the Truman Years, utilizing manuscript resources, political scholarship on the Harding-Coolidge-Hoover era appeared to be stagnating. Alleged destruction of papers and the apparent unwillingness of surviving politicians, but in most instances their heirs, to place valuable documentation at the disposal of the interested historical community often aroused suspicions that skeletons were lurking in the shadows which, once revealed, would make Tea Pot Dome and other known escapades pale into relative insignificance. Far from redeeming the somewhat spattered reputations of Republican leaders, denial of sources tended to perpetuate the tacky portraits that had filled so much of the literature.

In effect, the importance of the Hoover Presidential Library lies in the fact that it provides a repository where documentation pertaining to the Hoover Era is aggressively sought, collected, carefully processed, and made freely available for the use of scholars. Already, scores of manuscript collections have made their way to the Library in West Branch, supplemented by films, printed materials, oral history recollections, artifacts, and an impressive array of photocopies from relevant collections elsewhere. A competent staff has been assembled to make these materials useful to scholars who have been converging in increasing numbers from throughout the United States and many foreign countries.

Without much question, the vast nucleus of the Library's holdings consists of the Herbert Hoover papers. This collection as it now exists at West Branch, plus that portion mainly concerned with the First World War still reposing at the Hoover Institution at Stanford, California, may well constitute the single most important manuscript resource thus far for American political scholarship in the twentieth century. On its face, this statement may strike the reader as sheer hyperbole. Such value, I believe, can fairly be attributed not merely because of the dearth of other officials' papers for the 1920s (bearing in mind that numerous collections have been recovered by the Presidential Library since 1963), but because Hoover as secretary of commerce, 1921–29, and later as president, was more directly and deeply involved than was any other official in those deliberations affecting literally the entire spectrum of governmental activity. He occupied a pivotal position in matters pertaining to trade and transportation, manufacturing, agriculture, labor, and foreign policy, including loans and investments abroad along with the complicated, tangled legacy of Allied war debts. Moreover, my claim on behalf of the Hoover papers easily transcends the chronological bounds of the Republican era, 1921–33. As the articles in this volume bear partial testimony and visitors to the Presidential Library can readily observe through numerous museum exhibits, the Hoover Era embraced a full half-century of significant public activities, from the First World War almost to Hoover's death in 1964, at the age of ninety. Throughout these five decades, Hoover remained either at, or close to, the center of government authority in Washington. When, as in the years of the New Deal, he was on the outside often criticizing the Democratic administration of Franklin D. Roosevelt, he was a prophetic Jeremiah voicing serious concerns about the present and future national well-being.

Today's visitor to Hoover's native community, West Branch, Iowa, might well ponder what cultural advantages this midwestern rural community, unspoiled by the passage of time, afforded, that would compensate for the hostile climate. Drabness and an acute sense of isolation must have appeared even more pervasive during the last quarter of the nineteenth century when transportation and communication moved more slowly than has become the case in the age of automobiles, telephones, radios, and television. As one wanders about the still tiny village, observing the stark simplicity of the birthplace, his father's blacksmith shop, and the Quaker Meeting House, it is easy to ponder what inspiration could have provided the stimulus capable of transforming so many rural youth, nurtured in such environments, into intellectual, professional, and public leaders. Like Horatio Alger's many heroes whose youth was spent amidst adversity, Hoover's childhood was a continuous struggle to overcome privations. Again, following the pattern of Alger's fictional heroes, Hoover was able to rise above these limitations imposed by an impoverished and somber environment. Drawing upon exceptional ingenuity, exploiting opportunities that came his way, Hoover doggedly persevered to rise steadily up the ladder to positions of trust, leadership, and responsibility accompanied by material prosperity.

Orphaned at the age of ten, young Hoover went to live with a devoted aunt and uncle on a farm near Newberg, Oregon, dividing his time between the performance of chores and the pursuit of an education. He might not have been able to think of college had the costs of higher education been formidable. Fortunately, a new university, which Leland Stanford was building at Palo Alto, California, would not be charging tuition, and young Hoover was anxious to be considered for admission to the first class. Thanks to a sympathetic and perceptive interviewer, he won admission despite some recognized academic deficiencies. Stanford risked accepting the youth on condition that he arrive in the summer prior to formal matriculation in order to benefit from tutoring and other remedial instruction.

This opportunity to study at Stanford began what would be for Hoover a life-long romance with the university at Palo Alto. Setting his sights on the then developing profession of engineering, he soon gravitated toward a speciality in mining and minerals, which given the rising technological advances in transportation, the demands of industry for sources of energy, alloys, and various building materials, was undergoing a spectacular expansion. His studies at Stanford not only encouraged extensive reading, writing, and thinking, but along with much field work, they introduced the fledgling engineer to the real world of people, of affairs, and the serious commitment to improving the human condition. It is therefore no wonder that in his later years, Hoover would feel a keen sense of debt to Stanford which he credited with opening new vistas, stimulating his ambition, and encouraging latent talents. In short, the experience and training obtained at Stanford had transformed the previously callow youth into a confident, independent, and quite knowledgeable adult prepared to launch a career as a mining engineer. Also while at Stanford, Hoover met and would afterward marry fellow scientist, Lou Henry, a lady with congenial intellectual interests. In later years, the indebtedness to his alma mater would be acknowledged through many years of service on

Stanford's Board of Trustees, his organizing of the first Stanford Union, and most important, his leadership in the establishment, following the First World War, of the Hoover Institution dedicated to the serious study of war, peace, and revolution in the modern-contemporary world. During the Peace Conference in 1919, as the concept of the library was taking form, Professor Ephraim D. Adams and his assistant Robert C. Binkley, arrived in Paris to begin the collection of documentation covering the Peace Conference which would provide the nucleus for what has since become a distinguished center of research for international studies.[2]

Hoover's connection with Stanford proved to be auspicious for his successful career as mining engineer and consultant to mining companies during the next two decades. The years between his graduation and the onset of the Great War in 1914 found him employed by the British mining firm, Bewick, Moreing and Co., traveling about the world—to Africa, China, Russia, and throughout Europe—consulting governments and private firms, managing the company's extensive properties, and reporting on newly discovered mineral reserves. Hoover earned a reputation as an energetic, hard-driving, tough-minded manager. After 1908, he formed his own consulting firm, but there seemed no relaxation for the peripatetic engineer. At this time, while most Americans continued to be wrapped up in domestic concerns—conflicts between labor and management, municipal corruption, expanding industrialization, and the nation's admission of millions of new immigrants—Hoover remained essentially unkown to his countrymen. In the process of accumulating a sizable fortune, he had become essentially an expatriate residing in London, who only occasionally touched base in the United States. He had become the personification of the international capitalist, the precursor of the multinational entrepreneur whose interests and properties knew no political boundaries. By the time Hoover reached his fortieth birthday in August 1914, he was beginning to grow restless, anxious to change the direction of his life and apply his seemingly boundless energies to some different professional activity. He had reached the pinnacle as a mining engineer.

By happenstance, the onset of the Great War in August 1914 offered just the diversionary activity that Hoover was seeking. Sudden escalation of events in Europe found large numbers of Americans in belligerent countries anxious to return to the United States. Hoover volunteered his services in organizing, managing, and financing the repatriation of these overseas Americans. This demanding, voluntary, *ad hoc* effort on his part was observed closely and approvingly by the recently appointed American ambassador in England, Walter Hines Page, his staff, and by the American business community. Through them, officials in Washington quickly learned of the engineer whose tireless activities had turned what could easily have been a chaotic situation into an orderly evacuation of American civilians from the belligerent states. This display of administrative efficiency under fire quickly put him in line for an even more demanding responsibility.

Violation of Belgian neutrality by advancing German army divisions threatened wholesale starvation for the dense Belgian population. An urgent need existed for creating administrative machinery capable of organizing relief for the invaded state. In the collective wisdom of those who had observed him in action during the repatriation effort, European and American leaders who had known Hoover as an efficient engineering administrator identified him as the one man capable of leading the international mission to relieve the Belgian people threatened with mass starvation. As director of the Commission for Relief in Belgium, his would be no simple task. He would have to organize mammoth shipments of foodstuffs and conduct negotiations with the British, French, and German belligerent governments in order to assure that the supplies would safely reach the intended Belgian recipients. In accepting this difficult assignment, Hoover was to establish a pattern for relief administration, personnel management, and financing he would use repeatedly throughout his direction of several relief missions that would become his distinctive avocation during the era of the World War.

Hoover developed a staff composed primarily of persons, who, like himself, were engineers. These were professionals with whom he could easily relate, individuals who could comprehend the magnitude of tasks which would be undertaken. Like himself, Hoover's associates were volunteers, staff serving without remuneration. This was no merit system, for clearly the only persons who could afford to volunteer full-time labor without thought of salary were men of some considerable means. Affluence along with talent provided the chief prerequisites. Hoover seemed to believe that relief missions would be best administered by staff members who would themselves be making sacrifices. Responsibility for the tasks, he believed, had to be personal and indivisible. Hence, he came to distrust the efficacy of committees except those serving in advisory capacities. He also realized that for a relief agency to suc-

ceed in humanitarian endeavors, it would have to rely on a solid
base of public support. In order to mount public support for the
CRB, an extensive public relations program was conducted which
would sufficiently dramatize the need existing for the relief
endeavor.[3] Financing the program through governmental grants
and private philanthropy depended on the success of this public relations campaign. By taking direct charge of the entire Commission's activities, "the Chief," as Hoover came to be referred by
his associates, assumed virtually dictatorial powers. He tore
through bureaucratic red tape wherever it created obstacles; he
personally intervened with governmental representatives to break
down resistance to the Commission's efficient operations. In short,
by the spring of 1917, the Belgian nation had been delivered from
deprivation and starvation through efforts of the CRB. In the process, Hoover himself had earned the respect and admiration of
many persons, but at the same time he had also come to be distrust-
ed by some who found his directness grating. American ambassador to Belgium, Brand Whitlock, observed that even some
Belgian leaders came to dislike Hoover. They accused him of trying
to build himself politically through the efforts of the CRB, and
Whitlock admitted he was inclined to agree with these critics.[4]

Already by early 1917, reports of Hoover's successes had made
his name a veritable "household expression" in the United States.
Reports praising his leadership were reaching the White House
from American Ambassador Walter Hines Page in London and
from the president's close friend and adviser, Edward M. House.
His appointment as American Food Administrator, six weeks after
the nation's entry into the war, came as no surprise to close observers. It is from this period that the strange relationship between
President Wilson and Hoover can be dated. Their collaboration
during the war and the ensuing peace conference did not arise out
of personal friendship so much as it flowed out of their rather
widespread agreement over many fundamental questions relating
to the conduct of the war and arrangements for future peace. Few
if any of Wilson's wartime advisers were held in higher presidential
esteem than Hoover; no other sustained a higher measure of presidential confidence to the extent that Hoover's proposals were invariably approved, usually without any questions raised.

Hoover shared Wilson's concern that special, independent government agencies be established to cope with the urgent *ad hoc* problems posed by belligerency. In due course, a War Industries
Board, a War Trade Board, a Fuel Administration, transportation

boards, a Central Bureau of Statistics, and the American "Inquiry," to prepare the American briefs for the eventual peace conference, were formed. As one of these special wartime agencies, Hoover's Food Administration operated independently of the Department of Agriculture, its being authorized to mobilize the nation's food resources, formulate conservation policies, and provide shipments of foodstuffs to America's associates in the war. Hoover seemed to appreciate that the World War constituted total warfare involving whole national populations and resources, not merely the placing of soldiers and sailors in combat along with their weapons, supplies, ships, and planes.[5] The United States would be obliged to organize and maintain a propaganda campaign at home in order to remind Americans of the need to support the nation's war effort. Government sponsored public relations would underscore popular belief in the ideals for which the war was being waged, would not only assure the success of various Liberty Loan drives but would promote public compliance with the government's program to conserve foods, expand the production of commodities, and discourage hoarding of foods and other goods in short supply. Through voluntary compliance, he believed, the United States could meet its domestic food obligations and still provide adequate shipments to European associates in the war against the Central Powers without depending on statist devices like rationing and coercive measures. Although Hoover maintained a deep respect for American public opinion, he seemed to think government must take the initiative in providing appropriate leadership for a democratic society. Whatever success the Food Administration achieved, no little credit was due to the efforts of the public relations campaign. Whereas before the war American exports of grains to the United Kingdom, France, and Italy were by no means inconsequential—between 1909–13, the yearly average was nearly 55 million bushels—by 1917, grain exports per year had trebled.[6] Hoover kept a tight control over the food industry. In his view, food occupied a priority second only to trained manpower and munitions in deciding the outcome of the war.

The essays included in this volume cover a broad spectrum of activities in which Hoover was intimately associated during the World War, the Peace Conference of 1919, and subsequent American efforts to assist with European recovery extending into the early 1920s. For the most part, these eight essays concern American foreign affairs as they engaged Hoover's attentions from 1917 to about 1923. Although several articles interpret Hoover's activities sympathetically, readers will discern some serious criticisms as well. Criticism should be expected when reviewing the complicated career of a public official through the perspective of more than a half century. After all, Hoover's public life was nearly always in the thick of controversy. To ignore criticism would in a real sense do him and his work a serious injustice, for even the most honored of humans are not paragons of virtue. Historians have an obligation to strive to explain an official's activities as truthfully as is humanly possible on the basis of evidence at their command.

Although each article included here has its special subject, readers will observe that several articles do intersect. This overlapping is unavoidable and probably salutary given the many diverse functions which Hoover was performing often concurrently during these turbulent years. Following American intervention in the war, he continued as Commissioner for Belgian Relief while serving as Food Administrator of the United States. He was then also serving as chairman of the Sugar Equalization Board and chairman of the Grain Corporation, and member of President Wilson's *ad hoc* "war cabinet" of economic advisers. Later, at the Peace Conference, he combined these previously mentioned duties with his work as technical adviser on the American Commission to Negotiate Peace and member of the Supreme Council of Supply and Relief.[7] When it was formed in February 1919, the Supreme Economic Council would have Hoover as an American representative. Later, in one of his recollective volumes of the Peace Conference, Hoover would tell of his role on the numerous inter-Allied councils, boards, and commissions: "I was a member of twenty and chairman of half a dozen."[8] Allowing for some exaggeration, this statement does characterize the degree to which he was personally involved in various labors.

The need for foodstuffs and other essentials defined as relief could not legitimately terminate with the Armistice and the cessation of military hostilities. If anything, the threat to human life from European famine and epidemics, with its accompanying need for assistance to millions of suffering individuals living in enemy states, escalated sharply as the Peace Conference convened during December and January of 1918–19. Hoover would later write of this human condition:

Some 160,000,000 people in liberated and enemy nations were face to face with the most terrible famine since the Thirty Years War when a third of the people in those areas died. Their food supplies had steadily degenerated through the war, by blockade and diversion of man-power, until the consequent breakdown of morale in the civil population had contributed more than any other factor to their revolutions and subsequent surrender.[9]

Given the prostrate condition of European society, relief came to occupy a primacy directly affecting virtually all aspects of the peace negotiations.

The centrality of Hoover's responsibility for relief and economic recovery during the deliberations at Paris becomes obvious to students of the Peace Conference.[10] Supplying the populations of liberated, neutral and former enemy states with the means to sustain human life had a direct bearing upon the continuance of the Allied blockade of Germany and Russia and to the transfer of Germany's merchant fleet to Allied and American control. European relief and recovery could not be disassociated from Allied demands for indemnities and reparations. Even the fixing of national boundaries and the economic viability of national states, transit rights and control over Europe's principal rivers and railroads could not be resolved outside the framework of general relief and reconstruction. As the question of advancing bolshevism into East-Central Europe proceeded to occupy the attention of Allied and American statesmen, the relationship between economic recovery and political stability in both the liberated and former enemy states became increasingly apparent.

Hoover's important work was further complicated by virtue of the fact that while at the Peace Conference he was primarily a member of the American Commission to Negotiate Peace, hence responsible to the American government; he also held dual authority as director general of relief, an appointment made by the Supreme War Council of the Peace Conference. In this latter capacity, he became party to what the distinguished British secretary at the Peace Conference, Sir Maurice Hankey, referred to as the Supreme Control, the international executive authority of the Peace Conference.[11] This duality of authority under which Hoover operated in his several capacities can best be appreciated through the analogy of General Douglas MacArthur's command functions during the Korean War in the early 1950s. At one and the same time MacArthur was commander of United States Armed Forces in Korea and also commander of United Nations Forces. He was therefore serving his own national government and simultaneously an international organization, apparently without conflicting interests. In 1919, Hoover functioned at the Paris Peace

Conference as member of the American national delegation and also as servant of the Supreme War Council, later (beginning in February 1919) of the Supreme Economic Council, on which he also served as a United States representative.[12] If indeed Hoover thought much about this dual authority in conducting his activities, he does not so indicate in his several volumes recollecting these events. He appears to have operated consistently throughout solely as an officer of the American government calculating how whatever course of action would or would not serve the interests of the United States. Nevertheless, in order to appreciate Hoover's relative importance to the peace negotiations of 1919, it is incumbent to consider the magnitude of the Conference's organization and its agenda, bearing in mind the participation of the American Commission in these various endeavors.

Photographs and statistics become inadequate tools for comprehending what happened at the Peace Conference of 1919. At best, the many extant photographs capture the cultural atmosphere: hotels and villas where the nearly thirty national delegations congregated; conference rooms where the nearly sixty international commissions hammered out the draft recommendations for provisions to be incorporated in the treaties. From pictures we can yet see and identify individual statesmen, observe an entire national delegation, and perceive the seated Council of Four at its deliberations. Photographs can also depict scenes of the tumultuous ovations greeting President Wilson when he arrived in Paris on December 15, 1918, and his later visits to London, Rome, and other European cities. Through pictures we can still see the scene at the Hall of Mirrors in the Palace at Versailles where the Treaty with Germany was signed on June 28, 1919. The many pictures when joined with the welter of available statistical data simply fail to communicate the drama, the sense of idealism and lofty purpose, the air of controversy that often pervaded the deliberations. They cannot suggest the frustrations and disillusionment shared by many participants attending the "Sessions of the World." In essence, the Peace Conference was a verbal struggle and must therefore be contemplated in terms of the written documentation: minutes of several thousand commission meetings, a vast manuscript correspondence, archival records, personal papers, and the many volumes of personal recollections compiled by numerous participants.

Had the statesmen at Paris in 1919 been able to limit their deliberations to the creation of peace treaties with the defeated Cen-

tral Powers—Germany, Austria-Hungary, Bulgaria, and Turkey—
the difficulties of arranging boundaries, treating colonial dependencies, deciding on suitable reparation payments, military
disarmament or even military occupation and the like would have
been formidable. Had there been no Bolshevik revolution and a
continuing civil war in Russia with its threatened extension
throughout continental Europe; had there been no mass starvation
and deprivations affecting millions of Europeans victimized by the
protracted military struggle; had the Austro-Hungarian and
Turkish Empires not suffered dissolution as a consequence of the
war and had there not been successor states formed by the previously oppressed nationalities in East-Central Europe; had the Allied nations not entered into various secret treaties looking toward
their territorial aggrandizement, which treaties they felt committed
to honor; had there not been a general spirit of revenge, vindictive-
ness on the part of the Allies toward the defeated Central Powers;
and had President Wilson and other statesmen been willing to set
their sights lower than the goal of attaining permanent peace on
the bases of the Fourteen Points plus other subsidiary principles,
the tasks of the Peace Conference would not have been so onerous.
As fate would have it, all of these conditions intervened.

President Wilson's decision to direct the American Commission
and to participate in the actual negotiations at Paris reflected the
high priority he attached to this international undertaking. Besides
the five plenipotentiaries, the American Commission at its maximum size encompassed a staff approximating 3,000 persons.
Americans participated in virtually all phases of peacemaking,
ranging from implementation of the Armistice terms, arranging
boundary lines and holding plebiscites in disputed zones, regulating European waterways and railroad transportation, establishing
mandates for former Turkish and German colonies, deliberating
on the economic and reparations commissions to the creation of the
International Aeronautical Commission, the World Court, the International Labor Organization, and the League of Nations.
Throughout this near total participation, the extent of Hoover's involvement was impressive.

A partial inventory of Hoover's activities taken from the records
of the Supreme Economic Council indicate that the director
general of relief intervened in such varied activities as the administration of Austro-Hungarian railroads for purposes of ex-
pediting the transport of coal and other supplies; exercise of control over Czechoslovak and Polish coal mines; various programs for

feeding children; financing of food for Austria; Danubian shipping; estimating the harvest of various grain crops in Europe; alleged Georgian interference with food shipments intended for
Armenia; financing food to be sent to Germany; determining relief
requirements for Hungary; treatment to be accorded prisoners of
war; and measures to alleviate the typhus epidemic.[13] These activities, for the most part unpublicized, offer an imperfect sample
of those concerns to which Hoover and his relief organization devoted their attention. Because of his early recognition that human
distress in whatever guise required prompt response, Hoover conceived the value of a far-flung, continental-wide communications
network staffed largely by Americans who could quickly supply
current intelligence covering the shifting political and economic
conditions throughout Europe. This communications system, a
product of the U.S. Signal Corps' technical ingenuity, allowed
Hoover and his associates in Paris the capacity to respond almost
immediately as changing conditions required.[14]

Like other American delegates at Paris, Hoover had every reason
to expect the Allied governments would resist President Wilson's
American program for permanent peace. He was familiar with the
popular mood in France, Italy, and England bent on vengeance
toward the Central Powers, especially Germany. For Hoover, the
highest priority in constructing a durable peace settlement must be
the formation of liberal, economically viable nations. Germany
would have to be constructed on this foundation if the European
and also the world economies were to flourish. Stable, democratic
regimes stood the best chance to resist the political virus of
bolshevism and the economic collapse on which bolshevism could
easily spread, finding sympathetic hosts. Toward this end, Hoover
endeavored to enlist popular support for the relief and reconstruction of European society.

There is little question but that Hoover while at Paris lent his full
support to achieving the Wilsonian aspirations for peace. Yet, when
the Treaty of Versailles emerged from nearly six months of steady
deliberations, he would count himself among the American con-
tingent which exuded gloom and despair on reading its provisions.
The despondent disposition was so personally identified with
Hoover that Edward House in a postscript to a letter sent from
London to President Wilson, already back in Washington, tersely
characterized it:

Hoover, who has just left, is in one of his most pessimistic moods.
He is simply reveling in gloom. He gives Europe but thirty days

longer of orderly life—after that it is to be revolution, starvation and chaos. In his opinion the coal situation is the most menacing.[15]

In his memoirs, Hoover expressed the shared disillusionment in striking terms resembling a litany of Wilsonian diplomatic failures. There was the string of Wilsonian compromises which in large measure were accepted in order to obtain Allied concessions to modifications in the League of Nations Covenant. What disturbed Hoover most, however, was dismantling of the German economy through imposition of huge obligations in the form of reparations due the Allies. These still unspecified amounts when combined with the loss of Germany's merchant fleet, the transfer of coal and other valuable mineral resources to neighboring states threatened to make impotent not only Germany but the European economy as well. Bolshevism could seemingly fill this economic vacuum.

When Hoover and his associates examined the lengthy text of the Treaty they found trouble lurking in almost every section. The mandates system threatened to inhibit nationalistic movements in Arab states. Transferring the German leasehold over Shantung to Japan seemed reprehensible. This act "would keep Asia in turmoil."[16] In plain words, Hoover interpreted the Treaty to be nothing less than catastrophic. Allied statesmen, he insisted, Lloyd George and Clemenceau in particular, had never accepted or approved the Wilsonian terms for peace which they had signed into the Armistice with Germany. There had been insufficient American planning in advance for a peace settlement as all embracing as the one contemplated in late 1918. Wilson, who would continue to stir Hoover's deep admiration, was anxious to win support for the League of Nations, and in the process reluctantly conceded his principles elsewhere. The American government had made a grievous error in agreeing to the Treaty of Guarantee for France. To further compound this erroneous calculation, the United States, he believed, should never have considered the proposal for an American mandate for distant Armenia. It was the deteriorating condition of President Wilson's health which Hoover attributed to the poor judgments reached during the two months prior to the signing of the Treaty with Germany.

Two related criticisms found in Hoover's later writings capture the essence of his disillusionment. First, he believed it a cardinal mistake for the United States to commit its willingness to participate in the implementation of the European settlement.

Given its different traditions, orientation, and national interests, should America, Hoover wondered, have become involved in determining the political arrangements that would prevail in Europe? His second serious criticism proceeded from the first: he entertained grave reservations about the wisdom of what President Wilson was to term the "backbone" or "heart" of the League Covenant. Article X had committed members of the League "to respect and preserve as against external aggression the territorial integrity and existing political independence of all Members of the League. In case of any such aggression or in case of any threat or danger of such aggression the Council shall advise upon the means by which this obligation shall be fulfilled." Herein lay the crux of Wilsonian internationalism, the conception that the president had repeatedly expressed in public pronouncements since 1916. Modern political states had become so interdependent that no nation, certainly no self-respecting great power, could for long remain indifferent to military conflicts occurring anywhere in the world. If any rational justification were needed to underscore America's reasons for becoming deeply involved in a European war and a global peace settlement at Paris, it was this sense that America's interests had become truly universal, and hence the United States would be obligated to assume global responsibilities in maintaining the peace through the instrumentality of a League of Nations.

By his rejection of this fundamental principle of Wilsonian universalism, Hoover not only severed his personal ties to the Democratic president but at the same time denounced the mainspring for what would later be called collective security. Like other Republican reservationists who sought to tamper with Article X, Hoover was in the process of transforming the League into an organization neither contemplated nor desired by committed Wilsonians. This source of disagreement was probably as responsible as any single reason for prompting Hoover to feel that his political fortunes must lie with the Republican Party.

To characterize Hoover's developing ideas concerning America's role in the world community as isolationist would be unfair and simplistic. Within certain defined limits, he promoted trade, investments, and foreign assistance with the enthusiasm of the most zealous Wilsonian. He was an early leader in devising programs to achieve European economic recovery; he supported the concept of an international disarmament. From Hoover's experience in the war and conference years he learned that there were decided limitations on the application of political and military power. Po-

liceman for the world community was not in his judgment a proper function of American leadership. Bolshevism and other ills on
the world's body politic would in all likelihood prove to be self-
destructive due to their inner contradictions and irrationalities. To
oppose them through American intervention would serve only
questionable purposes but could conceivably threaten the very free
institutions at home which most Americans cherished. Hoover fully
appreciated the relationship between foreign military struggles and
their bearing on domestic institutional life. The French historian
Eli Halevi, in his Oxford lectures of 1929, would develop the theme
that the World War had turned into a titanic revolutionary
upheaval.[17]

In significant fashion, Hoover's public career provided an important transition from the turbulent universalism surrounding Wilsonian foreign policy to the not quite subdued or halcyon mood
that epitomized Harding-Coolidge normalcy. By late summer of
1919, even before the United States Senate rejected the Versailles
Treaty and with it American membership in the League of Nations,
the Wilson administration was already gradually withdrawing its
involvement in the continuing Peace Conference. No longer was
there serious consideration given at the State Department to the
possibility that the Senate would confer the necessary approval on
the Treaty of Guarantee.[18] Plans for an American mandate for
Armenia were quickly dropped at the White House as their realization appeared, practically speaking, an impossibility. Within the
Harding cabinet, Hoover offered the single human link with the
war experience. His reputation as food administrator and manager
of European relief was already firmly established and respected
among financial and business leaders on both sides of the Atlantic.
As secretary of commerce, Hoover assumed leadership in the United States for coping with the legacies of the late military conflict. He
participated in government agencies striving to resolve the financial complications wrought by the convergence of Allied war debts,
German reparations, and the extension of private American loans
along with other credits to European states. Future world peace, he
observed, rested on the renewal of Europe's, especially Germany's,
capacity to participate actively in the channels of world trade and
finance. European economic recovery was decidedly a prerequisite,
but it must not be accompanied by intense trade rivalry among the
commercial nations. Britain and France must acknowledge the
economic necessity for the Open Door, granting equal opportunities to all trading nations. Carl Parrini is probably correct in
appraising the reasons behind the failure of Hoover's political

economy. It wasn't that Hoover misjudged the social systems of Western Europe and North America but rather that he expected the business communities to act in a socially responsible manner, "eschewing short run profit and seeking the long run stabilization of the system." Unfortunately, with forewarning of the economic decadence and the crisis in the offing, too many bankers and entrepreneurs turned a deaf ear to the general interest.

For many an American who participated in the work of the Peace Conference of 1919, the experience was traumatic and indelibly fixed. By and large, personnel serving the American Commission were young men in their twenties and thirties. As one surveys the personnel roster, it becomes apparent that Hoover was by no means unique as a transitional figure of prominence who would link the Wilson era to the next generation of American foreign policy. In a real sense, the Peace Conference and the American Commission of 1919 offered a practical school affording a comprehensive education in statecraft to a rising generation of America's political leaders, statesmen who would guide the United States through world affairs for nearly the next half century. Besides Hoover, a sampling of Americans who received substantial apprenticeships in foreign affairs and who would later hold positions of responsibility in the American government included Bernard Baruch, Adolf Berle, William C. Bullitt, Allen W. and John Foster Dulles, Joseph Grew, Christian Herter, Edward Stettinius, and Robert A. Taft. This select list does not include persons who served at Paris in minor capacities and later rose to national prominence. As one adds the names of American academics, professors teaching modern history, geography, economics, and international law to a new generation of political leaders, the influence of this practical education in world affairs becomes even more apparent. Literally, the fundamental tone of American foreign policy during the second quarter of the twentieth century was altered by alumni of the American Commission. Quite obviously, the lessons perceived and mastered varied from individual to individual. However perceived, America's experience in the World War 1914–18 and the Peace Conference could not be ignored by these Americans who would shape the nation's foreign relations from the 1920s through the 1950s. As today's readers examine Herbert Hoover's numerous publications recounting the achievements and failures of those momentous years, it is hard to avoid the feeling that for him this experience had represented the central point of departure toward the later presidency.[19] The memories merge with the lessons, facts occasionally blur with fancy, but for Hoover the ordeal was a bully but serious endeavor.

NOTES

1   John D. Hicks, *Republican Ascendancy, 1921–1933* (New York: Harper, 1960), pp. 281–82.

2   Max Fisch, ed., *Selected Papers of Robert C. Binkley* (Cambridge: Harvard University Press, 1948), Introduction, pp. 3–6. See also Harold H. Fisher, *A Tower of Peace: The Story of the Hoover Library on War, Revolution and Peace* (Stanford: Stanford University Press, 1945).

3   For Hoover's promotion of public relations, see Craig Lloyd, *Aggressive Introvert: A Study of Herbert Hoover and Public Relations Management 1912–1932* (Columbus: Ohio State University Press, 1972), pp. 20–44.

4   Allan Nevins, ed., *The Letters and Journal of Brand Whitlock*, 2 vols. (New York: Appleton Century, 1936), p. 311. Whitlock's journal entry for October 29, 1916, states: ". . . Hoover, by his lack of tact, his tone of severity, has caused much of this trouble. Our Americans do not recognize that the position of the recipient of charity is so delicate that the donor should not add to the embarrassment by criticism and by intimations that there is lack of appreciation. Hoover would drive everybody with a bull whip; he is a strong man with a good heart, but lacks diplomacy. . . ." See also E. David Cronon, ed., *The Cabinet Diaries of Josephus Daniels 1913–1921* (Lincoln: University of Nebraska Press, 1963), p. 148. Daniels' diary entry for May 7, 1917, states: "Long talk with Hoover. There must be, he said, a Food Dictator, & no wheat or barley should go into intoxicants. . . .He wishes to be Food Dictator. Thinks it should not be under agriculture. People fear beaurocrocy [*sic*] & would wish dictatorship ended when war closes."

5   Herbert Hoover and Hugh Gibson, *The Problems of Lasting Peace* (Garden City: Doubleday, Doran, 1943), pp. 87ff.

6   Statistics of American grain exports to Britain, France, and Italy are cited in Frank M. Surface, *The Grain Trade During the World War: Being a History of the Food Administration Grain Corporation and the United States Grain Corporation* (New York: Macmillan, 1928), p. 23.

7   United States Department of State, *Papers Relating to the Foreign Relations of the United States: The Paris Peace Conference 1919* (hereinafter referred to as *FRPPC*) (Washington: Government Printing Office, 1945), 11:150–51, 485, 506.

8   Herbert Hoover, *The Ordeal of Woodrow Wilson* (New York: McGraw-Hill, 1958), p. 83.

9   Herbert Hoover, "The Economic Administration During the Armistice," in *What Really Happened at Paris*, ed. Edward M. House and Charles Seymour (New York: Scribner's, 1921), p. 336.

10   Later in his retrospective writings about the Peace Conference, Hoover was never modest in describing the relief program which he directed. In *The Ordeal of Woodrow Wilson*, p. 87, he indulges in self-appraisal: "Next to the Peace Conference itself, the most important American activity during the peacemaking and for some

time afterward was the Relief and Reconstruction of Europe, under my direction. Mr. Wilson often referred to it as the 'Second American Expeditionary Force to Save Europe.' "

11   Lord Hankey, *The Supreme Control at the Paris Peace Conference 1919* (London: Allen and Unwin, 1963). Although Hoover is mentioned, he and his work are not given any prominence. Lord Hankey is here concerned with how the machinery of the Conference functioned as an international entity.

12   *FRPPC*, 3:149. In *The Memoirs of Herbert Hoover: Years of Adventure 1874–1920* (New York: Macmillan, 1951), p. 297, the author refers to his international authority: "The President took up the question personally with Prime Ministers Clemenceau, Lloyd George and Orlando. They readily agreed that I should be appointed sole Director of Relief and Rehabilitation, directly responsible to the 'Big Four.' "

13   *FRPPC*, 10:396–98, 221–22, 278–79, 170–71, 522–25, 373, 462–68, 482–83, 477–78, 506–12, 502–06.

14   *FRPPC*, 11, p. 563. The Communications Division of the American Commission reported in May 1919: "This office handles all cipher and code messages in and out of the Commission. It is open twenty-four hours a day, and the men work in watches. It is purposely fully staffed in order to meet the maximum requirements. About one-third of the business of the communications office is devoted to transmitting and receiving messages to Mr. Hoover's organization. It is desirable that these communications be handled by this office, although Mr. Hoover's work is not wholly Peace Commission work, but is really international. If such work were eliminated, the personnel could doubtless be reduced by twenty men."

15   Colonel E. M. House to President Wilson, July 30, 1919, in *FRPPC*, 11:620–23.

16   For accounts of Hoover's objections to the Versailles Treaty and its provisions, see *The Memoirs of Herbert Hoover: Years of Adventure 1874–1920*, pp. 461ff; Hoover, *The Ordeal of Woodrow Wilson*, pp. 233–52.

17   Eli Halevi, "The World Crisis of 1914–1918: An Interpretation," in *The Era of Tyrannies*, translated by R. K. Webb (Garden City: Anchor Books, 1965), pp. 209–47.

18   For the text of the Agreement Between the United States and France, signed at Versailles, June 28, 1919, see *FRPPC*, 13:757–62. For further discussion of the Guarantee Treaty, see Louis A. R. Yates, *United States and French Security 1917–1921* (New York: Twayne, 1957), pp. 44–97, 116–45.

19   Hoover's published writings concerning the First World War and activities relating to the peace settlement of 1919 include the following: *An American Epic*, 4 vols. (Chicago: Regnery, 1959–64); *America's First Crusade* (New York: Scribner's, 1942); "The Economic Administration During the Armistice," in *What Really Happened at Paris*, ed. Edward M. House and Charles Seymour (New York: Scribner's, 1921); *The Memoirs of Herbert Hoover: Years of Adventure 1874–1920* (New York: Macmillan, 1951), pp. 135–482; *The Ordeal of Woodrow Wilson* (New York: McGraw-Hill, 1958); *The Problems of Lasting Peace* [with Hugh Gibson] (Garden City: Doubleday, Doran, 1942).

ROBERT D. CUFF

Herbert Hoover, The Ideology of Voluntarism And War Organization During the Great War

EDITOR'S INTRODUCTORY NOTE

Belligerency constitutes a state of national emergency resembling a crisis posed by some horrendous natural disaster. Yet, in modern warfare, not only are many citizens called upon to make the ultimate sacrifice on behalf of their country and its interests, but in 1917–18, thousands of American men were conscripted into military service, making personal sacrifices of lesser degrees. If indeed there existed some substantial national consensus favoring American belligerency, then the logic of this action would expect that leaders in the professional and business communities would come forward to offer specialized services in assisting the nation during the crisis. Herein lies the close relationship between civil voluntarism and military conscription.

The subject of Robert Cuff's paper, voluntarism, was certainly a central feature of personnel management for the many *ad hoc,* wartime agencies created by the Wilson administration, and Herbert Hoover was among its staunchest defenders and most consistent practitioners. Later commentators might judge voluntarism as an unqualified success. It was supposed, as Cuff here explains, "to promote planning without bureaucracy; regulation without coercion, cooperation without dictation." Presumably, voluntarism was also calculated to encourage the employment of persons with specially needed skills and intellectual resources who would not otherwise be readily recruited into government service. Also advanced on behalf of voluntarism is the argument that such a system allowed for persons, who were disinterested in the outcome of the agency's program, to make an easy transition from private employment to public service. This may possibly be the most spurious

Robert D. Cuff is professor of history at York University, Downsview, Ontario, Canada. Professor Cuff's paper was previously published in the *Journal of American History*, 64 (September 1977), 358–72, which controls the copyright.

feature of voluntarism. In Hoover's Food Administration, for instance, did persons who participated in the various and frequent
decisions that would have a vital bearing on the nation's economy
have potential conflicts of interest by virtue of their previous or
presumed future employment in the private sphere? Was there
some administrative advantage in recruiting personnel lacking professional and business expertise in order to avoid such conflicts
of interest? Was there wisdom in risking such conflicts for the advantage of recruiting staff members possessing the specialized
knowledge and experience?

Did voluntarism promote recruitment of the most competent
persons available, or did voluntarism tend to encourage a form of
cronyism in which bureaucrats brought their friends into staff positions? In a certain sense, voluntarism subverted the concept of a
merit system, substituting in its stead a kind of spoils system which
differed from the garden political variety in that volunteers would
not receive financial remuneration directly. Rewards from employment were not based on political services rendered but rather on
the volunteer's sense of patriotism supplemented by whatever business and professional friendships might yield future benefits.
Hoover obviously believed that this system promoted competence
in government. Nevertheless, Cuff's article does pose some sober-
ing questions and revises much conventional wisdom about the
utility of voluntarism.

For all of its advantages, voluntarism was hardly democratic,
favoring as it did the affluent over the needy, not necessarily the
qualified over the unqualified. Moreover, it tended to promote
personal loyalties in which "the boss," who was credited with at-
tracting the managerial personnel, could command the loyalty of
his staff. The system served to perpetuate a form of shared indispensability and independence on the part of the volunteers who
could presumably withdraw from government service whenever
some favored proposal failed to win approval. In this sense, government would become dangerously dependent upon the good will
of the volunteers. Most important, voluntarism tended to bring into the ranks of government agencies those persons who shared a
common world view, philosophy, fundamental economic values,
and by and large were not prone to question each other's assumptions very searchingly. This lack of criticism could potentially encourage arrogance in leadership.

Whether voluntarism should properly be understood as ideology
or as a practical device for administrative management, Hoover's

application was not lacking in significance. In his article, Cuff points to both the supposed advantages and disadvantages afforded by voluntarism. By eliminating salaries from budgetary calculations, voluntarism permitted the Food Administration to increase rapidly the size of its staff. Then, too, he maintains that the implications of voluntarism were essentially conservative rather than reformist and innovative. These and other claims for voluntarism might profitably be tested through comparing Hoover's adaptation in the Food Administration with the use made of voluntarism in other wartime government agencies. Cuff's article suggests several avenues that could stand close comparisons.

Herbert Hoover, the Ideology of Voluntarism and War Organization During the Great War

The theme of voluntarism pervades the literature on national mobilization during the Great War. The Wilson administration, according to this canon, achieved planning without bureaucracy, regulation without coercion, cooperation without dictation. To be sure, state agencies had had to plan, administrators to coordinate, enlightened statesmen to lead. But their administration had rested less upon manipulation and dictation than upon education, cooperation among civilian volunteers, widespread consultation among private groups, and a general spirit of patriotism. In this way the United States avoided the degree of state intervention, centralized administration, and persistent postwar bureaucracy evident in England and the rest of Europe. The challenge of mobilization, in sum, simply proved once again the exceptional nature of American institutions.[1]

There is some truth to this view. The structure of voluntarism as a system of thought reflects in fundamental ways the structure of American mobilization as a particular system of war organization. The unprecedented mobilization of national resources occurred in a vastly complicated and, in some areas, fragmented economy, with a paucity of prewar planning, a comparatively underdeveloped state apparatus, and a political culture still drawn to the doctrines of laissez faire. It is little wonder, therefore, that mobilizers turned to volunteer personnel, private sources of administration,

cooperative agreements, and great propaganda crusades for conservation and sacrifice.

There is evidence to support this view on a more personal level
as well. Herbert Hoover's remarkable wartime career, for example,
confirms such a perspective on the ideology of voluntarism in action. As head of Belgian Relief and as United States Food Administrator, Hoover projected his romantic view of the professional
man, a common cultural theme of the period and a central compo-
nent of the promise of voluntarism. The ideal of the professional
man combined the gentry tradition of the nineteenth century with
the technical requirements of the twentieth. In this way the
character, integrity, social consciousness, and proud individualism
of the gentleman might unite with the efficiency and technical
virtuosity of the modern manager. Though familiar with the in-
tricacies of modern business enterprise, this group of professionals,
it was hoped, could by virtue of their traditional moral superiority
rise above private interests to serve the commonweal. In Belgian
Relief, Hoover demonstrated his partiality for volunteer professionals like himself; and what is more, he proved his ability to
gather and hold such men. He would repeat his recruitment success as food administrator, the prototype of the private citizen in
public service.[2]

His views on appropriate forms of administrative organization
reinforced his image as the embodiment of voluntarism. Hoover
rejected the structure of such organizations as the military services
and the modern industrial corporation as models for his wartime
administration and drew rather from his private experience in
a mining-consulting firm. He chose a professional over a bureaucratic form of wartime organization. In a professional organization, in its ideal state, knowledge rather than office secures
authority. Men are professional equals rather than members of a
hierarchical chain of command and *ad hoc* problem solving
transcends routine procedures.[3]

From the start of his tenure as food administrator in May 1917,
Hoover intended to treat food questions "as one of a series of
problems"[4] and to regard his personnel as "problem managers"[5]
rather than as subordinates. He outlined his view in his first report:
"The United States Food Administrator . . . has called to his assistance specially qualified men from all parts of the United States.
The administrator selects an associate to handle each problem as it
arises, and this man in turn invites such other members of the Food
Administration to join him as he may require."[6] When Felix

Frankfurter of the War Labor Policies Board requested an organization chart from the Food Administration during the war, he was told that none had ever existed.[7] Hoover was belligerent on this point in his later reflections. "In setting up our organization," he commented on his postwar relief operations, "we had the usual plague of theorists, who wanted to make charts with squares and circles showing the relation of each job to the other, along with descriptions of particular functions and authorities. Nothing could raise my temperature faster than charts for an emergency organization which shifted daily."[8]

There was, then, a striking convergence between Hoover's own administrative capacities and principles on the one hand and the peculiar nature of national mobilization on the other. The wartime tasks both in European relief and American economic mobilization were unprecedented in size and scope and very much open to the kind of improvisation, flexibility, and elitist vision that lay at the heart of Hoover's approach. Moreover, in contrast to the years of permanent war after 1939, 1917–18 might better be regarded as war as emergency crisis; and Allen Barton's discussion of the function of voluntarism in modern disaster captures the affinities between Hoover's techniques and such a situation. "If mass mobilization for action is to be obtained [in disaster]," writes Barton, "it is up to those with special skills and knowledge to formulate intelligible versions of the facts and to construct organizations that give the public access to effective roles that are within their capacities."[9] From this perspective, Hoover was the very model of the modern disaster manager and a fitting symbol of how the structure of a system of thought—voluntarism—fundamentally reflected the structure of a particular system of war organization—the American mobilization effort.

But this is only one way to understand the relationship between the ideology of voluntarism and the structure and function of Wilsonian war organization. And it is by no means the most important, notwithstanding the fact that it dominates much of the secondary literature. Ideology may also be conceived and studied as a political weapon, manipulated consciously in ongoing struggles for legitimacy and power, as an instrument for creating and controlling organizations. And this second perspective on the ideology of voluntarism throws a quite different light on how Hoover's experience with the Food Administration exemplified underlying patterns of Wilsonian war organization.[10]

Hoover used voluntarism as an administrative tool from the start, when he made his case for a Food Administration independent of the regular cabinet departments. "People fear beaurocrocy [*sic*]," he warned Secretary of the Navy Josephus Daniels, "& would wish dictatorship ended when the war closes."[11] The emergence of Hoover's Food Administration should not be seen as simply inevitable since food administration, after all, remained firmly within the Department of Agriculture for most of World War II, and, even in World War I, the Department of Labor, among regular departments, managed to retain primacy in its traditional field. In Hoover's case, however, the arguments of voluntarism had a powerful effect; significantly, the agriculture department, Hoover's most obvious competitor, put up little resistance, for Secretary David F. Houston apparently did not believe that the new agency threatened his prerogative.[12] But not all departments were so accommodating, and a fledgling organization like the Food Administration had to be sensitive with them all in any case. Hoover's legal adviser cautioned him at one point: "It would be a mistake for the Food Administration at the beginning of its career to antagonize or appear to antagonize any of the established departments."[13] President Wilson himself, moreover, ever sensitive to congressional criticism of emergency departures from peacetime government and personally cautious toward forging the instruments of war power, also required persuasion for which the symbols of voluntarism were eminently suited.

It also fell to the ideology of voluntarism to justify the movement of private men into public places and to counter the charges of conflict of interest thus generated. The recruitment process troubled agrarian leaders in Congress from the first, and, though their criticism was most intense in the early stages, suspicions lingered on. Some commentators argued, moreover, that Hoover and the others should accept a salary in order not to embarrass those who could not afford to volunteer; others charged business volunteers with malfeasance. The structure and techniques of emergency administration required justification as well, and, in keeping with the gospel of voluntarism, Hoover and his men argued for administrative informality and unitary authority against congressmen who demanded detailed statutory prescriptions, strict accountability, and committee forms of emergency administrations.[14]

The ideology of voluntarism also served internal administrative needs. For one thing, the emphasis upon public service, character, and probity contributed to a pride of common association among a

diverse set of volunteers and may have functioned as well as an informal means, however tenuous, of social control in volunteer
agencies. Central administrators like Hoover were certainly concerned for the public reputation of their agencies and expected
those around them to act in good faith. To encourage this result,
and to head off congressional criticism, the administrators
sometimes searched for volunteers without connections to the product lines they would administer; in rarer cases still, they used the
criterion of voluntarism as a justification for asking a man to step
down. [15] But the heavy reliance upon voluntary personnel and disregard of the civil service rules held additional implications for a
new agency chief's administrative position. It provided him with a
personal base of power. One of Hoover's advisers touched upon
this kind of consideration in the course of setting up the Food Administration's legal department: "if the legal department of the
Food Administration is to be taken over by the Department of
Justice, you would undoubtedly lose your volunteer staff, and that
sympathetic cooperation which is essential. Lawyers employed in
the Department of Justice would owe no duty to you but would be
entirely subordinated to the Attorney-General." [16]

Administration and politics are never separate, of course, but the
ideology of voluntarism played a part in issues far broader than in-
teragency competition and internal administrative control. Groups
on both the right and left of Hoover debated the meaning of the
emerging administrative state and raised significant challenges in
the minds of the mobilizers. A current preoccupation among historians is to show how often demands from the left, both before and
during the war, pushed liberal reformers to action. This is an important point and undoubtedly true. But it should not obscure the
impact that right-wing opposition had on the emergence and
operation of Wilsonian war organization. In the daily round of
negotiations and regulation, Hoover and other administrators
dealt at least as much with politicians and businessmen who
thought they went too far toward federal control as with those who
thought they did not go far enough. The congressional battle to
establish the Food Administration in the first place is a good example of this point, as is the struggle Hoover had later to bring the big
meat packers within his administrative coalition. Hoover and the
other central administrators occupied an intellectual position very
close to that taken by Herbert Croly in *The Promise of American Life*
(1909). Their task, like Croly's, was not so much to restrain a
dynamic left as to convince private corporate and technical elites to

scuttle the tenets of laissez faire on behalf of minimal institutional change. The specter of greater state control that mobilizers held up to private business groups as the cost of recalcitrance may have been as much a rhetorical device on behalf of cooperation as a calculated response to any real threat from the left. Under the historical conditions of mobilization during World War I, voluntarism was far more the ideology of a liberal vanguard than one would suspect from the conservative uses to which it was put in the ideological debates of the 1930s and 1940s.

The ideology of voluntarism, then, can be viewed in two ways. It may be studied first of all as a structure of thought that reflected in varying degrees some of the underlying patterns of Wilsonian war organization, patterns inherent in the structural and historical conditions of the period and exemplified in part in Hoover's own wartime career. Voluntarism may also be understood as a tool in the administrative process itself, an ideology that sophisticated administrators like Hoover wielded in their general struggle for power and legitimacy. The first conceptualization has shaped much of the retrospective literature on the war experience; the second should receive more attention in future research.

But there is yet another aspect of voluntarism as an ideology that requires attention before its role as an administrative and political tool of mobilization can be fully appreciated, and this is perhaps the most important consideration of all. Though there is an obvious relationship between the ideology of voluntarism and some basic structural and social-psychological features of Wilsonian war organization, and though mobilizers like Hoover necessarily shared many of its tenets, it would be very misleading to regard the ideology as an accurate guide to the mobilization process in every particular. Like any organizational ideology, voluntarism was designed to resolve the tensions inevitable in administrative practice. Georg Lukács has written on this point: "On the level of pure theory the most disparate views and tendencies are able to co-exist peacefully, antagonisms are only expressed in the form of discussions which can be contained within the framework of one and the same organisation without disrupting it. But no sooner are these same questions given organisational form than they turn out to be sharply opposed and even incompatible."[17]

The ideology of voluntarism functioned, in other words, whether intentionally or not, to close off questions about the ambiguities and contradictions that emerged in practice around such polarities as cooperation-coercion, decentralization-centralization, civilian-state, and private-public. This was true during the war, of course, but it was even more the case in the interwar years as ideological and political partisans debated the relevance of the war experience for the various issues of their own day. The ideology of voluntarism thus shows how an integrated war organization was possible in theory, but only empirical research can determine the kinds of structural compromises on which it rested in practice.

With this perspective in mind, it may be found that in some areas of the war program no relationship at all existed between the ideology of voluntarism on the one hand and specific organizational arrangements on the other. It cannot be assumed, in other words, that action had its roots in ideology—that Hoover and others strove to bring structure into line with their ideological predispositions—any more than it is possible simply to dismiss the impact of ideology on their behavior altogether. The relationship between ideology and the structure and function of Wilsonian war organization is less a given than a question that requires investigation.

A closer look at Hoover and the Food Administration can illustrate some of the problems worth attention in determining the relationship between theory and practice in Wilsonian war organization. The ideology of voluntarism, first of all, obscures how bureaucratic traits invaded the mobilization process despite protestations among administrators to the contrary. The Food Administration, for example, notwithstanding an upper level of volunteers, obviously rested on a salaried staff that would necessarily have increased in both absolute and relative size had the war continued. Furthermore, administrative expansion, predictably enough, sometimes seemed to take on a life of its own. Edgar Rickard, Hoover's business manager, commented with dismay on the Food Administration's speaker division in early 1918: "It has grown without our appreciating its extent into an enormous organization, and as is bound to result, we have a whole lot of representatives that are not anything to be proud of. . . ."[18] The Food Administration's vertical structure increased in height, moreover, as the early volunteers relinquished detailed problem solving to others in order to take up broader policy questions.[19] Nor could private voluntarism on the local level be left without some kind of central direction, though this raised questions about the meaning of decentralized administration. After a nation-wide tour to study the impact of Food Administration propaganda, Ray Lyman Wilbur, its director, concluded: "There is a great and

powerful voluntary element in it. Nevertheless the ramifications of
the publicity in a population such as ours necessitate a large, expensive, thorough form of organization in each state. . . ."[20]

A closer scrutiny of the war agencies also suggests how the
ideology of voluntarism may have inhibited appreciation of the regional and class dimensions of wartime recruitment. Californians
and Stanford alumni were understandably well represented at the
Food Administration's center, and other agencies would no doubt
reveal similar regional biases in personnel. More significantly,
voluntarism, as its critics argued at the time, did imply placing
public power in the hands of men drawn from the top end of the
social structure.[21] It meant too that, even within this group, men of
large wealth, like Hoover or Bernard Baruch, could far more easily
enlarge their private staffs if salary did become an issue than could
administrators of more modest means, like fuel administrator
Harry Garfield, who had come to Washington from the presidency
of Williams College. The point here is not to question motive but
rather to consider the regional and class dimensions of national
mobilization and the implications they might have had in turn for
the struggle for power in wartime Washington.

That struggle was very real, after all, and not only between the
war agencies and Congress on the one side and private interests on
the other, but also among the administrators themselves. This is an
obvious and crucial fact, perhaps, but one not always evident from
the homilies about voluntarism in secondary accounts. Hoover's
own drive for personal control in these years is of course well
known, and it did not go unremarked at the time. Colonel Edward
M. House, who could appreciate such things, regarded Hoover's
persistent demands for "complete control" to be the food administrator's "besetting fault."[22] Hoover may have favored a col-
legial form of organization within the Food Administration, but the
thrust of his actions at the higher levels of policy making was
toward more centralized, executive power. In this respect Hoover
embodied two contradictory trends in the upper reaches of war administration. He sought greater autonomy for himself and the administrative network he headed while simultaneously pressing for
greater integration of all war agencies, his own included, under a
higher coordinating authority. But, to his opponents among business and political groups, of course, both initiatives represented
merely two sides of the same trend to oligarchy.

In that persistent conundrum of how to manage the managers,
problems arose on two levels, problems that were reconciled in

ideology but never solved in practice: how could the president control his subordinates and how could Congress bring the Executive to account? It is now almost a cliché to point out that the severe limitations of time and knowledge on presidential control result in a great deal of delegated authority, especially in wartime. Wilson was obviously a strong president who did not hesitate to restrain self-willed subordinates like Hoover when he felt it necessary. Nevertheless, he also found it necessary to defer to his food administrator on more than one occasion. In responding to one of Hoover's typically comprehensive and complicated schemes—for grain regulations in this case—he wrote: "I must frankly say that I have no judgement of my own about the matter. I do not feel that I am qualified to form one. I am quite willing to leave the decision in your own hands."[23] Hoover, moreover, was an aggressive administrator, unafraid to act first and consult later. Wilson wrote to Hoover with regard to milk negotiations under way in the fall of 1917: "I do not feel confident to judge the steps you have taken because, of course, I have not been at the conferences which led to them, but I take pleasure in approving what you have done."[24]

The authority relations between the food administrator and private interests were more complicated still. The ideology of voluntarism, of course, promised neutrality from the administrators and cooperation from private business interests, with both conditions designed to make independent state and federal coercion unnecessary. Hoover and the leading administrators were not, in fact, simply spokesmen in government for private interests, though in certain instances they did find themselves in that role. The administrators had additional purposes to serve, as is evident from the records of their negotiations with various business executives. Hoover, for instance, was an active participant in that larger international struggle against bolshevism, and he strove mightily to guide the American political economy to that end, especially in the post-Armistice days. His was a global vision that far transcended the more narrowly conceived views of many of his clientele, though, of course, this vision was by no means incompatible with America's overall prosperity. But, then, it is hardly to be supposed that Hoover would consciously seek to undermine the very economic structure his policies were designed to defend in this larger ideological struggle.

In fact, Hoover consciously guarded against proposals that in his judgment threatened this system. Though a wartime champion of price control, licensing, and other departures from peacetime orthodoxies, Hoover explicitly rejected the idea of seizing the war crisis as an opportunity to alter the structure of corporate capitalism and the distribution of power within it. He repeated his argument once again during World War II: "Reforms for making America over, no matter how attractive, cannot but dislocate the war effort."[25] And this view was embraced even more fervently by some of Hoover's more conservative colleagues. Those radicals in World War I who regarded the Food Administration and other executive agencies as the vanguard of a new cooperative commonwealth misunderstood the intentions of men like Hoover who occupied the command posts of war administration.[26]

From the perspective of structural economic change, the implications of voluntarism were profoundly conservative. Questions of distribution and conservation, not production and ownership, were Hoover's major domestic concerns, after all.[27] Success in the former, it was hoped, would obviate any alterations in the latter. As much as Hoover might argue and differ with major business executives, even to the point of requiring presidential authority to push them into line, the fate of his own administrative program both at home and abroad depended fundamentally upon them. Though intense negotiations and real bitterness characterized Hoover's early relations with the meat packers, for instance, he could hardly terminate that symbiotic relationship. George Soule touched upon this point when be observed: "Just because their monopoly is so nearly complete, their machinery must be utilized and their help secured."[28] Indeed in this particular case Hoover, despite the real grounds the industry had given him for taking punitive action, ultimately found himself defending the packers against those who sought to reduce their profits and dilute their power.

Hoover's stand in this instance might be cited as an example of how ideology affected administrative behavior. Yet, by contrast, it could also be used, as Soule suggests, to show how the structure and power of an industry partially determined the government's response. There can be no doubt about the dialectical relationship between the structure of an industry and the nature of that segment of the state designed to cope with it. It is arguable that had the American railroad industry been in better condition, for instance, the government would not have been forced to take it over. Had a strong American shipping industry existed it would not have been necessary to resort to outright state capitalism in that sector. Certainly, in the realm of daily wartime administration, a concentrated industry like sugar refining or steel was far more likely to yield up a "voluntary agreement" than a fragmented area like canning or lumber. In other words, the force of structural conditions may have far outweighed the impact of values in any one of a series of relationships between business and government during the war.

Nor is it altogether clear how much decisions against some measures, like rationing, sprang from ideology as opposed to a shrewd calculation of how much the political traffic would bear. In the case of food supplies, the problem was acquiring sufficient exports for the Allies, not feeding the American people; and it might be argued that under these circumstances rejecting compulsory saving was simply accepting discretion as the better part of valor. Hoover's stand in this instance is frequently interpreted as an example of his faith in the American people,[29] but it might indicate just the opposite. He wrote to Brand Whitlock in September 1917: "We have no real feeling as to the amount of sacrifice that must be made in the United States outside of a very limited class, and all of the measures which we undertake for furthering the war must be founded, in this republic, so much on voluntary self-sacrifice that it is of enormous importance to us to have that feeling stirred to the very bottom."[30] And, in explaining his reluctance to put the small flour millers under license, Hoover argued that the gains "are nothing comparable to the difficulties that will arise in the administration and to the noise and prejudice they can create...."[31]

There is ambivalence as well on the question of whether Hoover and the others wanted more authority than they possessed, or whether they possessed more than they wanted, or indeed whether they sought coercive means they never really intended to use. Lack of formal authority, after all, could provide an excuse to avoid something they opposed in any case, while references to voluntary cooperation could serve as a rationalization for the structural and political facts of life; alternatively, the mere existence of formal authority might stimulate the required voluntary behavior. Hoover outlined the latter strategy in one of his early presidential briefs: "It is proposed to accomplish as much as possible by stimulation to voluntary effort decentralized into the states as much as is feasible. Nevertheless some repressive regulations must be used and the existence of power to do the latter will stimulate the former."[32] Yet, as Hoover pointed out, such authority was often more than a matter of symbolic value; it was necessary to counter the opposition. In his first report as food administrator, Hoover emphasized the central role of voluntarism in securing many key agreements, but he

Food Section "Supreme Economic Council"

Left to right: Herbert Hoover, Lewis Strauss, Count Zucchini, Sir William Goode, M. Jules Max, Major Boykin Wright, Colonel J. A. Logan, Mr. Garvin, Colonel A. B. Barber, Alonzo E. Taylor, and Mr. Sherman. This photograph was made in Hoover's office at 51 Avenue Montaigne, Paris, about April 1919.

added: "The licensing system, however, is the backbone of all control. Without compulsion there will always be a few slackers in every trade who will profit by the patriotism of the majority and prevent any effective control."[33]

Yet simultaneously with seeking to extend his authority in some areas, Hoover discouraged statutory foundations in others. He objected to a measure of authority in the early stages of the debate over the Lever bill, for example, warning the president: "there are a great number of misguided faddists in the country who will bring constant pressure to bear upon us to take drastic action along these lines [wheat milling measures] and whose antagonism we will certainly incur if we have the powers and do not make use of them."[34]

What the war administrators like Hoover wanted most of all, of course, was to have the utmost freedom and flexibility of action. Since they believed themselves to represent the moral and technical superiority of the idealistic expert in public service they believed they might be trusted with wide-ranging delegated authority. And they were, in fact, a far more idealistic and sensitive group than the crisis-managers of recent times. But the obvious anti-democratic thrust of crisis management was present nonetheless. Columbia historian James T. Shotwell, a member of the Inquiry, caught the logic of the trend in a rather remarkable observation: "In proportion as the crisis becomes real, these specialized organs must free themselves from any other controls or bureaucratic impediments and act directly with or under the chief executive. . . . the most perfect model of the kind of government which all nations finally accepted in the World War was the Committee of Public Safety in the French Reign of Terror, an instrument of government, the precision and efficiency of which have been completely obscured in the popular mind because of that one activity—the Terror—with which its name is always associated."[35]

Questions of power, including the managers' own quest for autonomy, cut deeply through the concept pairs composing the ideology of voluntarism—centralization-decentralization, coercion-freedom, private-public, and so on. And without reference to them, the actual organizational structures in which the mobilizers attempted to embody these polarities cannot be fully understood.

Equally fundamental and obvious is the fact that if the ideology of voluntarism persisted into the interwar years and beyond as part of American political culture, it could never again have the same relevance for national action as it had during World War I. As an ideology of war organization, for example, voluntarism was keyed

to a conception of war as national emergency, which was, by definition, of very limited duration. And World War I, compared to
World War II and the permanent war of the Cold War years, can
certainly be conceived in these terms. But voluntarism was never
entirely congruent with historical conditions even then, so how
much less was this the case when war making became a continuing
function, and emergency management was built into the state itself.
In this altered context, the ideology of voluntarism, so deeply
rooted in an earlier historical era, could too easily become a misleading guide to a mythical past.

NOTES

1   This general view has been brought to bear on each wartime agency in turn, but
for references along these lines to the Food Administration in particular, see: Maxcy
Robson Dickson, *The Food Front in World War I* (Washington: American Council on
Public Affairs, 1944); Benjamin H. Hibbard, *Effects of the Great War Upon Agriculture
in the United States and Great Britain* (New York: Oxford University Press, 1919), p.
151; Herbert Hoover, *Memoirs: Years of Adventure 1874–1921* (New York: Macmillan,
1951), pp. 240–54; Will Irwin, *Herbert Hoover: A Reminiscent Biography* (New York:
Century, 1928), pp. 191–92; Eugene Lyons, *Herbert Hoover: A Biography* (Garden
City: Doubleday, 1964), pp. 100–01; Albert N. Merritt, *War Time Control of Distribution of Foods* (New York: Macmillan, 1920), pp. 5–7; Frank M. Surface and
Raymond L. Bland, *American Food in the World War and Reconstruction Period: Opera-
tions of the Organizations Under the Direction of Herbert Hoover 1914 to 1924* (Palo Alto:
Stanford University Press, 1931), pp. 15–16; Charles R. Van Hise, *Conservation and
Regulation in the United States During the World War* (Washington: GPO, 1918),
pp. 69–70; and William Franklin Willoughby, *Government Organization in
Wartime and After: A Survey of the Federal Civil Agencies Created for the Prosecution
of the War* (New York: Appleton, 1919), pp. 262–63, 270, 291. Harold J. Tobin and
Percy W. Bidwell, *Mobilizing Civilian America* (New York: Council on Foreign
Relations, 1940), can be regarded as consolidation of interwar thinking on the overall
problem of wartime mobilization. For the impact the ideology of voluntarism had on
various studies of the War Industries Board, see Robert D. Cuff, "Bernard Baruch:
Symbol and Myth in Industrial Mobilization," *Business History Review,* 43
(Summer 1969), 115–33.

2   For a discussion of the gentry tradition, see Stow Persons, *The Decline of
American Gentility* (New York: Columbia University Press, 1973). For a discussion of
the idea of professionalism and Herbert Hoover's particular relationship to it, see
Edwin T. Layton, Jr., *Revolt of the Engineers: Social Responsibility and the American
Engineering Profession* (Cleveland: Press of Case Western Reserve University, 1971),
pp. 53–78. It is worth noting that if charisma be defined as the belief of followers in
the power and capacity of their leader, then Hoover proved charismatic on this issue
through the war. For some young men, like Robert A. Taft, indeed, Hoover became
something of a father figure. See Lyons, *Herbert Hoover,* pp. 83, 91; William Hard,
Who's Hoover? (New York: Dodd Mead, 1928), pp. 108–09; and James T. Patterson,
Mr. Republican: A Biography of Robert A. Taft (Boston: Houghton Mifflin, 1972), pp.
79–80.

3 Walter I. Wardwell, "Social Integration, Bureaucratization and the Professions," *Social Forces*, 33 (May 1955), 356–59; Richard H. Hall, "Professionalization and Bureaucratization," *American Sociological Review*, 33 (February 1968), 92–104.

4 Committee on Agriculture, U.S. House of Representatives, *The United States Food Administration and United States Fuel Administration: Messages from the President of the United States, transmitting Reports of the United States Food Administration and the United States Fuel Administration* (Washington: GPO, 1918), p. 8.

5 Hoover to Theodore F. Whitmarsh, August 4, 1917, file 21-H, Box 56, United States Food Administration Records, Hoover Institution, Palo Alto, California.

6 Committee on Agriculture, *United States Food Administration . . .*, p. 8. As Hoover described it, the central Food Administration, with its informal team of highly motivated problem-solving experts, was not unlike the organizational structure of some electronic firms heavily engaged in research and development. Where a premium is placed on adaptation to a rapidly changing market and technology, the professional form of industrial organization has in these cases proved far more functional than the bureaucratic. See Tom Burns and G. M. Stalker, *The Management of Innovation* (London: Tavistock, 1966).

7 Felix Frankfurter to M. B. Hammond, June 17, 1918, and Lewis Strauss to Hammond, June 18, 1918, File 33-H, Box 64, Food Administration Records. See also "Tentative Organization of the Food Administration," September 11, 1917, *ibid.*; [Strauss] to J. J. Stream, Records of the Food Administration Grain Corporation, Box 240, *ibid.*

8 Herbert Hoover, *An American Epic*, 3 vols. (Chicago: Regnery, 1960), 2:301.

9 Allen H. Barton, *Communities in Disaster: A Sociological Analysis of Collective Stress Situations* (Garden City: Doubleday, 1970), pp. 101–02; Lyons, *Herbert Hoover*, p. 84.

10 How to conceptualize and study ideology is the subject of a vast literature in the social sciences. Since no single perspective on how ideology functions monopolizes the field, one can only make his assumptions clear. For purposes of this essay, three different yet complementary perspectives on the problem were used: ideology as a structure of thought reflecting underlying structural conditions, an approach that in this case helps situate much of the contemporary literature on Wilsonian war organization in general and on Hoover's Food Administration in particular; ideology as rationalization; and ideology as false consciousness. Among studies that approach ideology as rationalization in the politics of organization, see Michael Rogin, "Voluntarism: the Political Functions of an Antipolitical Doctrine," *Industrial and Labor Relations Review*, 15 (July 1962), 521–35; Grant McConnell, *The Decline of Agrarian Democracy* (Berkeley: University of California Press, 1953); and Philip Selznick, *TVA and the Grass Roots: A Study in the Sociology of Formal Organization* (New York: Harper and Row, 1966). For the classic approaches to the study of ideology, see George Lichtheim, *The Concept of Ideology and Other Essays* (New York: Random House, 1967). See also Norman Birnbaum, "The Sociological Study of Ideology (1940–1960), A Trend Report and Bibliography," *Current Sociology*, 9 (1960), 91–172; L. B. Brown, *Ideology* (Baltimore: Penguin Education, 1973); and Derek L. Phillips, "Epistemology and the Sociology of Knowledge: the Contributions of Mannheim, Mills, and Merton," *Theory and Society*, 1 (Spring 1974), 59–88.

11   E. David Cronon, ed., *The Cabinet Diaries of Josephus Daniels 1913–1921* (Lincoln: University of Nebraska Press, 1963), p. 148.

12   David F. Houston, *Eight Years with Wilson's Cabinet 1913 to 1920, With a Personal Estimate of the President,* 2 vols. (Garden City: Doubleday, Page, 1926), 1:329–33; Hoover, *Years of Adventure,* p. 243. For an alternative view, see Cronon, *Cabinet, Diaries of Josephus Daniels,* p. 149. For a bitter attack on the Food Administration, which refers to humiliation of the Department of Agriculture, see Alfred W. McCann, "The Hoover Food-Control Failure," *Forum,* 58 (October 1917): 381–90.

13   Curtis Lindley to Hoover, August 1, 1917, File 14-H, Box 45, Food Administration Records.

14   For the debate over a unitary authority, or food administrator, and a food board, see: Dickson, *Food Front in World War I,* p. 23n; Hoover, *Years of Adventure,* pp. 241–42; *Congressional Record,* 65th Cong., 1st sess., 4647–61 (July 3, 1917). This protracted fight, which included bitter personal attacks on Hoover himself, was one of the most discouraging periods for Hoover and his recruits. For evidence of Hoover's anger at his critics, see Hoover to Woodrow Wilson, August 23, 1917, Wilson Mss, Library of Congress. See also Lewis L. Strauss, *Men and Decisions* (Garden City: Doubleday, 1962), p. 11.

15   Joseph Cotton to Hoover, March 20, 1918, File 15-H, Box 47, Food Administration Records; Edgar Rickard to Lindley, February 21, 1918, File 14-H, Box 45, *ibid.* For other examples of Hoover's concern to maintain public confidence in Food Administration personnel, see Julius Barnes to Hoover, Box 245, Food Administration Grain Corporation Records; Hoover to Barnes, August 31, 1917, *ibid.;* and Hoover to G. W. McGarrah, August 13, 1917, Box 1-H, Food Administration Records.

16   Lindley to Hoover, August 9, 1917, File 14-H, Food Administration Records.

17   Georg Lukács, trans. by Rodney Livingstone, *History and Class Consciousness: Studies in Marxist Dialectics* (Cambridge: Merlin Press, 1971), p. 299.

18   Rickard to Lindley, February 8, 1918, File 14-H, Box 45, Food Administration Records.

19   For example, see "Memo," March 27, 1918, File 21-H, Box 56, *ibid.;* and Rickard to Lindley, April 10, 1918, File 14-H, Box 45, *ibid.,* both of which explain changes along these lines in the Food Administration's Distribution Division.

20   Edgar E. Robinson and Paul Carroll Edwards, eds., *The Memoirs of Ray Lyman Wilbur 1875–1949* (Stanford: Stanford University Press, 1960), p. 266.

21   See also Lindley's comment: "I, of course, do not mingle very much with the substratum of American life, but from what I can learn from all parts, Mr. Hoover is getting his reward in the appreciation of the grateful people." Lindley to Rickard, April 4, 1918, File 14-H, Box 45, Food Administration Records.

22   Quoted in Ray Stannard Baker, *Woodrow Wilson: Life and Letters* (Garden City: Doubleday, Page, 1939), 7:51n; Diary of Edward M. House, December 27, 1918,

February 10, 1918, June 17, 1918, House Collection, Yale University Library, New Haven, Connecticut. For a similar complaint, see Julius Rosenwald to Robert F. Brookings, September 20, 1917, File 21-Al, Box 28, Records of the War Industries Board, RG 61 (Federal Records Center, Suitland, Md.).

23   Hoover to Wilson, March 27, 1918, Wilson Mss.

24   Wilson to Hoover, November 26, 1917, *ibid.*

25   Herbert Hoover, *Addresses Upon the American Road: World War II, 1941–1945* (New York: Van Nostrand, 1946), p. 177.

26   Paul Bourke discusses the wartime views of some of the leading liberals and radicals in his "The Status of Politics 1901–1919: *The New Republic,* Randolph Bourne and Van Wyck Brooks," *Journal of American Studies,* 8 (August 1974), 171-202.

27   For this point in Hoover's overall professional ideology, see Layton, *Revolt of the Engineers,* p. 190.

28   George Soule, "The Control of Meat," *New Republic,* 14 (February 2, 1918), 14.

29   For example, Merritt, *War Time Control of Distribution,* p. 75.

30   Hoover to Brand Whitlock, November 5, 1917, Box 1-H, Food Administration Records. For his complaint about widespread profiteering, see Hoover to Walter Hines Page, September 22, 1917, *ibid.*

31   Hoover to Barnes, December 20, 1917, Box 246, Food Administration Grain Corporation Records.

32   Herbert Hoover, "Preliminary Note on the Organization of the Food Administration," June 1, 1917, Wilson Mss.

33   Quoted in Willoughby, *Government Organization,* p. 278.

34   Hoover to Wilson, May 31, 1917, Wilson Mss.

35   James T. Shotwell, *At the Paris Peace Conference* (New York: Macmillan, 1937), p. 13.

WITOLD S. SWORAKOWSKI

Herbert Hoover, Launching the American Food Administration, 1917

EDITOR'S INTRODUCTORY NOTE

Witold Sworakowski's paper is not so much another panegyric extolling Hoover's service as food administrator as it is a consideration of the circumstances that led to the formation of the United States Food Administration. Its time span focuses almost entirely on the interval from April 1917, when the United States intervened in the European War, through August 1917, when Hoover's appointment as food administrator was made official. The author takes it as uncontestable that Hoover's Food Administration was a resounding success. "This unanimity [judgment in the historiography]," he tells us, "makes it unnecessary to enter into a dialectical discussion of the success or failure of Hoover's assignment." Inasmuch as congressional committees did not venture to investigate the Food Administration, Sworakowski is content to accept the verdict of most contemporaries and most of his predecessors who have written on this subject. Somehow, the question lingers, by what criteria is the record of Hoover and his associates to be judged an unqualified success in the operation of the Food Administration?

Although the article mentions several times the Lever Act, the purpose of this statutory authority for the Food Administration might be explained here. Briefly put, the Lever Act (also known as the Food Control Act) as passed in August 1917, provided the nation's chief executive with rather sweeping, discretionary authority over food production and distribution even threatening extensive federal intervention in the entire agricultural economy. Such broad authority was favored by President Wilson and his advisers as a

Witold S. Sworakowski is professor emeritus at Stanford University and consultant to the Hoover Institution of War, Revolution and Peace, Stanford, California.

necessary means for offering financial incentives to farmers and as a device for stabilizing prices of American grains which at the time were in great demand. On August 10, 1917, in order to implement the Lever Act, Wilson issued an executive order creating the United States Food Administration and appointing Hoover to be its chief. Accordingly, Hoover's authority was made very broad, to include the following functions:

> . . . Said United States Food Administration shall supervise, direct and carry into effect the provisions of said act [Lever], and the powers and authority therein given to the President, so far as the same apply to foods, feeds, and their derivative products and to any and all practices, procedures, and regulations authorized or required under the provisions of said act, including the issuance, regulation and revocation in the name of said Food Administrator, of licenses under said act; and in this behalf he shall do and perform such acts and things as may be authorized or required of him by the President from time to time. . . . [1]

Utilizing this authority, Hoover made a deliberate attempt to decentralize the Food Administration's bureaucratic structure through the formation of units in all states and principal localities in order to enforce the government's fiat. The magnitude of the operation was truly remarkable. Within the United States alone, the Food Administration utilized the services of several hundred persons, and the overseas program required thousands more. Whether the Food Administration relied essentially on voluntary compliance by farmers and the public in conserving foodstuffs, as suggested by Sworakowski, has been questioned by commentators. As food administrator, however, Hoover stimulated food production by devising the means for managing a pricing structure for farm commodities. Seen from this perspective, the success of the Food Administration derived more from the substantial financial incentives offered by the government supported agricultural program and less from the patriotism of the farmers. It would seem therefore that Hoover was most seriously concerned about postwar American agriculture as it related to world agricultural production and to the commodity pricing structure. Did Hoover anticipate a decline in farm prices, or did he expect the continued need for government price supports? At the time, there was much concern about the future of agriculture expressed in the influential *Wallace's Farmer*. What must be appreciated is that Hoover's task was by no means limited to providing incentives to the nation's farmers for increased agricultural harvests or to encourage homemakers in the conservation of foods already in short supply. His assignment also came to include responsibility for shipments of food surpluses to meet the urgent needs of America's cobelligerents in Europe.

1   For text of the Executive Order, see Appendix B, "Executive Order Establishing the United States Food Administration, August 10, 1917," in Frank M. Surface, *The Grain Trade During the World War: Being a History of the Food Administration Grain Corporation and the United States Grain Corporation* (New York: Macmillan, 1928), pp. 517–18.

Herbert Hoover, Launching the American Food Administration, 1917

When the United States entered World War I in April 1917, it considered as one of its primary obligations the mobilization of the nation's food resources. The man who directed this mobilization was Herbert Hoover, and his spirited resoluteness and resourcefulness in carrying out the job was a principal contribution to the American war effort, a gigantic national endeavor that in large measure made victory possible in November 1918. Deeply believing in the moral strength of the American people, he entrusted to them the saving of this country and its European allies from a disastrous food shortage. Hundreds of thousands of men and women, inspired by the example of "the Chief" as a tireless volunteer, offered their time and energy in answer to Hoover's call to selfless service to the nation.

History books on World War I describe, frequently in great detail, many skirmishes, battles, and campaigns in the European theater that had minor importance for the final victory. In a war in which hunger was used with callous deliberation as a strategic weapon, the crucial battle fought and won on the American home front under Hoover's leadership—one that prevented internal collapse in the Allied countries as a result of deficient food supplies— has all too often been either overlooked or underestimated by historians.

The Food Administration and Hoover, its head, were not only eminently successful, but they were also remarkable in that no serious accusations were raised at any time against them. Not a single investigation by Congress, so numerous in the case of other wartime agencies of the Wilson administration, was undertaken against this agency or its chief. The dozens of articles and books published in the past fifty years on the activities and achievements of the Food Administration and its administrator have had nothing but praise and recognition for a job well done.[1] This unanimity makes it unnecessary to enter into a dialectical discussion of the success or failure of Hoover's assignment. From the perspective of more than fifty years, with the knowledge of the trials and errors of another food administration during World War II, and in the midst of a crippling energy crisis in our day, this study will focus on the ideological concept, the ways and means by which Hoover won the battle for food supplies on the home front and piloted the Food Administration to redoubtable accomplishments.

From its founding days, the United States either as a whole or in its particular regions had experienced difficulties in food provisioning as a result of bad crops, floods, inadequate transportation, and the calamities of the Civil War and the Spanish-American War. But none of these created as critical a situation for the entire population of the country as did the food shortage in the spring of 1917. The gap between supply and demand widened suddenly on the American market, and the prices of grain, bread, meat, oil, sugar, and milk rose uncontrollably from week to week. With wages and other earnings well stabilized, the purchasing power of the blue- and white-collar workers diminished painfully and threatened to unbalance seriously the prevailing economic equilibrium.

This upward trend of food prices reached an alarming level just as the United States was entering the war. The skyrocketing cost of food meant fewer calories at the dinner table of the average American family; it meant reducing the energy of the working people who became so important for the war industry. In the absence of some remedial action, a serious crisis involving hunger could well have developed, with crippling side effects for the war effort.

Under these calamitous internal economic conditions, on April 6, 1917, Congress overwhelmingly passed the declaration of war against Germany. Seven months later, in November 1917, the United States also declared war against Austria-Hungary. Congress, seriously concerned about the critical food situation, immediately began to search for ways of controlling the growing food shortage and preventing further increases in food prices. On April 21, the chairman of the House Committee on Agriculture, Asbury

F. Lever, introduced a bill on food control. Despite the urgency of this legislation, it took until August 10 for the Lever Food Control Act to become law. Democracy works slowly—even in time of war.

In the last days of April the press reported that President Wilson had asked the head of the Commission for Relief in Belgium, Herbert Hoover, to return as soon as possible to the United States. Taking advantage of leaks in official Washington, the press noted that the president wanted to consult Hoover on his experiences and observations in establishing the food administration in German-occupied Belgium and northern France. Having traveled freely to countries on both sides of the front lines, Hoover was familiar with the efforts of the warring nations to cope with their food scarcity.

Even before Hoover's return, the press speculated in early May that Wilson would appoint him "food controller," "food dictator," or "food czar." This all developed during a time when the broad American public knew little if anything about Hoover. His successful repatriation of thousands of American tourists stranded in England at the outbreak of the war had been favorably mentioned in the American press in 1914, but since then there had been only infrequent news items on his accomplishments in feeding the Belgians.[2] Only starting in May 1917, biographical sketches and articles on Hoover and his "Belgian adventure" began to appear in American newspapers and magazines. The American public at last learned details about the man, about his success in mining enterprises, about his skillful negotiations with the British, French, Belgians, and Germans that made it possible to save millions from hunger.

On May 3, 1917, Hoover landed in New York. His intensive work on the solution of America's worst food crisis was about to begin.

Since the summer of 1914 the United Kingdom, France, and Russia had been at war with the Central Powers. Italy joined the Allies in May 1915. Owing to wartime transport difficulties, Russia, the major European wheat exporter, disappeared from the markets of Western Europe in mid-1914. Rumania, a much smaller food exporter, followed soon after. The mobilization of farm labor into the armies of all the belligerent nations caused a sudden drop in the size of the 1915 grain crop of these countries. The fastest to recover was the country with the smallest grain production: the United Kingdom in 1917 had a larger wheat crop than its prewar average. Yet it still produced less than one-quarter of its needs.

Italy recovered its former production in 1918, but its once large grain import from Russia and Rumania had been blocked since late 1914, when Turkey's entry into the war closed the straits. France, deprived of its northern provinces, which were under German occupation, did not recover its prewar grain production until after the hostilities ended. United States wheat exports to the United Kingdom, Italy, and France before the war had not been of great consequence. In early 1915, however, the situation had changed radically. The United Kingdom, France, and some neutrals whose Russian deliveries had been cut off turned to the American commodities market to obtain as much foodstuffs as were feasible and that limited transport facilities could handle.

During the period 1906–13, the United Kingdom obtained an average of 78% of its wheat consumption through imports; France obtained 14%, and Italy, 24%. The Russian and Rumanian wheat exports to these three countries during the years 1906–13 averaged 14% to the United Kingdom, 27% to France, and 76% to Italy. Whereas at the start of war these countries were able to replace most of their former Russian deliveries by imports from Argentina, Australia, and India, by 1916—with the loss of ships in the war at sea—they had to partially abandon these distant sources. So they turned to the United States. The upshot, as shown in the tabulation below, was that by the critical year 1917, the once-insignificant wheat imports from the United States to these three countries had soared.

U.S. wheat exports to:	1909–13 average (in million bushels)	1917 total	1909–13 average (percentage of import)	1917 total
United Kingdom	49.0	121.9	22.3	59.0
France	2.5	36.0	6.4	41.0
Italy	3.1	29.5	5.4	38.2
Total exports	54.6	187.4		

Source: Frank M. Surface, *The Grain Trade during the World War* (New York: Macmillan, 1928), p. 23.

The increase in United States wheat exports to these three countries by 133 million bushels not only came during a bad 1917 crop year but drained the national reserve. The bidding on the American market by buyers from the three countries against one another, against buyers from neutral Europe, and against the

American consumer resulted in an increase in the price of the 1916 wheat harvest from $1.42 a bushel in late 1916 to $3.25 in May 1917. The index of farm products rose from the basic 100 in 1913 to 117 in July 1916, and to 235 on July 1, 1917.[3] It was not the farmer, but the middleman and the stock-market speculator who made the big profit at the expense of the American consumer.[4]

Animal products and oil, in great demand by the countries at war, also became scarce on the American market and their prices began to rise. Compared with the prewar annual averages, exports of beef, pork, and dairy products increased considerably. The foreign buyers were ready to pay the higher prices and the American consumer had to go along, further inconvenienced by scarcity on the home market. The market became demoralized and chaotic.

This was the food situation in the United States when on May 3 Hoover landed in New York.

Three months earlier, on February 1, 1917, the German government had declared unlimited submarine warfare. On February 3, President Wilson recalled the American ambassador from Berlin in protest against this violation of freedom of the seas for neutrals. These developments found Hoover in the United States, where he had come to settle certain matters of the Commission for Relief in Belgium. Hoover conferred in New York with Colonel Edward M. House, a confidant and chief adviser of President Wilson. House asked for a memorandum on what immediate steps the United States should take in case of involvement in the war against Germany. Torpedoing of ships from neutral countries, particularly American vessels, sharply exacerbated American-German tensions. Hoover delivered the requested memorandum to House on February 13.[5] Seven points of this memorandum dealt with political, financial, shipping, and other measures to be taken in order to help the Allies win the war. The eighth point discussed the possible food shortage and how it should be approached. On the same day, House forwarded the memorandum to Wilson who thought it provocative and, through Secretary of the Interior Franklin K. Lane, an old friend of Hoover's, and fellow Californian, invited its author to the White House. Hoover was in Washington on February 14 and 15, and visited the president who discussed the memorandum suggesting that it would be helpful if Hoover, on his return to Europe, could study the Allies' wartime economic organizations. On this occasion Lane told Hoover that in case of America's entry into the war he would be needed in Washington for food organization.[6]

Hoover left for Europe on March 13. On his return to Paris and London, he and his trusted staff members of the Commission for Relief in Belgium undertook, as suggested by Wilson, the study of Allied economic wartime measures. But his plans telescoped on April 2 when President Wilson requested that Congress declare war on Germany. Hoover quickly began preparations for his return to America. He cabled an intimate friend in Washington, Hugh Gibson,[7] that "the Belgian Relief will be fully organized within ten days and I shall be available for any appropriate service if wanted."[8] On April 6, the day the United States declared war on Germany, Gibson forwarded copies of this cable to House, Lane, and Frank Polk of the State Department.[9] A few days later, the American ambassador in London, Walter Hines Page, notified Hoover that the president wanted him to return to Washington "to organize the American food activities."[10] Gibson's message had obviously reached the president. Hoover accepted Wilson's invitation on condition that he also could continue to conduct the Belgian Relief, and asked that he be allowed to postpone his return in order to wind up current Relief work and also to complete the study of Allied wartime economic measures, including food needs.[11]

Everyone who at some time had dealings with Herbert Hoover was aware of how fast his orderly mind worked, how plans for complicated actions were set up by him in short order, sometimes in a few seconds. So it was not too surprising that, even before he left Europe, Hoover had definite plans for organizing a food authority in the United States. On April 18 Norman Hapgood, an American writer and war correspondent in London, alerted his friend Colonel House that Hoover was sailing for the United States: "He [Hoover] is somewhat worried: does not wish to undertake the work unless enough independence goes with it to make it successful: that is, he would not want to be under any department. I am writing this more tactfully to the President and Secretary Houston,[12] but to you I may speak without indirection."[13]

On the afternoon of his arrival in New York on May 3, Hoover talked to House, who noted in his diary: "He has a well-thought-out and comprehensive plan, if he can only put it into execution. . . . Hoover knows the question of food control as no other man does, and he has energy and driving force."[14] The next day House wrote a letter to the president about his conversation with Hoover:

Hoover, as you know, is just back. I hope you will see him. . . . He has some facts that you should know. He can tell you the whole story in about forty minutes, for I timed him.

I trust Houston will give him full powers as to food control. He knows it better than anyone in the world and would inspire confidence both in Europe and here. Unless Houston does give him full control I am afraid he will be unwilling to undertake the job, for he is the kind of man that has to have complete control in order to do the thing well.[15]

On arriving in Washington on May 4, Hoover must have discussed the food control problems with Agriculture Secretary Houston and reached an agreement with him. As Houston preferred not to get his department entangled in the economic aspects of the food crisis, he was willing to see Hoover handle them.[16]

On May 7 Hoover appeared before the House Committee on Agriculture, which was considering the Lever bill. At Hoover's request, this meeting was held behind closed doors, but the next day the *New York Times* gave a short report on the two-hour deliberations. According to the *Times*, Hoover told the committee that "he believed a special Commission should be created to aid the Department of Agriculture and the President in conserving the food supply, encouraging production, and bringing about equitable distribution." Hoover also had urged that Congress act immediately on the Lever bill.[17]

The following day Hoover appeared before the Senate Committee on Agriculture. He again asked for prompt action on the Lever bill, advised that a separate department of the government should deal with the food question, and proposed government control of grain and sugar distribution.[18] The *New York Times* report on this meeting was brief and rather vague. In his writings Hoover himself never mentioned these two appearances before the congressional committees, obviously not ascribing much importance to them.

On the afternoon of May 9, Hoover was received by the president.[19] There is no official record of this conversation. (Its contents, reconstructed from Hoover's later writings, are summarized below.) As Hoover was leaving the White House, press reporters asked him whether he would accept a position as food dictator. "I don't want to be food dictator for the American People. The man who accepts such a position will die on the barbed wire of the first line entrenchments."[20]

To other questions, Hoover replied that during his hour-long conversation with the president he had reported on food conditions abroad, on what the foreign governments had done about their food crises, and on the Allied governments' estimates of their food requirements from the United States.[21] Obviously he said not a word about the food crisis at home and how it should be met.

Later the same day Hoover conferred with the six cabinet members who comprised the Council of National Defense. Like other meetings of this council, it was secret. The *New York Times* again professed to know that "at this conference he [Hoover] cited the need for food control and told what the Allies are doing in this direction."[22]

On May 12 the newspaper carried an editorial entitled "The Food Question," which supported the president's plans for the solution of the food crisis and commented on Hoover's possible role in it.

On May 13 Hoover was again received by Wilson.[23] No record of this conversation is available, but it can be assumed that details on the future Food Administration were elaborated and the necessary changes in the Lever bill were discussed.

During the evening of May 15, President Wilson had a conference with Houston and the members of the House and Senate Committees on Agriculture. According to the president's official biographer, Ray Stannard Baker,

He [Wilson] emphasized the imperative necessity for prompt action on food control legislation, discussing "the food situation in the United States, in the allied countries, and in neutral countries which the United States must at least help to feed," and stating emphatically "that it would be difficult to express in parliamentary language what should be done with anyone who would speculate in food products in a situation like the present."[24]

The *New York Times* on May 16 brought out a dull report on the meeting but was still able to disclose:

The President told the committeemen that, in his opinion, the three factors that would control the war situation, in the order of their importance, were the actual fighting forces, control of the food situation, and control of transportation facilities of the country.

But by the next day, obvious leaks on Capitol Hill enabled the *Times* to carry more detailed information. Under the headline "Hoover Will Head New Board," it reported that the congressional committees were adjusting the Lever bill to the president's demands. The bill, if enacted, would establish a new agency that would be headed by one man who, along with a staff of assistants, would work without pay and would be authorized to use the services of other departments. The paper mentioned Hoover as the president's choice for head of this agency.[25] Clearly, these events on Capitol Hill were the effects of the May 15 conference in the White House. The president was able to influence both committees to go along with the plans he had adopted from Hoover. The necessary changes in the Lever bill demanded a tedious redrafting of its text, and this in turn resulted in new delays.

On May 18 the press reported opposition of "some senators" to the Lever bill and to the appointment of Hoover as head of the future food agency. However, it added, that the effects of this opposition were minimal.[26]

By now Wilson had obviously become annoyed by the leaks to the press and by sluggishness of Congress in passing the Lever bill. He asked Hoover to draft for his approval a public announcement in which the president would place before the American public the facts that motivated his request to Congress for immediate legislation giving him authority to establish a Food Administration for handling the food crisis and to appoint Hoover to head this agency.[27] This presidential announcement was issued on May 19 and appeared in the press on May 20. It contained an outline of the strategy agreed upon by Wilson and Hoover for the handling of the food crisis. It took Wilson and Hoover ten days to elaborate and to agree upon the details of their food-mobilization plans. It took Congress three more months to provide the legal basis—the Lever Food Control Act of August 10—for the implementation of their plans.

Hoover's writings provide the main source for reconstructing the Wilson-Hoover conversations that led to the president's acceptance of Hoover's food-mobilization proposals. It is impossible to establish at which conversation specific features of the strategy were agreed upon. The main questions and their proposed resolution are clear.

The pivotal problem—the future distribution of food—was solved in a manner that rejected the methods applied in the six European countries involved in the war. Hoover, who had had a ringside seat in observing food rationing in these countries, advised the president that the United States could and should avoid the pit-

falls of food rationing with its many "Prussianizing" ironclad regulations, its unavoidable bureaucracy, and the legal prosecution of
abuses. Hoover had firm confidence that American society was willing to cooperate, without coercion, in reducing consumption and
in conserving foodstuffs. Simple patriotism, he was sure, would be
far more effective than elephantine government regulations. He
was convinced American housewives would respond so vigorously
to his appeal to conserve food that surplus supplies could be delivered to the Allies. The press reported this daring approach in
one sentence: "Hoover puts it up to the women of America to conserve the food supply and win the war."[28]

Indeed, Hoover's proposal for voluntary food conservation by
the women of this country was not only daring, but it involved a
tremendous risk. The general American public, which accepted
without demurral Hoover's appeal for this system of food conservation, certainly did not realize the risk involved were the plan to fail.
It seems that not even the president was fully aware of the disastrous consequences that a failure of this voluntary system could
precipitate. Hoover, however, was well aware of the risk. He had
seen in Europe the miseries of people who lived on short, uncertain
food rations. He had had reports on the effects of food shortages
on the morale of the people in Germany and Austria-Hungary,
where in 1916 food rations had to be further curtailed. He knew
that the fall of the Romanov Empire in Russia, just a month before
he sailed for the United States, had been preceded by food
shortages and bread riots in Petrograd. He was well aware that by
the spring of 1917 morale behind the front lines in France and Italy
had reached a point close to the limits of endurance because of food
deficiencies. He realized that food was as important in the European war as were bullets. Hoover grasped that, owing to the new
technological inventions in armaments and the involvement of
Eastern, Central, and Western Europe in the war, for the first time
food could play a decisive role in the outcome of a war. Nevertheless, his confidence in the moral values of American society was so
strong and real that he pushed aside as nonexistent the risk involved in his voluntary system of food control. He had no doubts
that the system would be fully successful. His solid belief in America
brought Wilson around to his point of view.

The second major question was price regulation—in order to
protect both the producer and the consumer. Hoover proposed to
entrust this problem to the voluntary self-control of the producers,
distributors, and retail merchants in cooperation with the future

Food Administration. Reasonable wholesale prices and fair markups for distributors and local merchants, all reached through the cooperation of those concerned, would end hoarding, speculation, and overcharging of the consumer. Moral pressure and—if needed—reprisals by the Food Administration against those who would abstain from or oppose voluntary cooperation would correct their resistance. The creation of the Food Administration Grain Corporation as the agency that would buy the farmer's grain crop at a guaranteed price would protect the farmer and stimulate greater production. Finally, the centralization and control of all food exports by the Food Administration would put an end to the devious work of speculators on the commodities market. Again, by proposing a voluntary means of price control, Hoover was avoiding the pitfall of "Prussianizing" the relationship between producer, distributor, consumer, and federal authorities.

The third question was to determine the type of administration that would direct and supervise food conservation and price control. Before Hoover returned to the United States, during the first three weeks of the war, President Wilson, following the democratic practice of this country, created several "committees" and "boards" which were to direct and control in a collective manner particular sections of the nation's war effort. Thus production of armaments and munition, shipping, railroads, and a few other sectors were dealt with. These collective bodies with officers selected without regard to party affiliation were to make decisions in the best democratic tradition, after thorough study and discussion of the upcoming problems.

Hoover, who had had dealings with similar boards of divided responsibility in England and France, reached another conclusion:

> From observation of the host of such Allied failures in organization, I felt there must be a single head to the food problem and that his authority must cover every phase of food administration from the soil to the stomach. That included direct or indirect control over production, farm policies, conservation, exports, imports, buying for our military forces and those of the Allies, prices, rationing, processors, distributors and consumers.[29]

Hoover believed that unusual times demanded unusual measures. Rapidly changing situations demanded promptness and elasticity in decision-making. As a successful businessman, he was aware of the advantages of decision-making by a sole executive. Finally, the American system of government, with the broad executive powers of the president, justified his recommendation for a one-man executive for the Food Administration. His recent experience as the sole executive of the Committee for Relief in Belgium, and the successful conduct of its affairs under most complicated conditions, were valid arguments in his conversations with the president. His presentation was obviously strong enough to convince Wilson.[30]

He also convinced the president that his title as head of the Food Administration should be simply food administrator. Thus, he eliminated the undemocratic titles invented by newspapermen—"food dictator" or "food czar"—which he detested. The title "Food Administrator" was certainly an unprecedented novelty but it accurately described the functions of its bearer.

Hoover agreed to head the future Food Administration "on condition that he is to receive no payment for his services and that the whole of the force under him, exclusive of clerical assistance, shall be employed, so far as possible, upon the same volunteer basis."[31] This again was an innovation proposed and obtained by Hoover. To attempt to organize an embryonic nationwide service (and to do so in the shortest time possible) on a voluntary basis was a daring and courageous intention, again motivated by Hoover's confidence in the moral integrity and patriotism of his countrymen, and his experience with volunteers in the Committee for Relief in Belgium.

In a statement to the press on May 19, released the same day that President Wilson issued his announcement on the future Food Administration, Hoover explained his appeal to the American people for voluntary work:

> My intention is to see my own people solve their own problem. Those men and women who cannot serve in the trenches or the shops can show their patriotism in no way so fully as in this service, and I feel that we have as much right to call upon them to serve in the administration as we have a right to call upon our men to serve in the trenches.[32]

Countless press comments emphasized and supported Hoover's forthright appeal. And in those early days nobody could even dream of the numerical proportions that Hoover's volunteers would reach in the future.

The last question for which Hoover wanted to obtain the president's approval concerned the organizational principles for the Food Administration. He wanted to be responsible directly to the president. He was not concerned with details but wanted to have it clearly established that he had full responsibility for the operations of the Food Administration without any "board" that would hamper his activities, and that he was authorized to delegate responsibilities to decentralized local administrations. He explained to the press that he did not intend to draw up organizational charts in advance but to build up the organization, the central office in Washington as well as any regional or local divisions, as the need arose. In his statement to the Senate Committee on Agriculture on June 19, Hoover voiced a principle which he followed and applied thereafter: "Our theory of administration is that we should centralize ideas and decentralize execution."[33]

These were the policy principles worked out by Hoover during his conversations with the president and certain cabinet members, among whom Secretary of Agriculture Houston played a prominent role. At first they were not intended to be made public before the Lever bill was accepted by Congress. However, as mentioned before, leaks in official Washington revealed many details—true as well as distorted—that appeared in the press and that were repeated on Capitol Hill. Wishing to put an end to these rumors, and also irked by the halting progress of the Lever bill in Congress, the president decided to issue his announcement of May 19 on the future Food Administration and Hoover's role in it.[34]

On the same day Hoover distributed a press release in which he amplified the president's description of the future food agency and his tasks as head of it. The release contained also the following presentation of his concept of the Food Administration:

> I have presented to the President five cardinal principles of food administration.
>
> First: That the food problem is one of wise administration and not expressed by the words "dictator" or "controller" but "food administrator."
>
> Second: That this administration can be largely carried out through the co-ordination and regulation of the existing legitimate distributive agencies of the producers, distributors, and consumers.
>
> Third: The organization of the community for voluntary conservation of foodstuffs.
>
> Fourth: That all important positions, so far as may be, shall be filled with volunteers.
>
> Fifth: The independent responsibility of the food administration directly under the President, with the co-operation of the great

and admirable organization of the Department of Agriculture, the Department of Commerce, the Federal Trade Commission, and the railway executives.[35]

After May 19 a paradoxical situation developed. There was a detailed plan for handling the food crisis and for preventing hoarding, price increases, and speculation. A chief for the future food agency had been nominated and was anxious to start working. The time of the 1917 harvest was approaching and the crops had to be secured both for Americans and the Allies. But a key element was still missing: the legal basis for the activities of the future Food Administration. Chaos on the market and disorientation of the American public continued while the politicians on Capitol Hill were still delaying passage of the bill.

Both Wilson and Hoover realized that further idle waiting for the passage of the Lever bill would be highly damaging to the interests of the state and its public. On June 12 Wilson wrote to Hoover:

It seems to me that the inauguration of that portion of the plan for food administration which contemplates a national mobilization of the great voluntary forces of the country which are ready to work toward saving food and eliminating waste admits of no further delay.

The approaching harvesting, the immediate necessity for wise use and saving, not only in food but in all other expenditures, the many undirected and overlapping efforts being made toward this end, all press for national direction and inspiration. While it would in many ways be desirable to wait complete legislation establishing the food administration, it appears to me that so far as voluntary effort can be assembled, we should not wait any longer, and therefore I would be very glad if you would proceed in those directions at once. . . .

I trust . . . that the women of the country will not only respond to your appeal and accept the pledge to the Food Administration which you are proposing, but that all men also who are engaged in the personal distribution of foods will co-operate with the same earnestness and in the same spirit. I give you full authority to undertake any steps necessary for the proper organization and stimulation of their efforts.[36]

Hoover immediately appealed to American housewives to come forward and announce their pledge to join the future Food Administration in its efforts to save food and eliminate waste. The press, particularly the local papers, gave full support to this campaign, and the names of women who made the pledge started to appear in the newspapers. Within five months about twenty million Americans, mostly housewives, signed pledges that made them "members" of an agency that at first did not legally exist.[37] With the pledges snowballing, Hoover's tenacious belief in the patriotism of the American public passed its first test. The Hoover staff started to issue occasional instructions to the zealous housewives on how to preserve food. The Hoover motto for this campaign was "Eat plenty, wisely and without waste."

During discussions with representatives of producers, distributors, and processors of grain, Hoover explained the intentions of the future Food Administration and met with their willingness to cooperate. Plans were set up that would be implemented after the Lever bill became law. Businessmen and representatives of farmers' organizations were well aware of their responsibility in the mobilization of the United States for war and responded enthusiastically to the call for patriotic service. Many of the most helpful suggestions for the Food Administration's future actions came from them.[38]

After successfully jumping all the congressional hurdles, the much-amended Lever bill was accepted by the House on August 3 by unanimous vote. The Senate passed it on August 8 by a vote of 66 to 7. On August 10, 1917 (which also happened to be Hoover's forty-third birthday), the president signed the act into law, and presented to Hoover the pen with which he signed it.

Now the road was open for the full application of Hoover's knowledge, wisdom, and skill to lead and direct the American people and the trades of the nation in their voluntary efforts to cooperate with the government in the solution of the war-emergency food problems.

By presidential executive order on August 14 the U.S. Grain Corporation was created as a commercial subsidiary of the Food Administration. Its purpose was the buying, selling, and storing of grain and cereal products. Founded shortly afterward was the International Sugar Committee, which in July 1918 was transformed into the Sugar Equalization Board; both handled the regulation of sugar distribution in this country and for the Allies, who faced a severe sugar shortage.

Then, still in August, was started the organization of Food Administration branches in each state, in each county, and in thousands of localities. The women who earlier had pledged cooperation with the Food Administration played a prominent role in these subdivisions, particularly in the local branches. The entire executive personnel of these subdivisions and branches were volunteers. Only clerks and office help were salaried. The purpose of this country-wide network of Food Administration organizations was not only to promote conservation of food, but also to observe conditions on the local level and report to the Washington central office the execution of the Food Administration's rules and regulations. More than 750,000 volunteers manned these branches of the Food Administration.

No attempt can be made here to condense all the measures taken by Hoover and his Food Administration that assured the successful execution of the agency's aims and tasks. They are excellently described and fully documented in William C. Mullendore's *History of the United States Food Administration, 1917–1919*. Mullendore was one of the Food Administration's legal counsels and remained in its service during its entire time of operations. Created as a war-emergency agency, the Food Administration was partially disbanded after the signing of the Armistice on November 11, 1918, and finally dissolved immediately after the signing of the Versailles Peace Treaty on June 28, 1919.[39]

Hoover's major contribution to the tremendous war effort of the United States during World War I was the full success of the Food Administration that was his brain child. At home, in 1917 and 1918, enough food was saved to provide the Allies with foodstuffs that enabled them to feed their armies and their civilian population—sparingly but adequately. Unequivocably, American women helped to win the war. Thanks to their drive and enterprise, Hoover's demand and hope passed the supreme test. Hoover achieved what he wanted: "My intention is to see my own people solve their own problem."[40] He judged and evaluated his countrymen by his own standards. Demanding and obtaining the voluntary self-denial of millions of Americans and thereby subjugating the specter of hunger for America and its associates, Hoover had the great satisfaction of finding that his faith in his countrymen was justified. The great risk that he took in May 1917 by basing his "cardinal principles of food administration" on the voluntary services of the American people proved to be no risk at all. Growing up to his high stature in 1917 from humble orgins as one of the people, he knew well his country and its people. He trusted and relied on the American people, and was not disenchanted.

Herbert Hoover's performance as "Chief" of the Commission for Relief in Belgium, and of the American Relief Administration after World War I, made him known the world over as the Great Humanitarian. His devoted and selfless service to the nation as food administrator during the war, when by personal example he stimulated the patriotism of millions of Americans, established him as the Great American Patriot.

NOTES

1   Frank M. Surface and Raymond L. Bland, *American Food in the World War and Reconstruction Period: Operations of the Organizations under the Direction of Herbert Hoover, 1914 to 1924* (Stanford: Stanford University Press, 1931), pp. 990–94, contains a large bibliography on the Food Administration. There is also a chapter on this agency in an unpublished bibliography by Thomas T. Thalken, "American Overseas Relief Operations, 1914–1924" (manuscript in possession of its author).

2   Hoover's first experience as food controller took place not in Belgium but in China. At the age of twenty-six, as a mining engineer residing with his family in Tientsin, he was caught in the month-long siege of Tientsin during the Boxer Rebellion of 1900. To Hoover, already respected for his common sense and his knack for improvisation, fell the responsibility of strengthening the barricades and of organizing and distributing the food and water supplies of the beleaguered city's foreign compound. Eugene Lyons, *Herbert Hoover: A Biography* (Garden City, N.Y.: Doubleday, 1964), pp. 50–52.

3   William Clinton Mullendore, *History of the United States Food Administration, 1917–1919* (Stanford: Stanford University Press, 1941), p. 5.

4   Frank M. Surface, *The Grain Trade during the World War* (New York: Macmillan, 1928), pp. 28–29.

5   Herbert Hoover, *The Ordeal of Woodrow Wilson* (New York: McGraw-Hill, 1958), pp. 5–6 (full text of memorandum).

6   *Ibid.,* pp. 7–8.

7   Hugh Gibson, first secretary and chargé d'affaires at the American Legation in Brussels, collaborated with Hoover on Belgian Relief matters and they became close friends. In April 1917 Gibson was temporarily in Washington.

8   Edward M. House, *The Intimate Papers of Colonel House,* arranged as a narrative by Charles Seymour, 4 vols. (Boston: Houghton Mifflin, 1926–28), 3:16.

9   Gibson to his mother, April 6, 1917, Hugh Gibson Collection, Box no. 8, Folder April 1917, Hoover Institution Archives, Stanford University.

10   Hoover, *Ordeal,* p. 8.

11   *Ibid.*, pp. 8–9.

12   David F. Houston, secretary of agriculture.

13   House, *Intimate Papers,* 3:16–17.

14   *Ibid.*, p. 17.

15   *Ibid.*

16   Herbert Hoover, *The Memoirs of Herbert Hoover,* 3 vols. (New York: Macmillan, 1951–52), 1:241, 243.

17   *New York Times,* May 8, 1917, p. 3, and Ray Stannard Baker, ed., *Woodrow Wilson: Life and Letters,* 8 vols. (New York: Doubleday, Page, 1927–39), 7:53.

18   *New York Times,* May 9, 1917, p. 5, and Baker, *Wilson,* 2:57.

19   Baker, *Wilson,* 7:61.

20   *Ibid.; New York Times,* May 10, 1917, p. 4.

21   *New York Times,* May 10, 1917, p. 4.

22   *Ibid.*

23   Baker, *Wilson,* 7:66.

24   *Ibid.*, p. 70.

25   *New York Times,* May 17, 1917, p. 6.

26   *Ibid.*, May 18, 1917, p. 8. After he was named food administrator, Hoover was bitterly attacked in the Senate by Senator James A. Reed of Missouri. One of his highly publicized charges was that Hoover and some others had profited personally from the Commission for Relief in Belgium. This unsubstantiated accusation was effectively demolished by John White, an official in the Belgian Relief. The opposition of a few congressmen, who were appalled by the very idea of any sort of interference with the people's food rights, gave Hoover a hard time before the opponents were convinced of the soundness of his proposals. Hoover, *Memoirs,* 1:248.

27   Herbert Hoover, *An American Epic,* 4 vols. (Chicago: Regnery, 1959–64), 2:32.

28   *Evening Record* (Boston), May 17, 1917, in a dispatch from New York.

29   Hoover, *Memoirs,* 1:241.

30   Hoover, *Epic,* 2:29–30.

31   President Wilson's statement on the Food Law, May 19, 1917, in Ray S. Baker and William E. Dodd, eds., *The Public Papers of Woodrow Wilson, War and Peace* (New York: Harper, 1925–27), 2:43.

32   *New York Times,* May 20, 1917, pp. 1–2.

33   Mullendore, *Food Administration,* p. 70.

34   Full text in *Public Papers of Woodrow Wilson, War and Peace,* 1:42–44; also *New York Times,* May 20, 1917, p. 1.

35   Mullendore, *Food Administration,* p. 52; and *New York Times,* May 20, 1917.

36   Francis W. O'Brien, ed., *The Hoover-Wilson Wartime Correspondence, September 24, 1914 to November 11, 1918* (Ames: Iowa State University Press, 1974), pp. 28–29.

37   Lyons, *Hoover,* p. 101.

38   Mullendore, *Food Administration,* pp. 54–55.

39   The food supplied by the United States to its Allies during the Food Administration's period of operation totaled 23,103,266 metric tons. This massive contribution was made without cost to the American taxpayer. Of the $10,000,000 appropriated for administration of the agency, $7,862,669 was spent. Not only was all the money advanced the Food Administration by both congressional and presidential appropriation (including $150,000,000 as working capital) returned to the taxpayers, but the agency's two subsidiary organizations—the U.S. Grain Corporation and the Sugar Equalization Board—gave to the Treasury an additional sum of over $52,000,000. Mullendore, *Food Administration,* pp. 41, 355; Hoover, *Memoirs,* 1:270–71; and David Hinshaw, *Herbert Hoover: American Quaker* (New York: Farrar, Straus, 1950), p. 96.

40   Hoover's statement to the press on May 19, 1917, *New York Times,* May 20, 1917, pp. 1–2.

ROYAL J. SCHMIDT

Hoover's Reflections on the Versailles Treaty

EDITOR'S INTRODUCTORY NOTE

Although Herbert Hoover was not one of the five United States plenipotentiaries attending the Paris Peace Conference, his involvement in the general European settlement was nevertheless extensive. As a principal economic adviser with special responsibility for food and other kinds of relief, Hoover became involved in virtually every political as well as conventional economic question confronting the Conference. This was true because the need for relief and reconstruction for countries devastated by protracted warfare impinged upon nearly every other concern: controversies over territorial boundaries; the future status of Germany and the successor states in East-Central Europe; the potential expansion of bolshevism; the Russian civil war; the continuing Allied blockade; and the disputes over reparations.

Hoover's responsibilities were compounded further by the several functions that he performed concurrently. He served as economic adviser, American representative on various international economic commissions including the Supreme Economic Council when it was formed in February 1919, and as director general of relief and reconstruction in which capacity he was directly responsible to the Supreme War Council. Hence, by virtue of these different authorities under which he conducted business, Hoover was not only a servant of the United States government, but also served in an executive capacity as part of "the Supreme Control" of the Conference. In order to direct these often diverse operations, he found it expedient to recruit a sizable staff drawn mainly from American military personnel then in Europe and to develop an efficient intelligence network throughout the continent with stations and an elaborate communications facility linking them. Probably no other American leader excepting President Wilson, and possibly the other American plenipotentiaries, could

Royal J. Schmidt is professor of political science and history at Elmhurst College, Elmhurst, Illinois.

potentially affect the outcome of the proceedings at Paris to the extent that Hoover could.

Royal J. Schmidt's article that follows maintains that Hoover did exercise considerable influence during the Peace Conference. Yet, the reader should also bear in mind Hoover's subsequent disclaimer, criticism, and even profound disillusionment with the settlement of which he was supposedly an influential architect. This influence was later denied in Hoover's letter to President Wilson of June 4, 1919, wherein he instead claimed that he had had "no part in the Treaty making." It is indeed difficult to reconcile these subsequent statements disassociating himself from the collective American effort at Paris with Hoover's record of participation in the work of the Conference. For the historian, the problem of interpretation is further complicated by Hoover's singling out the economic provisions of the settlement for special opprobrium. Presumably, whatever influence he would have contributed would have applied chiefly to the economic provisions. Whereas many members of the American Commission to Negotiate Peace expressed private disappointments with the emerging treaties, few actually joined William C. Bullitt in resigning as a means for registering protest.

Hoover's expressions of critical dismay on reading Article X of the League of Nations Covenant present additional difficulties for the historian. Many persons, including thoughtful Americans, objected for good reason to Article X, sincerely believing it would be a mistake for the United States to "undertake to respect and preserve as against external aggression the territorial integrity and existing political independence of all Members of the League." The element that seems strange in Hoover's response is that at no time prior to the appearance of the whole draft of the peace treaty did he express any indication of his personal disenchantment with this "heart of the Covenant." Verbiage in Article X was nothing novel; it represented the logical culmination of President Wilson's public statements since May 1916. It is therefore difficult to believe that Hoover could have been innocent of Wilson's pronouncements on the function of the embryonic League in maintaining permanent peace. Like many Republicans who had supported the League as some purely juridical body capable of settling disputes between states, Hoover apparently had failed to grasp the fundamental innovation of Wilsonian universalism, namely, the doctrine of collective or mutual security. When he did so, in May 1919, he found it wanting.

When interpreting Hoover's retrospective writings about the Peace Settlement, Schmidt emphasizes the didactic values. By diagnosing the reasons for the failures of the Versailles Treaty, Hoover hoped the American people and their Allies during the Second World War would be able to avoid the errors of their fathers. From a close examination of Hoover's analysis, it is possible to perceive his values and philosophy of international relations. One lesson is clear: Hoover apparently had no regrets that the United States had not joined in the League of Nations.

Hoover's Reflections on the Versailles Treaty

"No document or treaty is worth more than the good will behind it. The whole of history goes to prove that mere signing of treaties alters nothing unless the causes of war have been allayed."

Herbert Hoover, November 6, 1943

The basic objective of the following study is to ascertain the views held by Herbert Hoover regarding the Versailles Treaty and his estimate of its general significance to postwar America and the world. The main sources have included the substantial collection of Hoover's unpublished papers at the Hoover Presidential Library, West Branch, Iowa, mainly for the 1918–25 period, and his published books, speeches, and articles. While Hoover's own writings have necessarily been stressed, many other sources have been scrutinized to discern whether they offer added and worthwhile information or relevant interpretations of Hoover's views of the Treaty.[1]

Hoover, a highly successful mining engineer, had been living abroad for eighteen years prior to World War I. During this period and for some years prior to it, he had traveled extensively and had become a world citizen as well as a citizen of the United States. In October 1914, he was instrumental in the founding of the Commission for Relief in Belgium, a voluntary private organization with himself as chairman. He subsequently made many visits to war-torn

Belgium and could never forget the horrors of war which he witnessed at first hand. Eventually he succeeded in securing agreements with the British to permit food, clothing, and medical supplies to pass through the Allied blockade. The Germans, for their
part, promised to give protection to the distribution of these supplies to the people of Belgium and northern France.[2]

To underwrite the cost of Belgian relief, Hoover ultimately received subsidies from the governments of France, Britain, and the
United States. Later, as food administrator in President Wilson's
administration, he directed the distribution of 18,500,000 tons of
food to the Allies and famine-stricken areas of Europe. Subsequently he served as alternate chairman of the Supreme Economic
Council and as a member of the advisory economic committee of
the U.S. delegation to the Paris Peace Conference of 1919. Located
in the Hotel Crillon, he had frequent opportunities to meet and
converse with delegates to the Conference. Here he coordinated
the continuing work of the Food Administration, the Belgian and
Northern France Relief Mission, and the Relief and Reconstruction
of Europe Commission of which he had been appointed director
general by the Allied governments. His operations, which spread
over thirty-two European countries, involved the development of
an extensive organization covering these countries and eventually
recruited nearly 4,000 personnel from the American armed forces
in Europe. Hoover and his relief organization probably exercised
considerable influence and power in Europe during the course of
the Peace Conference and after. It is possible, as he alleges, that his
organization in Europe had considerably more accurate information than was available to the Peace Conference delegates. In any
event, it is quite germane to this study to note that during the
course of his relief work Hoover undoubtedly gained many of the
impressions which motivated and influenced his reactions to the
Versailles Treaty.[3]

A letter to President Wilson, April 11, 1919, expresses some of
Hoover's concerns with regard to the European situation while
negotiations with Germany were still in progress:

> It grows upon me daily that the United States is the one great moral
> reserve in the world today and that we cannot maintain that
> independence of action through which this reserve is to be
> maintained if we allow ourselves to be dragged into detailed
> European entanglements over a period of years. In my view, if the
> Allies cannot be brought to adopt peace on the basis of the 14

points, we should retire from Europe, lock, stock, and barrel, and we should lend to the whole world our economic and moral strength, or the world will swim in a sea of misery and disaster worse than the dark ages. If they cannot be brought to accept peace on this basis, our national honor is at stake and we should have to make peace independently and retire. I know of nothing in letter or spirit of any statement of your own, or in the 14 Points, that directly or indirectly ties the United States to carry on this war through the phase of enforcement, or the multitudinous demands and intrigues of a great number of other governments and their officials. It does appear to me that your conception of the League of Nations was with view to the provisions of a dominant Court, where the difficulties could be thrashed out and if we sit as one of the prosecutors, the Court will have no judge.[4]

On May 14, 1919, Hoover wrote to Wilson on a subject which suggests the intricate pattern of economic and political problems involved. Hoover hoped that Wilson could agree that the United States "should not be led into joining with the Allies in a food blockade of Germany as a method of forcing peace." Although he granted that a blockade might secure the German signature to the Treaty, he seriously doubted "whether when the world has recovered its moral equilibrium that it would consider a peace obtained by such a device as the starving of women and children as being binding upon the German people."[5]

Hoover wrote to Wilson again on June 4 expressing the hope that the president would not "take it amiss" if he forwarded some comments on the Treaty. Hoover noted that he had had "no part in the Treaty making," and for this reason and due to the "independent sources of information which he had enjoyed," he felt that he had had "a useful opportunity in objective observation." He wanted Wilson to know, however, that he was prepared in any event to "stand by" any course which the president chose to take. Hoover was apparently convinced that the Germans would not sign the Treaty without considerable modification. He felt that even if Germany did sign and accept the stated terms this would not secure stability. If she refused, she would probably extinguish the possibility of democracy in favor of either communism or reaction. In the process, the very foundation of the League of Nations would be wrecked.[6] Hoover's concern for the development of democracy and a representative governmental system appears to be a recurring theme in his observations of the peace settlement.

Hoover's first look at the draft Treaty had come on May 7 when he was sent a copy. This was the precise day on which the draft was to be handed to the Germans. At that time, he "was convinced that the terms set up in this draft of the Treaty would degrade all Europe and that Peace for the long run could not be built on these foundations." He strongly believed that the Treaty "contained the seeds of another war." It seemed to him that the economic provisions alone would "pull down the whole continent and, in the end, injure the United States." In discussing the Treaty with the British economist, John Maynard Keynes, and the South African leader, General J. C. Smuts, there seemed to be an agreement among these three that the consequences of many parts of the proposed Treaty would "ultimately bring destruction." According to Hoover's later writings, he and Keynes "agreed fully on the economic consequences of the peace."[7]

Joseph C. Grew, secretary-general of the American Commission, who was assigned the thankless task of parceling out tickets to a limited number of guests, anxious to witness the signing of the Treaty in the Hall of Mirrors at Versailles, described Hoover as "one ray of sunlight in a dark atmosphere who said he had never expected to be included and expressed surprise and gratification at receiving a card." "A great man with a child's modesty," observed Grew, "is to be appreciated yea much." Apparently other aspiring observers of the ceremony had made Grew bear the brunt of considerable abuse and recrimination. During the signing of the Treaty at Versailles, Hoover had some difficulty keeping his mind on the ceremony. He was thinking of "the fearful consequences of many paragraphs which these men were signing with such pomp."[8]

Clemenceau and the French were strongly opposed to any modification of the Treaty. Recognizing this fact, President Wilson apparently concluded that the world must be "saved from chaos" by signing the Treaty with the hope that its wrongs might, in time, be ameliorated by the League.[9]

Hoover and his staff were inclined to recall that in the past European statesmen had periodically dismembered Germany only to live to see it unified in the explosion of war. They were also "completely agreed" that the provisions for monetary and commodity reparations required from Germany by the Treaty would bring speedy disaster. They were certain that ceaseless claims for damages without setting some fixed sum within Germany's capacity to pay would inevitably stifle her ability and incentive to maintain production. There was also a conviction that the initial reparations payment of five billion dollars in cash, coal, machinery, tools, and ships would strip Germany of working capital. This obligation alone would prevent her from regaining industrial productivity from which reparations could be paid. Germany's coal supply would be cut nearly in half by her loss of Alsace-Lorraine, the Saar for fifteen years, and part of Silesia. The Germans would have no fuel for household use if they were to keep their industries going. There were additional shortcomings noted. Hoover and his staff detected elements of empire building in the mandates system, an observation which history would tend to substantiate. Although Hoover staunchly defended the Covenant of the League, he had fears with respect to the probable outcome of Article X and the coercive provisions. Whether these fears became serious concerns for Hoover in May and June of 1919, or developed later cannot be wholly ascertained. It seemed clear that the Germans could, with considerable truth, claim that the Treaty was far removed from Wilson's "basis of peace" on which they had surrendered. The staff was convinced that if the Germans did sign without substantial re-laxation in terms, there would be no recovery in Germany and the Treaty would, sooner or later, need to be revised. Hoover and his colleagues in the relief organization sought, with limited success, to use their influence to improve the Treaty. Some, like Vance McCormick, who directed controls over imports, exports and blockade matters, refused to accept Hoover's critical analysis of the Treaty and expressed an opinion that his pessimism was exagger-ated. To this Hoover replied, "Just wait about five years and see."[10]

While supporting the League, Hoover had doubts about Article X of the Covenant, which guaranteed the boundaries of all the signatory states and made provisions for economic and military sanctions in case of aggression. He was doubtful whether an or-ganization so revolutionary and so young could successfully carry the burdens imposed by this controversial article. Colonel House advised Hoover, however, that President Wilson considered Article X and the provisions for coercion to be the heart of the League Covenant. Whereas Wilson and House were against separation of the Covenant from the Treaty, Secretary of State Robert Lansing told Hoover that such a separation might actually facilitate ratifica-tion. Rightly or wrongly, the heart of the resistance to the Treaty seemed to revolve around Article X. Opposition in the Senate and the country to ratification was concentrated mainly on this article.[11] Wilson's convictions to the contrary, Hoover and his staff felt that the Covenant would really be more effective without the controversial article. They believed that the Covenant provided a powerful organization; that its provisions for determining aggression and its authority to use economic and military sanctions were adequate. For Hoover the major purpose of the League was "to serve as a medium of pacific settlement of controversies among free nations." On the other hand, he and his staff had grave doubts about guaranteeing the boundaries of all the thirty-two signatories to the League inasmuch as some of them were already at war over boundary disputes.[12] It seemed to Hoover that the tendency of Article X was toward emphasis on a status quo, whereas the lessons of history suggested the inevitability of change.

Aside from serious misgivings about Article X and other aspects of the Treaty, Hoover and his staff felt that Europe had to have peace at once in order to halt the drift toward economic and social degeneration. Hoover announced to the press, July 28, 1919, that the Treaty was "an absolute necessity if this war were to be ended." As for the League, it was "our one hope of our correcting the dangers of the Treaty." On the other hand, Henry Cabot Lodge and many of the opposition in the Senate demanded amendments that would make it clear the United States would assume no obligations to interfere in controversies between nations as set forth in Article X or to employ armed force without authority of Congress. Hoover advised the press that "whatever the reservations implied, they did not in my mind destroy the great major functions of the League and except for Article X they could possibly be modified." On November 19, 1919, prior to the Senate's vote, Hoover wrote Wilson to urge the acceptance of a compromise. The letter was never acknowledged. At this time, Hoover wanted Wilson to accept the reservations with few exceptions. Hoover regarded some of the reservations as constructive—especially the one which placed emphasis on the war power being exercised by Congress. He actually did not believe that any of the reservations tended to imperil the principle of the League of Nations working to prevent war. David Hunter Miller, who had a large part in the drafting of the Covenant, agreed with Hoover that Wilson was attaching too much importance to the reservations. Miller, in later years, argued that "So far as the Lodge reservations made changes in the League, they were of a wholly minor character; they left its structure intact, and they would have interferred with its workings not at all.[13]

On November 19, 1919, Hoover expressed his belief that "with the League once in motion it can within itself and from experience and public education develop such measures as will make it effective." He was apparently impressed with the desperate necessity for early ratification. Delays, he felt, had "already seriously imperiled the economic recuperation of Europe." "In this," he observed, "we are vitally interested from every point of view." Hoover saw a need for putting the Covenant "into constructive operation at once because the American public would not appreciate the saving values of the Covenant as distinguished from the wrongs imposed by the Treaty." "These wrongs," Hoover argued, "will day by day become more evident to the entire world and will be confused with the Covenant itself." He felt that it could only be a matter of days until actual starvation would begin in Vienna. In his opinion, "the insistence by England, France and Italy upon political isolation of Austria from Germany must bear the fundamental responsibility." Hoover also was concerned about the possibility of the Treaty becoming a political issue in the coming 1920 election year. He feared that it would become confused with American domestic issues and racial prejudices. It would be difficult to "secure the clear voice of the American people on the Covenant itself." The shades of difference between Democratic and Republican reservations were "too fine for alignment of public opinion."[14]

In a June 5, 1919, memo to Wilson, Hoover stated that an impression existed in his mind that one objective of the proposed Treaty "seemed to be to take all the economic surplus of Germany for a generation." He warned that if more than the surplus were taken the population would either die, migrate, or plunge into economic chaos that would engulf Europe. Hoover observed that the coal to be furnished the Allies for reparations and lost to Germany by cession of coal territory such as the Saar, Silesia, and Teschen would, in total, reduce Germany's supply to little more than the household consumption, leaving nothing for railways, utilities, and manufacturing establishments. Hoover's sharp criticism, however, apparently produced an angry response from Wilson and the break between the two men seems to have been fairly complete thereafter. Another objective of the Treaty appeared to Hoover to set up a regime and control which would strip Germany of her power of political and military offensive. He thought that this assumed the desirability of establishing a stable democracy in Germany, for otherwise "she will turn to Communism or Reaction." Hoover was "not sure how far we ought to sacrifice the United States to the objectives of the European Allies." He thought that the opportunity had arrived for President Wilson to "absolutely insist on his original contentions (the fourteen points and supplementary addresses) even at the risk of disruption of the [Peace] Conference."[15]

World War II and the need for looking ahead to the peace which would follow it ultimately led Hoover to refer frequently to the record of the Versailles Treaty and its implications. He felt that the world had been poorly prepared for peacemaking in 1919. In describing his own reactions to the Paris Peace Conference, he begins by referring to the Armistice which had lasted for nine long months. During this period, says Hoover, a thousand diplomats of forty nations, in daily sessions, wrangled and struggled to settle the gigantic problems which had been thrust upon the world. After this there was a long period of uncertainty in the ratification of the Treaty. In connection with the Conference, Hoover's main job as relief commissioner was to face the gaunt realities of hunger and pestilence which threatened to destroy the very foundations upon which a lasting peace must be built. At the Conference, Hoover daily witnessed the impact of "age-old forces of nationalism, imperialism and militarism acting under the direction of subtle diplomacy." He saw "the rise of selfish interests, the clash of ideals and the competition of personalities and selfish ambitions." The bringing together of vindictive forces tended to intensify the old conflicts and to generate new ones. It created "countless nests of intrigue." Attempts to solve over a hundred problems at once provided "infinite opportunity for dark corner operations in trades and combinations." Hoover, writing in 1942, recalled that the whole Conference ultimately had degenerated into "a gigantic struggle for power." In this conflict the spiritual forces of idealism, conciliation, and justice were gradually driven back by the forces of destruction. Peacemaking was "swept down the terrible stream of intrigue, power politics and conflict." It was wrecked in a "whirlpool of destructive compromise and upon the rocks of selfish interest and emotional action." Hopes for a negotiated peace gave way to an "imposed peace" by the powerful.[16]

The Peace Conference and the Versailles Treaty not only failed to allay or still the destructive and dynamic ideological and economic forces present at the peace table, but also failed to control the excesses of nationalism and related forces. It actually stimulated many of these forces. Hoover, in later life, looking back on these years and thinking ahead to the need for peace following World War II, felt that unless the forces of fear, hate, and revenge between peoples and nations could be "turned aside, the world will again enter upon the ceaseless treadmill of war." Hoover felt that "the purpose of peace making must be to establish a regime of law and justice, not regimes of hate." He believed that unless such forces were dealt with vigorously by the nations, the "seeds of war will again be planted which no organization can for long curb."[17]

In a speech given at Minneapolis in 1943, Hoover insisted that no lasting peace could be made as was attempted at Versailles in the middle of a military armistice. Such an armistice "simply suspends the whole world between war and peace." The machinery and routines of both war and peace are out of action. Such a situation involved "a period of economic and political degeneration with an agonized world crying out for haste." The end product tended to be "a hasty compromise of principle and justice," not a real and viable solution. Versailles, "the greatest tragedy in modern history," according to Hoover, provided a lesson which suggested that no abiding and successful peace could ever be written in a few weeks or months under such pressures.[18]

Looking ahead toward the possibilities for a lasting peace following World War II, Hoover insisted that peoples of the world would need to face the fact that "a period of disturbing years must inevitably elapse after the next victory over our enemies." Whether this transition period resulted in degeneration and a third world war or whether it involved a period of transition from war to lasting peace depended upon "what we do during that period." Hoover differed strongly from those who visualized another general conference after World War II like that held at Versailles in 1919. This, he argued, should be avoided. Men were "no greater today than in the past nor could they see any further into the future than they have done before." It was likely, no matter what pomp and circumstance heralded a new treaty, that the "forces of change would put it again in the wastebasket."[19]

On the strength of his analysis of the Versailles Treaty, Hoover came to believe that "no document or treaty is worth more than the good will behind it." He felt that all history tended to prove that the "mere signing of treaties alters nothing unless the causes of war have been allayed." At Paris in 1919, "the things that should have been done quickly and imposed on the enemy to start the world again to political life and economic productivity were delayed nine months while the economic world degenerated." On the other hand, "long view problems that should have been given years of development were settled in nine months and settled wrong." As a result, "the world was once again to move into war."[20]

Hoover was critical of the lack of preparedness for peacemaking which characterized the situation by 1918. "We went to the Peace

Conference in 1919," he recalled, "animated by the loftiest and most disinterested ideals, but were totally unprepared for the specific problems and the ambushes that had to be met at the peace table." In any event, Hoover was convinced that very little real or lasting peace was secured. There should be "just as much preparedness for peacemaking as there was for war."[21]

The economic consequences of Versailles were, in Hoover's judgment, disastrous. They not only failed to heal the economic wounds of the world but opened up and irritated new ones. The continuation of the blockade during the armistice period, in violation of a pre-armistice agreement, which had led Germany to believe that the peace would not be unconditional but would be based on Wilson's fourteen points, caused steady economic degeneration. The creation of a host of new small nations with many new boundaries and "no restraints on their barriers to trade" ultimately contributed to impoverishment and despair. Trade barriers were increased rather than eliminated. Hoover referred to the "preposterous method of collecting reparations" as conducive to "periodic world jitters over its periodic readjustment." These "impossible inter-governmental obligations," he argued, "were a running sore for 20 years." Little was done toward relieving the world of the cost of arms; no effort was made to stabilize the currencies. The whole economic field, in Hoover's opinion, was largely neglected. The consequent destructive economic pressures "had much to do with the violence of the hurricane of economic depression and revolution that came ten to fifteen years later." On the other hand, Hoover maintained that the most constructive economic action at Paris was "the relief of several hundred million starving people and action to restore communication and transportation." He also felt that the Peace Conference was correct in its belief that representative government provided the best hope for securing peace.[22]

Hoover proposed that after World War II we have "no armistice" and "no general peace conference" such as the one at Versailles. His suggestion was to "set the peace-making in two stages." First, there should be a "conditional peace" that would "turn the world toward political, economic, and spiritual recovery without the delays of last time." Second, the world should then "take time to cool off and work out, one by one and separately, the solutions for lasting peace."[23]

Hoover detected and deplored an assumption that nationalism and government must necessarily be based on and tied up with race. Such extreme racialism did prevail in the states of Eastern Europe. These states, Hoover felt, were set up without regard to their economic life or defense. They erected new trade barriers, built large armies and huge fortifications along their frontiers and entered into conspiracies and intrigues against each other. This friction had arisen long before the emergence of Hitler. Excessive racialism led to efforts to curb the cultural expression of minorities. Mother countries began to clamor for the return of their minorities.[24] The Sudeten example was only one of several.

Hoover also came to believe by 1942 that one of the major failures of the Treaty was that it permitted Germany to keep an army of 100,000 men and a small navy. In these forces even the privates were potential officers. Their generals and their staffs, as visualized by Hoover, "sat plotting war again." The continuity of the General Staff was insured along with their know-how to make war. Hoover favored complete disarmament of the defeated nations. He assumed that, after World War II, the victors would not make "the major mistake of Versailles," but would demand the absolute disarmament of Germany so that they would not be able again to engage in aggression. Only a constabulary force would be maintained which would exclude all Nazis or previous army officers. Disarmament should be continued for a generation or two.[25]

Outstanding in its threat to the peace of Europe were the hates and fears which developed between France and Germany. Hoover came to feel that French policies during the interwar years produced an impression upon the Germans which tended "to heighten every German hatred and confirm every fear of encirclement and destruction." In Hoover's opinion, France had a choice between two courses. One would involve holding Germany down by sheer force of arms. The other was the more conciliatory policy of sustaining a democratic regime in Germany which would give her an economic chance. Hoover felt that France actually followed neither course consistently and the conciliatory one least of all. During the whole period from 1918 to 1938, "France tended to be a stumbling block to every proposal for world advancement, constantly demanding guarantees for her own security as a price of cooperation with other nations in any direction." At the same time, she tended to alienate her major and natural enemies. Both Hoover and his colleague Hugh Gibson came to believe that French conduct helped to alienate the United States from all European problems. Writing in 1942, Hoover referred to the whole course of French diplomacy as "incredible" and described it as governed by "the age-old forces of fear and hate doing their suicidal worst." The incorporation of the Sudeten Germans into Czechoslovakia, for example, was described by Hoover as the result of French pressure at Versailles regardless of the expressed misgivings of President Masaryk and Dr. Eduard Benes.[26]

Hoover and Gibson argued that there could be "no doubt that the preponderant judgment of the world was that provisions in the Treaty of Versailles," formulated in the heat of war, with its violations of Wilson's Fourteen Points and his subsequent addresses "were destructive of peace and recuperation in Europe." Whereas Wilson and Hoover had both hoped that the cooling of war emotions would permit a wider vision of reconstruction and a possible correction of Treaty weaknesses by the League, this proved to be a vain hope. The veto power of the Allies over every League action restricted it largely to a tool for the preservation of the status quo.[27]

Hoover pointed to the poor judgment of those defenders of the status quo who regarded the Treaty as immutable and sacrosanct. Arguments raised by this group suggested that any attempt to reconsider a single article of the Treaty was nothing less than "a sinister attempt to undermine its whole fabric." Many people came to believe implicitly that all change must be resisted on high moral grounds. Hoover felt that these persons could apparently not see that change, "instead of being the enemy of peace," was in reality "essential for its preservation." Hoover insisted that history was "a story of growth, decay, and change." If no provision nor allowance was made for peaceful, evolutionary change, it would "come anyway and with revolutionary violence." Treaties should not be regarded as being on a superhuman plane. Furthermore, treaties which were forced upon nations were "not upon the same plane as those that are entered into freely and willingly." Though the war was mainly responsible for preparing the soil for later totalitarian revolutions by its contribution of destruction, untold miseries, disillusionment, and moral degradation, the Treaty also bequeathed other destructive legacies. The conduct of the dominant powers in the years following the Treaty contributed greatly to driving peoples to further desperation.[28]

Referring to history, Hoover noted that earlier treaties such as that of Westphalia (1648) and Vienna (1815) had not tried to punish vanquished nations or put them into economic bondage. Possibly, he suggested, this explains why they were more durable than the Versailles Treaty. Hoover and Gibson came to contend that "no nation can be punished as a whole, and at the same time leave any hope of lasting peace." They felt that the "endless tread-mill of punishment must be stopped in the world if there is to be real peace." Victory dominated by vengeance "spelled ultimate defeat in the modern world." "We can have peace or we can have revenge," they suggested, "but we can not have both."[29]

In an article written in 1943, during the middle of World War II, Hoover stressed the futility of alliances and suggested that the "ghastly display of scraps of paper behind us" might suggest that "we might try some other approach than the Treaty of Versailles with its 613 precisely worded paragraphs which attempted to anticipate and fix the world to come, together with the conduct of the peoples in it." Whatever the regional or world structure to preserve peace might be, it would be "futile unless the foundations were properly laid." Referring to the sins of omission and commission in the Versailles Treaty, Hoover noted that of the 613 paragraphs of the Treaty only 26 dealt with the League Covenant. He believed that the remaining 587 paragraphs had done the most to kill the League. The sins of omission and commission in these 587 paragraphs had "laid some of the kindling for this war." "If we make a good peace," Hoover insisted, "it will largely preserve itself. If we make a bad one like Versailles, we shall simply be laying the kindling of World War III and no machinery for preserving peace will stop it from taking fire."[30]

Hoover's critical views of French policy in the postwar years undoubtedly received considerable stimulus from policies connected with the French decision to occupy the Ruhr industrial area of Germany in 1923 and the debatable contention that this was entirely in line with sanctions as outlined in the Treaty. It should be recalled at this point that the postwar atmosphere of distrust, hatred, desire for revenge, and lust for territorial expansion obviously contributed to the built-in weaknesses of the Versailles Treaty which Hoover deplored and about which he expressed such serious misgivings. He also was concerned with the general failure to abide by some of the pre-Armistice and Armistice promises. The emotional *Zeitgeist* of the postwar era, needless to say, was more conducive to a spirit of revenge, on both sides of the Rhine, than to a spirit of conciliation. Although the bitter Germanophobia of these years began to decline somewhat in England and the United States by 1922, it was carefully nurtured by nationalist politicians and other pressure groups in France. In January 1923, Premier Raymond Poincaré, pressed by nationalist and militarist forces in France, including influential leaders of the French Steel Trust, the *Comité des Forges,* which was seeking control of a guaranteed supply of high grade coke from the Ruhr area of Germany, sent French troops into the region ostensibly to insure a flow of reparations payments to France. Actually France had moved earlier in this direction under Millerand in 1920 and Briand in 1921. The cities of Düsseldorf, Duisburg, and Ruhrort remained occupied until the summer of 1925. In 1923 the Belgians, although uneasy with Poincaré's new coercion policy, felt obliged to support the policy of their French allies, but did so reluctantly.[31]

There is little reason to doubt but what the germs of the ensuing Ruhr conflict were firmly imbedded in the Versailles Treaty— especially in its reparations, sanctions, and war guilt clauses. The vague and indefinite statements on reparations had, as Hoover had correctly prophesied earlier, led to unlimited wrangling and much bitterness.[32]

Article 231, the war guilt clause of the Treaty, fixing sole guilt on Germany for the war, was both inaccurate and unjust. It set the stage for virtually unlimited demands upon her with little or no serious effort to ascertain her capacity to pay. The Treaty made it possible for the French dominated Reparation Commission and the Rhineland High Commission to have their own way in determining reparation and occupation policies. In instigating the Ruhr occupation in 1923, Poincaré represented himself as the dedicated champion of strict interpretation of the Treaty. Actually, he was adopting a revisionist course which proceeded to stretch the interpretation of the reparations and sanctions clauses to suit his own purposes.[33]

Poincaré recognized that the Ruhr area was the key industrial area of Europe by 1923 and of fundamental importance to Germany as a power. Control of the area would not only provide a steady supply of high grade Ruhr coke needed for French metallurgical development, but would probably insure France and the *Comité des Forges* a dominant metallurgical role on the continent. It might also hasten French control over the preponderantly German Rhineland and perpetuate a disunited, dismembered, and decentralized Germany. Poincaré's minimum objectives probably included the possibility of permanent French control of the Rhineland, a revival of France's historic Rhine policy. His maximum goals probably envisioned permanent French control of the Ruhr and the political disintegration of Germany. French aid to separatist movements in Germany was very extensive and designed mainly to hasten the emergence of permanent French control in the Rhineland, Saar, Palatinate, and probably the Ruhr. It was also designed to prolong chaos in Germany, promote her dismemberment and to perpetuate her weakness.[34] All of this was, of course, highly detrimental to policies favored by such leaders as Wilson and Hoover who preferred a policy which sought to encourage the speedy reintegration of Germany into the total European system and to support the efforts of the Weimar Republic to make a success of representative government.

The French Ruhr policy was not successful in bringing large amounts of reparations to France, in securing permanent French control of the Rhine-Saar-Ruhr areas, or in bringing about the disintegration of Germany. Neither did it safeguard the sanctity of the Versailles Treaty. The Ruhr occupation, in a strictly legal sense, was actually contrary to the Treaty and was tantamount to a renewal of war. The policy served mainly to unite German opposition and to inflame bitter hatred for France among Germans of all classes.[35]

Historians have tended to overlook the need for a careful scrutiny of the French Rhine-Saar-Ruhr policy, its relation to the Treaty and its impact on the resurgence of fanatical German nationalism. This may, of course, be partly due to the failure of the French to open their national archives for this period. Kept within bounds by the statesmanship of a moderate nationalist, such as Gustav Stresemann, this spirit need not have paved the way for an extremist such as Hitler. The death of Stresemann and the coming of the Great Depression, however, pushed the pendulum toward extremism. During the early 1930s, the younger generation of Germans refused to bear the stigma of sole war guilt and listened eagerly to the diatribes of the Nazi Fuhrer against the Treaty. The Ruhr controversy is significant as a case study which tended to support Hoover's contention that sooner or later there would be serious troubles stemming mainly from the weaknesses of the Treaty—especially in the area of reparations. The controversy provided a seedbed in which the dragon's teeth of suspicion and hatred were sown, to blossom eventually into the power struggle which was to culminate ultimately in the coming of World War II. While the Ruhr imbroglio was by no means a sole cause for the renewal of armed conflict, it was probably a major contributory factor.[36]

When the French moved into the Ruhr in January 1923, Hoover was serving in the Harding cabinet as secretary of commerce. The United States, through Secretary of State Charles Evans Hughes, tended to follow a somewhat cautious policy and refrained from direct intervention. Hoover, in his capacity as secretary of commerce, was probably inclined to see the economic fallacies of the move more clearly than other aspects. Needless to say, as a cabinet member he could not speak out too bluntly on his own or act in an outspoken fashion. While it would be most interesting to know his views as a mining engineer on the implications of the French move to the possible emergence of a French continental metallurgical monopoly, he did not put his thoughts on this subject down on paper. There can really be little doubt, however, that he was strongly critical of major aspects of French policy which he believed could only alienate Germany completely and obstruct her reintegration into the European and world economies. The following response to a citizen's request for his views on the possibility of League action in the Ruhr controversy suggests some hesitancy to go into specific details and an almost fatalistic view of the situation:

> For your confidential information, the forces that are moving the French people at the present time are beyond the control of any sort of international organization. The League of Nations, with America in or out, or any other form of international cooperation or conference could not stop the present action of the French Government. I am convinced that this form of activity has been in storage ever since the Armistice and it has simply got to express itself by action which must exhaust itself through experience. I have no doubt that this experience will be disastrous to both Germany and France but it will at some stage offer an opportunity when the rule of reason can be brought to play. Therefore, I simply can add nothing to comfort your mind until this brainstorm has expended itself for I am certain that any lightening rod we could put up at the present moment would draw the lightening into our own house.[37]

Hoover's sources of information with respect to developments in the Ruhr following January 11, 1923, were usually helpful. Alan Goldsmith of the Bureau of Foreign and Domestic Commerce relayed a Berlin cable on that very day:

> The penetration of the Ruhr, besides disturbing what still remains of German morale and willingness to attempt a partial fulfillment of Peace Treaty obligations, causes the gravest concern with regard to the domestic coal supply, over 80% of which is of Ruhr production. German industry and transportation have no longer stocks of coal, and even a temporary interference with Ruhr shipments might paralyze German economic life.

Goldsmith apparently recognized that Poincaré probably had more extensive objectives in his Ruhr policy than just the acquisition of reparations. France had earlier, under Briand (1921), established a customs cordon, of dubious legality under the Treaty, which had largely isolated Germany from the outside world. Apparently, France visualized an economic stranglehold as the guarantee for forcing the German government and German industry to disgorge foreign assets. Goldsmith pointed out that "neutral observations" were practically unanimous in the belief that such a control could not further a reparations policy, although it might easily facilitate an alternative and apparently major French policy of "annexation or dismemberment." The present writer feels that this may be a fairly realistic appraisal of French objectives which were quite separate and remote from French pretensions to the role of defender of the Versailles Treaty.[38]

As the scope of the French occupation steadily expanded, Charles E. Lyon, acting chief of the Western European Division of the Bureau of Foreign and Domestic Commerce, informed Hoover on March 6 that the French had occupied Darmstadt, Mannheim, Karlsruhe, and the small towns of Lorch and Knielingen. The French called their action a "reprisal" against continuing German sabotage in the Ruhr and especially the sabotage of the Rhine-Hoerne Canal. France now had complete control of both banks of the Rhine from Alsace-Lorraine to the Dutch border and, in addition, all railroad lines from the interior of Germany to the Rhineland. In Darmstadt the French seized the railroad shops and roundhouses.[39] While Poincaré was still informing the world that he had sent only a limited number of technicians into the Ruhr, it seemed likely to Hoover and his staff that a far more extensive intervention was underway.

The Dawes Report of April 1924 could be regarded as a partial revision of the Treaty in the area of reparations. Hoover's public reaction to it, like that of Hughes, was to praise it highly. It is possible, however, that he was secretly dubious as to its adequacy. The final Dawes Report was actually presented with little attention to the suggestions of British and American technical experts who were united in condemning it. The American experts were certain that no real productivity could be gotten out of the Ruhr district until the military occupation was ended. The Dawes plan did not provide for evacuation. According to one of the expert advisers, the consensus of opinion among the experts, who were supposed to advise the Dawes Committee, was that Germany would find it difficult to exist as a nation. These critics argued that the Dawes schedule of payments for Germany involved sums which were onerous and a manner of supervision which was too humiliating.[40]

Although it is not clear what was Hoover's candid judgment of the Dawes Report, he was definitely aware of the sharp criticism voiced by the experts. A copy of a detailed statement dated April 30, 1924, by a leading member of the British economic staff is filed among the Commerce papers at the Hoover Library in West Branch. The writer of the statement did not think that the Dawes Plan was workable or that it would last long enough to be of any real importance.[41] In any event, it seems likely that there is need for considerable re-evaluation by historians of the contemporary praise for this dubious revision of the Treaty's reparations arrangements.

As previously suggested, one other aspect of the Versailles Treaty, which raised doubts in Hoover's mind, involved the provisions for mandates. He could find little real difference between mandates and colonies. Hoover felt that Wilson's attitudes on the mandates were mainly due to a lack of familiarity with old world diplomacy and to Wilson's over-confidence in General Smuts, who cornered a sizable area for the Union of South Africa. Hoover also felt that Wilson was "just fooled" and under an illusion as to the ultimate effect of the mandates. On February 28, 1919, Wilson proposed that the United States accept a mandate over Armenia, Constantinople, and the Dardanelles. By that time the total area under mandate involved 1,132,000 square miles, one-third the area of the United States. To Hoover, the imperialistic tendency was obvious. He was directing the relief of Armenia and Constantinople during May 1919. Colonel House advised him that Wilson planned a mandate in this area with Hoover as governor. Although Hoover did not want to see the Bolshevik regime in Russia take over in Armenia, he realized the difficulties involved in preventing this. He proposed that a mission be sent under General Harbord to study the situation. The mission eventually reported that it was doubtful whether such a mandate could be made stable and defensible. Subsequently, Armenia fell into Russian hands. Hoover recognized possibilities for empire building among the mandates. He feared that the repression of independence movements among the Arab states could only lead to trouble. He also saw a great injury to China in the assignment of German titles in Shantung province to Japan. In his *America's First Crusade* (1942), Hoover referred to the mandate system and the secret treaties as main elements in a "secret division of the world." He felt that the British,

French, and Italians had determined to bring about a peace treaty by which they would dominate Europe politically and economically. They were planning to divide the German colonies, Persian oil, and the Turkish Empire among themselves. Germany was to be reduced to economic and military impotence.[42]

Having introduced this resumé of Hoover's reflections on the Versailles Treaty by referring to his contacts with Woodrow Wilson's ideas and attitudes, I would like to conclude by referring to a revealing and confidential letter sent to William Allen White, Kansas newspaper editor, in 1924. On this occasion, Hoover was responding to White's request for clarification of Hoover's opinions concerning Wilson. He wrote under date of June 13, 1924, as follows:

> I have some very serious doubts about ventilating any question of my disagreements with Woodrow Wilson. They hinge entirely around my objection to many of the terms of the German and Austrian treaties and my further somewhat vigorous objections to our being involved in the multitude of items set up under these treaties. I delivered numbers of verbal protests in an endeavor to secure what I thought was a more intelligent action (since justified) and wrote several memorandums for the President to reinforce them.
>
> Taking it altogether, it seems to me that these questions of personal relations are trivialities, for Wilson had a large proportion of the parts of a very great man and did extra-ordinary service for the American people.
>
> I supported the Treaty, although I did not like it and had protested against it, because I believe that it was essential to stop the killing of men; to give the world a turning point to peace and reconstruction; to set up the technical relations of commerce and industry; and that it was not possible to remedy every ill in the world at one go. I contended then and still contend that no international agreement is immutable; that the forces which run through peoples are infinitely more powerful than every written document, especially one formulated in such an atmosphere; that eventual peace could not be brought about by a collection of words and that the service of impressive documentation was mainly to change the currents of men's thoughts, to start the forces of peace—all of which was badly needed.
>
> From all this I do not want to be put in the position of criticizing Woodrow Wilson. I believe men should be judged for the good they do. The whole tendency of modern public criticism is to damn men for their very minor accomplishments. That immortal son of Holland who saved his native land by keeping his fist in a

leaky dike no doubt sassed his mother. My personal view has always been that the failure of Mr. Wilson was pathological and began with his first physical shock in April or May, 1919. (He was laid up ten days some time thereabouts from some sort of shock). I felt then that he suddenly gained a stubbornness, tended to rely upon his previous decisions, was less open to conviction, resented opposition of opinion, all of which I am told are pathological symptoms. Therefore, his real history ought to end right there. In my mind the development of this condition led to the great tragedy—his refusal to accept the reservations to the Treaty. The petty incidents of his personal relations with myself or Colonel House or any other of the men with whom he got out of patience and refused to cooperate are in my mind not worth consideration, for I believe they were part of the same pathology.[43]

Judging from Hoover's comments in *The Ordeal of Woodrow Wilson,* it is apparent that he shared some of the president's idealism and faith in concepts of representative government. At the same time, Hoover tended to have a less ingenuous and more realistic conception of the basic character of human nature and its contribution to the weakness of the Treaty. His fears for the future were real ones and were largely justified by the subsequent course of history.

Hoover undoubtedly saw serious sins of omission, hasty compromise, too little awareness of the basic causes of war, a highly cynical disregard of ethical and moral principles, considerable injustice in the establishment of boundaries and treatment of ethnic groups, a general lack of preparedness for peacemaking at Paris, a neglect of the economic dimensions by the Treaty, too much adherence to the secret treaties negotiated during the war, stimulation rather than mitigation of extreme nationalism, and a reparation policy guided more by a desire to keep Germany down than to conciliate her or reconstruct the economy of Europe. Whereas Hoover supported the League in 1919 as an institution which might possibly serve to correct some of the abuses of the Treaty, he came to feel in later years that the Allies had converted the League into a tool for preserving the status quo—a policy which was often accompanied by a tendency to consider the League sacrosanct and impervious to change. This tendency, Hoover believed, ran contrary to the lessons of history which suggest that political change is inevitable.

The outstanding importance of Herbert Hoover's role during the period from 1918 to 1925 is likely to be realized more fully as modern scholarship proceeds to draw attention to Hoover studies. One contemporary scholar, for example, has suggested another specific area in which Hoover was critical of the Versailles Treaty. Seizure of enemy-owned property within the borders of an Allied country was legitimized by Article 248 of the Treaty. An illustration of this occurred when the Bank of England took over the property of Anglo-Austrian banks. Hoover wrote to Henry Stimson during March 1920, fiercely denouncing the clause in question. Professor Carl Parrini has pointed out that Hoover and the U.S. government's policy-makers were actually attempting to reduce German reparation burdens and win the readmission of Germany to the world economy. This has been described elsewhere as a reintegration policy for Germany. Still another Treaty clause questioned by Hoover was that which denied Germany most favored nation treatment for the first five years of the Treaty while at the same time forcing her to grant such treatment to the Allies. Parrini also points out that the Harding administration actually believed that German investments seized by the Allies in Southern, Eastern, and Central Europe, as well as in Turkey, along with the preferential trading agreements imposed on the weaker nations, were more than sufficient payment for the costs of the war.[44]

In the midst of World War II, Hoover wrote to the journalist Arthur Krock, June 22, 1942, characterizing the Armistice period after the First World War as "one of total degeneration all over the planet." In this same year Hoover and his friend Hugh Gibson were attempting to develop a formula in their *Problems of Lasting Peace* which would "avoid the confusion of such assemblies as Versailles." Suffice it to say, in closing, that many of Hoover's views of the Treaty seem to have been largely vindicated by the passage of time. As Arthur Krock has succinctly put it: "He was a great American, a great citizen of the world. On these high and solid pedestals Herbert Hoover takes his place in history."[45]

NOTES

1   This study draws mainly from the following published writings of Herbert Hoover: *Addresses Upon the American Road 1941–1945* (New York: Van Nostrand, 1946); *Addresses Upon the American Road 1945–1948* (New York: Van Nostrand, 1949); *America's First Crusade* (New York: Scribner's, 1942); [with Hugh Gibson] *The Problems of Lasting Peace* (Garden City: Doubleday, 1942); *The Memoirs of Herbert Hoover: Years of Adventure 1874–1920* (New York: Macmillan, 1952); *The Ordeal of Woodrow Wilson* (New York: McGraw-Hill, 1958); *An American Epic*, 3 vols. (Chicago: Regnery, 1959–61).

2   Edgar E. Robinson, "Herbert Clark Hoover," *Encyclopaedia Britannica* (1973), 11:674–77.

3   *Loc. cit.* See also Seth P. Tillman, *Anglo-American Relations at the Paris Peace Conference of 1919* (Princeton: Princeton University Press, 1961), p. 263. Hoover contends that his Relief Organization had more contact with what was currently going on in Europe than did any of the national delegations at the Peace Conference. He saw his mission as having large political as well as humanitarian implications. See *The Memoirs of Herbert Hoover: Years of Adventure 1874–1920,* p. 433. The manuscript for this volume was drafted during 1922–26.

4   Letter from Hoover to Wilson, April 11, 1919, in the Hoover Mss, Pre-Commerce Series, Herbert Hoover Presidential Library, West Branch, Iowa.

5   Letter from Hoover to Wilson, May 14, 1919, Hoover Mss, Pre-Commerce Series.

6   Letter from Hoover to Wilson, June 4, 1919, Hoover Mss, Pre-Commerce Series. In stating that he had had "no part in the treaty making," Hoover tends to ignore the actual record which suggests a more active role. The denial may be technically correct in the most literal sense, but that Hoover exercised a weighty influence on the peace negotiations can hardly be denied. See U.S. Department of State, *Papers Relating to the Foreign Relations of the United States, Paris Peace Conference 1919,* notably in 11:100–01, 485, 506, 550–51.

7   Hoover, *The Ordeal of Woodrow Wilson,* pp. 233–34.

8   Joseph C. Grew, *Turbulent Era: A Diplomatic Record of Forty Years 1904–1945* (Boston: Houghton Mifflin, 1952), 1:392–93. See also, Hoover, *Memoirs: Years of Adventure,* p. 468.

9   Hoover, *The Ordeal of Woodrow Wilson,* pp. 249–50.

10   *Ibid.,* pp. 236–38. Hoover and his staff were well aware of the promises involved in the pre-Armistice agreement, which stated that surrender would not be unconditional in either a moral or legal sense. The Germans interpreted this to mean their surrender on the basis of Wilson's Fourteen Points and subsequent public pronouncements. See Charles Seymour, ed., *The Intimate Papers of Colonel House* (Boston: Houghton Mifflin, 1928), 4:148, 174, 187, 202, 267, 272, 321, 343, 381, 408–09, 434, 479. For additional comments regarding the pre-Armistice agreement, see Ferdinand Czernin, *Versailles 1919* (New York: Putnam, 1965).

11   Hoover, *The Ordeal of Woodrow Wilson,* p. 184. The text of Article X reads as follows: "The members of the League undertake to respect and preserve as against external aggression the territorial integrity and existing political independence of all members of the League. In case of any such aggression the Council shall advise upon the means by which this obligation shall be fulfilled."

12   *Ibid.,* pp. 184–89, 266.

13   *Ibid.,* quoted p. 284.

14   Quotes in this paragraph are from letter, Hoover to Wilson, November 19, 1919, Hoover Mss, Pre-Commerce Series.

15   Hoover, *America's First Crusade,* pp. 57–62. According to Hoover, the manuscript for this book was based on notes for memoirs prepared during 1934–35.

16 Hoover, "The Approaches to Peace," Chicago, December 16, 1942, in *Addresses Upon the American Road 1941–1945,* p. 6.

17 Hoover and Hugh Gibson, "Further New Approaches to Lasting Peace," in *ibid.,* p. 42. This series of articles was originally published in *Collier's Weekly,* June 5, 1943; June 12, 1943; June 19, 1943; June 26, 1943. See also Hoover and Gibson, "An Approach to a Lasting Peace," in *New York Times Magazine,* April 4, 1943, pp. 3, 37–38.

18 Hoover, "New Approaches to Peace," Speech at Minneapolis, September 3, 1943, in *Addresses Upon the American Road 1941–1945,* pp. 76–77, 83.

19 Hoover, Speech at Kansas City, October 28, 1943, in *ibid.,* p. 91.

20 Quoted passages in paragraph are from Hoover and Hugh Gibson, "The Futility of Military Alliances," in *ibid.,* pp. 104–06. This article was originally published in *Collier's Weekly,* November 6, 1943.

21 Hoover, "The Limitations on Freedom in War," Address, New York City, May 20, 1942, in *Addresses Upon the American Road 1941–1945,* p. 170.

22 Hoover and Gibson, "Further New Approaches to Lasting Peace," in *ibid.,* pp. 35–36.

23 Hoover, "The Approaches to Peace," Address in Chicago, December 16, 1942, in *ibid.,* p. 8.

24 Hoover and Gibson, "Further New Approaches to Lasting Peace," in *ibid.,* pp. 38–39.

25 Hoover and Gibson, "History's Greatest Murder Trial," in *ibid.,* pp. 64–70, originally published in *This Week Magazine,* August 29, 1943. See also Hoover, *Addresses Upon the American Road 1945–1948,* pp. 85–86, 101.

26 Hoover and Gibson, *The Problems of Lasting Peace* (New York: Doubleday, Doran, 1942), pp. 143–44, 167; John Maynard Keynes, *The Economic Consequences of the Peace* (New York: Harcourt, Brace and Howe, 1920), pp. 23–33; see also Hoover, *America's First Crusade,* p. 33.

27 Hoover and Gibson, *The Problems of Lasting Peace,* pp. 165–67.

28 *Ibid.,* pp. 126, 170–71.

29 *Ibid.,* p. 248.

30 Hoover and Gibson, "The Futility of Military Alliances," *Colliers,* November 6, 1943, in *Addresses Upon the American Road, 1941–1945.* Hoover and Gibson, "An Approach to Lasting Peace," *The New York Times Magazine,* April 4, 1943, in *Addresses Upon the American Road, 1941–1945,* pp. 57–63.

31 Royal J. Schmidt, *Versailles and the Ruhr: Seedbed of World War II* (The Hague: Martinus Nijhoff, 1968), pp. 231–32.

32 *Loc. cit.*

33   *Ibid.*, p. 232; p. 2, for Annex II, paragraphs 17 and 18, which were presumably the parts of the Treaty cited by Poincaré in order to sustain his actions. They are here quoted, as follows:
Annex II, Paragraph 17: "In case of default by Germany in the performance of any obligations under this part of the present treaty, the Commission will forthwith give notice of such default to each of the interested Powers and may make such recommendations as to action to be taken in consequence of such default as it may think necessary."
Annex II, Paragraph 18: "The measures which the Allied and Associated Powers shall have the right to take in the case of a voluntary default by Germany, and which Germany agrees not to regard as acts of war, may include economic and financial prohibitions and reprisals and in general such other measures as the respective Governments may determine to be necessary in the circumstances."

34   *Ibid.*, pp. 232–34.

35   *Ibid.*, p. 235.

36   *Ibid.*, p. 243.

37   Hoover to Charles F. Scott, January 13, 1923, Hoover Mss, Commerce Series–Germany, Ruhr Occupation, Box 137, Hoover Presidential Library.

38   Alan Goldsmith to Hoover, January 12, 1923, Hoover Mss, Commerce Series, Box 137, Hoover Presidential Library.

39   Secretary of Commerce, Official File, Box 132, Folder, "France 1921–24," Charles H. Lyon, Memo, March 6, 1923. Lyon was acting chief of the Western European Division, Bureau of Foreign and Domestic Commerce.

40   *Versailles and the Ruhr,* pp. 219–43. See also "The Diary of Colonel L. P. Ayres," unpublished manuscript, Hoover Institution on War, Revolution and Peace, Stanford, California. Ayres's Diary is the source for the criticism of the Dawes Report. Ayres was a financial adviser to the Dawes Commission.

41   Secretary of Commerce Papers, Personal "Reparations–Dawes Plan," Excerpts from a personal letter of one of the leading members of the British Economic Staff assigned to the Reparation Commission, British Delegation, April 30, 1924. Hoover Mss.

42   Hoover, *Ordeal of Woodrow Wilson,* pp. 222–36; Hoover, *America's First Crusade,* pp. 26–27.

43   Hoover to W. A. White, June 13, 1924, Commerce Series, Personal File, Hoover Mss.

44   Carl P. Parrini, *Heir to Empire: U.S. Economic Diplomacy 1916–1923* (Pittsburgh: University of Pittsburgh Press, 1969), pp. 123, 129, 139, 223, 250.

45   Arthur Krock, *Memoirs: 60 Years on the Firing Line* (New York: Funk & Wagnalls, 1968), pp. 139, 143.

MURRAY N. ROTHBARD

Hoover's 1919 Food Diplomacy In Retrospect

EDITOR'S INTRODUCTORY NOTE

Murray Rothbard's article that follows is a severe interpretation of Hoover's activities as United States food administrator and director general of relief during 1918–19. Rothbard seeks to demolish the popular characterization of Hoover as humanitarian by arguing that relief was a thinly disguised instrument which allowed the American government to enrich American farmers who had expanded acreage under cultivation and had amassed huge food surpluses by the time of the Armistice. Demand for food during the war had led the American government to guarantee minimum farm prices. These government assurances had in turn encouraged banks to extend liberal credits to farmers. Thence, when the war ended, American farmers were confronted with stockpiles which if not exported to the recent European belligerent states would presumably rot in storage bins. Farm prices would fall precipitously, banks would be losers with the result being a severe agricultural depression in the United States. Hence, Rothbard insists, Hoover's chief concern in 1918–19 was not with supplying food to the destitute of Europe; he was chiefly actuated by the need for finding markets in Europe that would relieve the farm surpluses and thus prevent economic dislocations in the United States, hardly an act of altruism, philanthropy, or humanitarianism. In such context, Hoover functioned as international broker assisting his clients to achieve the highest possible profits and avoid financial ruin. Whatever concern Hoover and other American leaders may have felt for starving Europeans was purely secondary. While Hoover was disguising his own crass motives with eloquent pleas for relief to Europe's starving millions, he hypocritically assailed the motives of Allied leaders who opposed American attempts to relax the Al-

Murray N. Rothbard is professor of history at the Polytechnic Institute of New York. This paper was contributed to the Fourth Centennial Seminar in October 1974.

lied blockade of Germany and Russia. With appropriate moral out-
rage, Hoover bitterly criticized those who would permit the ravages
of war to continue after the Armistice by depriving whole populations in East-Central Europe from receiving American food shipments.

Rothbard proceeds to strip away further remnants of Hoover's
moral armament by relating how the director general of relief (with
the presumed connivance of President Wilson, the American Commission, and also the Supreme Council of the Peace Conference in
Paris) resorted to making the relief program a political tool for opposing bolshevism of the Left and also containing reaction of the
Right in East-Central Europe. By being able to supply or deny relief, Hoover could assist anti-Bolshevik nationalists as well as oppose reactionary regimes in Hungary, Rumania, Poland, and the
Baltic states. Through the stillborn Nansen Mission, Hoover
planned to orchestrate the civil struggle in Russia toward the ultimate goal of encouraging liberal democratic government.

This analysis is by no means lacking in evidentiary support. Actually, much of the documentation derives from Hoover's own
recollective writings. It would seem rather obvious that massive
supplies of food could not be produced overnight. In order to have
supplies on hand at the end of military hostilities the American
government enlisted the services of farmers through financial incentives in the form of guaranteed prices. Clearly, Hoover felt
obliged to find markets for the huge surpluses that American
agriculture assembled during the fall and winter of 1918–19. Not
only did Hoover expect to supply the needs of the Allies and the
neutrals, he also expected to provide American food for populations in the defeated Central Powers. Hence, his strong appeal to
end the Allied blockade. Without necessary foodstuffs, populations
in Europe would be prone to turn to political extremism, and
bolshevism would hold considerable appeal. At least this was how
Hoover and other American leaders came to perceive relief as the
best means for resisting political extremism from the Right and
Left. Given this analysis, food relief became a commodity which
Hoover thought it possible to trade for a cessation of violence and
civil war as well as the establishment of liberal, democratic states.
No serious writer commenting on the crisis of 1918–19 has denied,
Hoover least of all, that food was an important diplomatic tool. Cer-
tainly, the historian is justified in asking whether the humanitarian
motive should have received higher priority.

Hoover's 1919 Food
Diplomacy in Retrospect

A scant six days after the Armistice ending World War I, Herbert
Hoover set sail for Europe, where he was to add to his powerful
wartime role as U.S. food administrator by serving also as director
general of relief and reconstruction. Arriving amidst the political
and economic chaos of post-Armistice Europe, a chaos aggravated
by the power vacuums in Eastern and Central Europe and by the
continuing Allied blockade of food and other necessary supplies to
the Continent, Hoover, stationed in Paris, served as virtual pro-
consul and food diplomat on behalf of President Wilson's grand design for a reconstituted Europe. Essentially that design was to fish
in the troubled waters of the Continent, to impose upon the war-
borne turbulence a centrist political order, democratic in form and
liberal corporatist in content, under the guidance of a United States
government that had developed much the same institutions. Concretely, Wilson saw two distinct and competing threats to that design: attempts to re-establish old-fashioned monarchical institutions as well as the older imperialism of the Allied governments;
and the new wave of proletarian Marxism or bolshevism under the
inspiration of the new Soviet Republic.[1] Throughout much of the
crucial year 1919, Herbert Hoover energetically used his control of
vast supplies of food to further the Wilsonian design. Fortunately,
several autobiographical works by Hoover, written after World
War II, enable us to examine Hoover's account of his role as food
diplomat and how close that account came to reality.[2]

From the very first, Hoover exhibited a remarkable capacity to
attribute a high-flown moralism to his own activities, while seeing
with crystal clarity the selfish beam in the eyes and activities of other
nations. While only two years earlier he had had some reservations
about the impending war "to save democracy," by the Armistice he
was convinced that the war had simply been fought "to establish
liberty," and that "the purification of men, the triumph of democracy would bring a new golden age. We were indeed proud
that we had had a part in this rebirth of mankind."[3]

No sooner did he arrive in Europe, however, than he found the
Allied governments reeking with "selfishness," "nationalism," and
"heartlessness," a reflection of the fact that these nations had
"always had class government," serving solely "the selfish and

greedy" "nationalist interest" of their particular country, each serving its own "Empire First." In contrast, Hoover asserted, the
American State was the only one acting purely out of "morals" and
"idealism"; Hoover even went so far as to declare that "Ours was
the only nation since the time of the Crusades that had fought
other peoples' wars for ideals."[4] A truly remarkable American ex-
ceptionalism!

Concretely, the Allied "selfishness" was then manifested chiefly
in continuing the food blockade of Europe, not simply as a means
of coercing the enemy powers into accepting Allied peace terms,
but "to bring pressure upon us to accept the reduction in prices" of
American food "by closing the outlet for our surpluses until we
gave way."[5] If the Allied desire to see the prices of their imported
food lowered was "selfish" and "greedy," what then constituted
American "idealism" in this matter? Simply, to keep up the
artificially high food prices which the U.S. government had
guaranteed to American farmers. As Hoover wrote, "we had a
special problem to avoid a break in our guaranteed farm prices
which would ruin our farmers and the country banks which had
extended credit to carry our surplus."[6] Hoover might call this
policy "justice to our farmers," but the food-starved Allies may be
pardoned in branding as selfish as well as hypocritical a U.S. policy
of cartelizing food so as to keep the American farmers in the
artificial wartime prosperity to which they had rapidly become
accustomed.[7]

In his *Ordeal of Woodrow Wilson,* Hoover presents the letter of
December 15, 1918, which he wrote for Wilson's top foreign policy
aide, Colonel House, to present to the Allied Council of Prime
Ministers. In the letter's call for ending the Allied blockade, and
thereby converting pent-up American food surpluses into
shortages, Hoover laid greatest stress not upon the alleviation of
starvation in Europe, but upon the economic situation in the United States. Hoover wrote:

> There must be instant expansion of marketing of American sur-
> pluses or there will be a great financial reaction in the United
> States. A review of the very large stocks [of food] now held and
> the large amount of banking credit advanced against these stocks
> creates a situation of the utmost danger. Any failure to find solu-
> tion to this situation . . . would possibly precipitate financial
> difficulties in the United States, ...[8]

Hoover's reaction to the Allied decision to repudiate their tentative agreement to relax the blockade in response to American

pressure was a curious but characteristic blend of moralizing and an almost studied incomprehension of the Allied economic position. On the one hand, the Allied blockade was a "horror," "most insensate," and "wicked," seemingly an incomprehensible expression of wartime vengeance. On the other hand, Hoover reports without comment the explanation of the Allies that the blockade was being continued "as a measure to reduce world food prices in the interest of all mankind." Yet, while Hoover did not seem to understand the Allied desire for lower prices of American food imports, he was most alive to the American political desire for guaranteed high farm prices. For his initial reaction to the Allied continuance of the blockade was to complain that "Our warehouses were already overloaded and a flood of grain and food animals was coming hourly to the processors in the United States. With no European outlet, the processors would be unable to continue buying at the guaranteed prices." Hoover goes on to detail his prompt maneuvers in the purchase of American food by the U.S. government, as a result of which

> the pressures of the farmers' shipments to the central markets had relaxed. We had held our guarantees, but at the cost of many sleepless nights for our Washington and New York staffs and myself.[9]

In his *Memoirs,* Hoover explodes at the apparently wicked British desire for prices of their imported food to fall from their artificially high levels; he can only expostulate that this "would have represented a gigantic breach of good faith between men and governments." Hoover noted the high prices which the U.S. government had guaranteed the American farmer, in such products as wheat, hogs, dairy products, and sugar. Pork and dairy products, being perishable, were pressing on U.S. storage capacity. Noting that "in 1918 we had assured the American farmer an increase to $17.50 per hundred pounds for hogs," he added that the guarantee was supposed to continue until March 1919. Without a trace of irony, Hoover records that the farmers' response was to produce pigs in unprecedented numbers: "The valiant farmer, in response to patriotic appeal, and assured price, produced and sent to the market 26,000,000 hogs in this period." We might guess that the assured price loomed a bit larger than patriotism in the farmers' "valiant" response. "The only answer" to this massively induced production of pork was "a steady movement into Europe." For, Hoover lamented in retrospect:

The moment our storage was filled the packers must stop buying hogs and not only would the price of hogs crack but cattle prices would come down with them, then animal feeds and every other product except wheat (provided we could find storage for it). Ten thousand country banks had made loans to the farmers and merchants to produce and handle these products upon the basis of our prices. They would crash also. And the immorality of breaking faith with the farmer was unbearable.[10]

Hoover added that "during these months I had nightmares of the collapse of the American farmer and the country banking system." In the midst of these nightmares, and of the "hysterical cables" to the same effect coming from Washington, Hoover adds, with an uncharacteristic note of sarcasm, that "to add to our joys, Secretary [of the Treasury Carter] Glass got into a panic to reduce prices on food by taking off our guarantees."[11] But Hoover prevailed against Britain from without and Carter Glass from within.

In short, Hoover, while all too keenly alive to the American policy of guaranteeing high food prices to American farmers, and holding such a policy of the first importance, could not seem to comprehend, in any terms but villainy, the Allied desire for lower food prices, and he could only see the consequent Allied blockade as purely "insensate." Professor Gordon Levin's assessment is scarcely an exaggeration when he states "that one of Herbert Hoover's concerns in establishing American control over relief operations in postwar Europe was to make certain that America's glutted farm markets would be cleared at advantageous prices." This was in line with the general Wilsonian program, as Levin points out, for "a world commercial system [which] would also be made to order for what Wilsonians had always seen as America's need to expand her exports in order to maintain domestic prosperity."[12]

With American farm prices secured in early 1919, Hoover could concentrate even more intensively on one of his major themes in the battle against the Allied food blockade in Germany, as well as of his food diplomacy in general: the supply of food in order to block the spread of "anarchy" and communism in Europe. Hoover recalls his repeated statements to that effect. Thus: "What is desired most now is for Germany to get on some sort of a stable basis"; "Famine is the mother of anarchy . . . anarchy is infectious, the infection of such a cesspool will jeopardize France and Britain, will yet spread to the United States."[13] Hoover did not include in any of his retrospective accounts his clearest statement of this view, expressed in a policy statement on November 12, 1918:

> this mass of [German] people is now confronted with engulfment in absolute anarchy. If we value our own safety and the social organization of the world, if we value the preservation of civilization itself, we cannot sit idly by and see the growth of this cancer in the world's vitals. Famine is the mother of anarchy. From the inability of governments to secure food for their people, grows revolution and chaos. From an ability to supply their people, grows stability of government and the defeat of anarchy.[14]

More specifically, Hoover recalls his repeated argument that relaxation of the blockade and the shipment of food was vital to check the threat of a Bolshevik Germany. On January 1, 1919, he wrote Wilson of the necessity to relax the blockade, because "even a partial revival of the ordinary activities of life within enemy territories will tend powerfully to [check rising] Bolshevism and [bring] the stabilizing of governments."[15] By early March, Hoover writes, "the situation in Germany became desperate. The Communists were making steady progress. The feeble German Government was threatened with quick collapse." In a conference with Lloyd George on March 7, Hoover sternly "recited a list of cities in Germany which had already gone Communist (Spartacist). I handed him a telegram from our staff representative stating that machine guns were chattering in Berlin streets at that very moment." Pointing to the Communist governments in possession of Munich, Hamburg, and Stettin, and at other times of the state governments of Bavaria, Saxony, and the Ruhr, Hoover "recalled that during these months I had been warning of the steady advance of the Communists among a hungry people and of the weakening of the new German representative government."[16]

After the Allies relaxed the blockade under Hoover's and America's pressure, "We moved some 200,000 tons of food into Germany in ten days," "hoping our supplies would arrive in time to save the new German Republic under Ebert." As a result, the "dangers of Communist revolution considerably abated." Still, "We had been so delayed in opening the blockade that it was nip and tuck keeping ahead of Communist movements"; as Hoover wrote to Wilson on April 3, "it is a neck and neck race as to whether food will maintain stability as against the other forces that have grown out of hunger in the meantime."[17]

In his policy of political support for the Social Democratic Ebert regime in Germany, Hoover successfully defended the regime from two very different Allied thrusts: a British proposal that Ebert include some Spartacists in a coalition government, and a French plan to create separatist republics in Bavaria and the Rhineland. On the Bavarian scheme, Hoover perceptively but scornfully remarks that "Whoever controlled the food would control the state. The French-Bavarian conspirators wanted to be assured of food independently from the central government." But Hoover was more anxious to send food to northern and eastern Germany, thereby "keeping ahead of Communist movements" there. Similarly, Hoover blocked a French plan, or, as Hoover puts it, "a conspiracy between French and German industrialists to set up a Rhenish Republic." Hoover notes with some satisfaction that "President Ebert ended this conspiracy by locking their industrialists up in jail."[18]

Omitted from all of Hoover's accounts are some of the crucial sources and implications of his food diplomacy in Germany as well as the rest of Europe. For example, there is no mention of the remarkable series of pre-Armistice memoranda by which the bright young State Department official William C. Bullitt formulated the Wilson administration's line on the question. Surveying the spectre of the spread of bolshevism and revolution throughout Central and Eastern Europe, Bullitt had declared that " 'economic disorganization and famine were the parents of Bolshevism,' " and "that if Central Europe were allowed to dissolve into economic chaos and to starve, no leaders on earth [could] prevent the establishment of a dictatorship of the proletariat with attendant pillage and murder." The major American antidote, asserted Bullitt, should be its abundant supplies of food, by which the United States could support moderate Social Democratic regimes and suppress bolshevism. Thus, in the defeated Austro-Hungarian Empire, Bullitt urged "immediate action by the United States and the Allies . . . to prevent famine and economic disorganization from driving Austria and Hungary to Bolshevism."[19] Therefore, Bullitt proposed that Herbert Hoover be sent to Berne to "organize the provisioning of Tyrol, Vienna, and Bohemia," since there and in the rest of Europe the "roots of Bolshevism could be cut only by food and restoration of economic life. . . ."[20]

By November 25 Bullitt was mainly worried about Germany, and the rise of the Spartacists, and he urged that Ebert be given prompt economic aid, and "immediate supervision by Mr. Hoover of food distribution. . . ." Secretary of State Lansing proposed that Hoover personally be sent to Berlin "to get in touch with the actual situation, both political and economic." But the American officialdom agreed that a Hoover visit would reap too much publicity, and so instead Hoover's aides, Vernon Kellogg and Alonzo Taylor, were sent on a mission to Germany.[21] Hoover recalls that the Kellogg-Taylor Mission reported to him "that the new Ebert Government was weakening under Spartacist (Communist) uprisings, . . . and that there was real danger of the Government's being overthrown by either the old military or by the Spartacists, who were playing on the emotions of the hungry."[22]

Hoover does not mention, however, the significant findings of the Dresel Mission to Germany. From December 27 to January 5, the American government sent Ellis Loring Dresel on a mission to Germany, where the Dresel Mission spoke with a number of important German leaders. Not one of these leaders urged immediate food shipments; indeed, they declared that Germany had enough food until March or June. Instead, they urged the United States to contribute to the probably successful battle against Spartacism by telling Germany that the Allies would only send food to a "stable and democratically based government"; in other words, they urged an Allied policy of food blackmail against Spartacism.[23]

The Dresel trip was followed by the establishment of a quasi-permanent American mission headquartered in Berlin, and headed by American naval captain Walter R. Gherardi. The function of the Gherardi Mission, again not mentioned by Hoover, was to gather information on the explosive German political situation, and to recommend measures to help stabilize the Ebert-Scheidemann government. Gherardi joined Kellogg and Taylor in urging relaxation of the food blockade to Germany as the most necessary measure to stem the Bolshevik tide. By early March, as the Spartacists gained in strength, their calls gained in urgency, and Hoover was able to break the Allied food logjam.[24]

From the American point of view, Austria and Hungary, the two major centers emerging out of the other leading wartime enemy, were in even more precarious condition than Germany. Famine was far more severe in Austria than in Germany, and Bullitt's pre-Armistice memoranda concentrated on food and the menace of Bolshevism in Austria. Bullitt had urged the president to ship food to Vienna immediately upon an armistice, "to be distributed by an American directorate" through the Austrian government of Friedrich Adler; in that case, Bullitt declared frankly, "the ad-

ministrative agencies which controlled the food distribution would
automatically obtain the greatest power over the proletariat and
the American directors would control the Governments." We have
seen that Bullitt urged that Hoover be sent to Berne to organize the
provisioning of the Tyrol, Vienna, and Bohemia.

America's shakiest moments in Austria came in late March, when
the Communist government of Bela Kun took power in Hungary.
The Kun regime expected the Austrian Marxist government of
Friedrich Adler and Karl Renner to join Hungary in quickly
establishing a Soviet-type system. While publicly expressing their
friendship and sympathy, however, the Austrian Marxist leaders
were happy to use the American control of food as an excuse not to
join their Hungarian comrades. As a government-inspired
editorial in the Vienna *Arbeiter Zeitung* put it:

> Because of their food reserves the Hungarians can survive the
> withdrawal of the Allied missions from Budapest. We could not
> survive. We have no flour of our own and are at the mercy of Al-
> lied supplies. Should Allied food trains be withheld we would be
> without bread . . . . We are slaves of Paris [the Allied govern-
> ments] because only Paris can supply us with bread. . . .[25]

Despite this rebuff, the Allies and the Austrian Social Democratic
government were alarmed to find the threat of a Communist revolt
growing, and the Austrian officials were particularly worried
about the suggestion of a British officer to ship food to Communist
Hungary, for the Austrians had kept the revolution in check "by
arguing that if Austria went Bolshevik, food supplies would cease,"
and now this argument was being undercut by the Allies
themselves. One Austrian official expressed alarm that the Social
Democrats were being "deprived of one of their best arguments for
keeping people quiet."[26] In response to this problem, and to
Austrian reports of an impending Communist uprising, Herbert
Hoover had the Vienna authorities post a proclamation warning
that:

> Any disturbance of public order will render food shipments im-
> possible and bring Vienna face to face with absolute famine.
> Herbert Hoover.[27]

Other threatening statements by Hoover were approvingly quoted
in the Austrian press as warning that rioting would endanger Al-

lied supplies. In his retrospective accounts, Hoover writes that the food relief operation in Austria "was indeed a race against both death and Communism," but that "fear of starvation held the Austrian people from revolution." His account, however, is inadequate, in stating only that a Communist uprising was expected for May Day, and that, perhaps as a result of his proclamation, "May 1 came and went quietly."[28] May Day may have been quiet, but the Communist uprising did come earlier, on April 17, and was quelled by the Austrian People's Militia.[29]

If Austria was troublesome for American policy, still more so was Hungary, where the Bolshevik regime of Bela Kun took power on March 22. Hoover successfully opposed the immediate Allied response led by the French, to blockade all food into Hungary. In his recollections his motives for this action were mixed; on the one hand, he termed them, in a letter to Wilson on April 15, "purely humanitarian," and with "no relationship to the settlement of any political questions"; combined with the fact that Hungary had already paid for the trainloads of food which the French were holding up at the frontier. On the other hand, he drove a hard bargain for continuing food shipments, insisting that Kun "permit us to operate our trains over the Hungarian lines and we would sell him some food," in short, "we arranged with the Communists that the supplies should be distributed under American control." Furthermore, he transmitted with approval to the president the report of his aide in Hungary, Captain T. T. C. Gregory, to the effect that the continuing food shipments "created most favorable feeling for Americans as demonstrating their integrity in carrying out their engagements, more particularly among the anti-Bolshevik labor element in Budapest." Another practical consideration was that food shipments to Poland and Czechoslovakia depended on rail shipments through Hungary.[30]

In his April 15 letter, Hoover spelled out the severe limits of the "purely humanitarian" considerations in view:

If we put Hungary on precisely the same food basis as the other states, we shall lose our control of the situation in the surrounding states. We have ample indication that the restraining influence that we hold on these governments is effective but if the disturbing elements in Austria, Czecho-Slovakia, Jugo-Slavia, etc., consider that they will be as secure as to food supplies after disturbance [Communist revolutions] as before, our present potentiality to maintain the status quo of order is lost.

Hoover went on to propose that the Allies "do not at present intend to accord the same consideration to Hungary as they are according to liberated countries and German Austria today. To these latter countries they are sending a constantly increasing flow of food supplies. . . ."[31]

In the continuing discussions among the Allies on how to deal with the Kun regime, Hoover recalls that he persistently opposed the idea of Allied (including American) military intervention, but he did spell out a program of active economic warfare. By early July, Hoover warned the Allied leaders that the Kun regime had become an "economic danger to the rest of Europe," since Communist "ideas were impregnating the working classes throughout the area. Unless some means could be devised of abating the infection, the economic regeneration of Central and South-Eastern Europe would be difficult." The means that Hoover devised, as a superior alternative to military invasion, was "by offering decent treatment to Hungary if she would throw off the Communist yoke."[32]

Specifically, Hoover proposed a public declaration to Hungary "to the effect that economic assistance would be given to a properly constituted government" (i.e., a non-Communist government). The French premier, Georges Clemenceau, was enchanted, and bluntly declared that

> He believed Mr. Hoover held the key to the situation. The offer of food in return for good behavior would be a very effective weapon. . . .   The action exercised by Mr. Hoover would therefore have, he thought, greater chances of success than military intervention. . . .[33]

Accordingly, Hoover drafted, and the Allied leaders issued, a tough declaration of July 26, to the effect that the economic revival of Central Europe was impossible "until there is in Hungary a Government which represents its people, and carries out in the letter and the spirit the engagements into which it has entered with the Associated Governments. None of these conditions are fulfilled by the administration of Bela Kun. . . ." The Allies concluded that "if food and supplies are to be made available, if the blockade is to be removed, if economic reconstruction is to be attempted, if peace is to be settled it can only be done with a Government which represents the Hungarian people and not with one that rests its authority upon terrorism."[34]

While Hoover indeed had devised his alternate means of exerting severe pressure upon Hungary by July 10, he completely omits from his recollections his ardent advocacy of Allied military invasion during June and early July. For in early June, Captain Gregory had urged Hoover to recommend "an immediate combined advance from all quarters," that the Allies promise food and coal to Hungary "as soon as the city of Budapest was taken or the present government ousted," and that this policy be promptly carried out "to support a new and more conservative government when it goes in." On June 9, Hoover forwarded this dispatch to Wilson with a supporting note of unqualified approval. Hoover wrote the president:

> As much as I dislike to suggest it, I can see but one solution and that is for the French troops which are now in Yugoslavia to advance on Budapest without delay. Otherwise, it appears to us, that both the Czechoslovakian and the German-Austrian Governments will surely fall. [35]

On July 1, moreover, Hoover urged the Allied leaders to "throw out [Kun] by force of arms." According to the Minutes of the American Commissioners Plenipotentiary meeting on that date:

> All of the British and American economic and food relief experts were strongly of the opinion that he should be thrown out. . . . Hoover was convinced that the two French divisions at present in the southeast of Europe were fully capable of accomplishing this act. [36]

At any rate, the Hoover-Allied declaration of July 26 was swiftly followed by the internal overthrow of the Kun regime; Hoover happily responded by resuming large-scale shipments of food: "Immediately I ordered [August 2nd] large food shipments in accord with the Allied promise." Hoover recalls that the Allies adopted his draft proposal to remove the blockade of Hungary and the Danube, but with the warning that "the Danube shall be opened and shall remain opened so long as the present Hungarian Government gives practical evidence of its intention to comply promptly with the conditions of the Armistice." In supporting his proposal to the Allies, Hoover noted that "the new [Socialist] government, though very radical, represented the trade unions. Trade-unionism was an instrument used to upset Bolshevism . . . the Hungarian Government should be encouraged as a very important reaction might result on Russia." [37]

But this centrist idyll was not to last; in just a few days, the invad-
ing Rumanian army was able to take advantage of the chaotic conditions in Hungary to complete its conquest of the country and
quickly agree to a coup which installed the Hapsburg Archduke
Joseph as head of state in Hungary. Both actions, harkening back
to the "reactionary," pre-Wilsonian political order, were anathema
to Hoover. On the Rumanian invasion, Hoover was horrified at the
systematic plundering of the country by the invaders; but, more
important, as he wrote Clemenceau, was "that this must mean a
great setback in the evolution of self-government in Hungary."
Hoover's response was swift, and in keeping with his carrot-and-
stick food diplomacy: using food relief to reward favored political
regimes and to punish the unworthy. As he wrote Clemenceau: "I
cannot recommend either to my own government or to the Allied
governments, for whom I act, that they should incur any expen-
diture or effort in endeavoring to provision the city of Budapest in
the face of these [Rumanian] demands and the existing situation."[38]

The installation of the Archduke was even worse, from Hoover's
point of view, bringing up as it did the spectre of the return of the
Hapsburg monarchy and of the "reactionary" pre-World War I
political order. Twelve days later, on August 12, Hoover urged the
State Department to have the Allies quickly "demand Archduke's
retirement and the formation of a ministry representing labor and
. . . middle classes and peasants," and to deny any form of recognition to the Archduke's regime. At a meeting of the Supreme Council of the Allies over a week later, Hoover developed the reasons for
his implacable hostility to the new regime:

> This event had immediate repercussion throughout Poland and
> Eastern Europe and the Bolshevists were making much of it and
> claiming that the . . . [Allies were] trying to reestablish reac-
> tionary government in its worst form and this had done more to
> rehabilitate the Bolshevist cause than anything that had hap-
> pened for a long time.[39]

Hoover thereupon drafted a telegram that the Allies sent to
Budapest, demanding that "the present claimant to the headship of
the Hungarian State should resign, and that a Government in
which all parties are represented should . . . [be elected by] the
Hungarian people." Otherwise, the Allies would not recognize or
negotiate with the Hungarian government, and, furthermore, as
long as the existing government continued in office, "nor can the

Allied and Associated Governments give it the economic support which Hungary so sorely needs." The result of this Allied pressure was the immediate resignation of the Archduke, an event celebrated in a telegram of August 23 from Captain Gregory to Hoover in slang code: "Archie on the carpet 7 P.M. Went through the hoop at 7:05 P.M."[40] Hoover thereupon resumed the systematic shipment of food relief for Hungary.[41]

But the Rumanians were still looting and occupying Hungary, and Hoover records that the Allies first stopped all shipments of supplies to Rumania, and then blockaded Rumania, until, as Hoover simply states, "the Rumanians withdrew."[42] In this way, Hoover managed to omit all mention of the method by which the Rumanians withdrew, and of what happened to his and the Allied demand for representative elections in Hungary. Had he done so, his tale of success might well have been blunted, for the Rumanians turned over Hungary to the repressive dictatorship of Admiral Nicholas Horthy, who proceeded to institute a White Terror which made the Red Terror of the Kun regime pale by comparison.[43]

Apart from the Rumanian invasion of Hungary, Hoover had his troubles with food relief in Rumania. He found the government inefficient and corrupt, and used considerable pressure to establish American control of food distribution in Rumania, including employing a threat to expose Rumanian graft to the outside world. That Hoover's motivation was, again, not solely humanitarian is revealed in the message at the end of April to Hoover by his aide in Rumania, Colonel William N. Haskell, to the effect that "the dangers of Bolshevist insurrection have been greatly lessened if not entirely obviated by the arrival of our food cargoes . . . ."[44]

One of the boldest and most curious examples of Hoover's food diplomacy in 1919 was the case of Poland. This new country had declared independence under its military hero, the revolutionary nationalist Marshal Joseph Pilsudski. From Hoover's point of view, a Pilsudskian military dictatorship violated all of the centrist American ideals of Wilsonian democracy. And so he quickly adopted the suggestion of his emissary to Poland, Dr. Vernon Kellogg, to urge President Wilson to withhold food aid from starving Poland unless Pilsudski made the Polish-American pianist Ignace Paderewski, premier of Poland. Wilson made the threat, and Paderewski was promptly made premier. Herbert Hoover had succeeded via food diplomacy in foisting his old friend Paderewski as premier of Poland. Hoover promptly sent a staff of expert advisers to administer and virtually run the Polish government, in particular its administration of food and railways. Other American advisers were seeded into the Polish departments of public health, mining, commerce, and finance. To complete the circle, Hoover's old friend Hugh Gibson was made American ambassador to Poland.

Why the imposition of Paderewski? Hoover insists that the pianist was "beloved by all Poles," but this is belied by his admission that "the Polish people knew little of his [Paderewski's] immense service and sacrifice, which had made possible the independence and greatness of Poland." On the other hand, "Pilsudski had gained wide popularity through his welding an army from Polish recruits in the three partitioned provinces and establishing a re-united Poland."[45] A more important reason in Hoover's account was Paderewski's devotion to the Wilsonian ideals of democratic and representative government, and liberal land reform, in con-trast to Pilsudski's revolutionary and militarist nationalism. It might be ventured, too, that Paderewski, as a Polish-American who had organized the "Freedom for Poland Committee" of overseas Poles during the war, would clearly be far more amenable to American guidance than the intractable nationalist general. In the light of Polish reality, however, what Hoover termed the "tragedy" of Paderewski's ouster and exile at the end of 1919 seems inevitable.[46]

An important omission in Hoover's account is his references to Paderewski's closest Polish associate, Roman Dmowski, as simply "able," "shrewd," and "hard-headed." Hoover neglects to point out that before the war, Dmowski, an old enemy of Pilsudski, had been the veteran leader of the pro-Russian party of large Polish landlords; after the Russian Revolution, Dmowski had shifted his allegiance to the Western powers. It is unlikely that a Paderewski-Dmowski regime would have instituted any meaningful land re-form in Poland.

Hoover played an active military as well as relief role in the com-plex struggles in the newly-created Baltic states. The Baltic na-tionalities, formerly part of the Russian Empire, had been invaded and occupied by Germany during the war, and, in a bizarre twist, the Allies, at the Armistice, urged the German occupying army, headed by General von der Goltz, to remain temporarily in charge of the Baltic countries. Hoover's explanation was that the Allies feared "general chaos" should von der Goltz withdraw, but more likely the phrase was a euphemism for Communist control, which was threatened by Soviet armies and native Communist forces.

Hoover then faced the complex task of succoring the fledgling
Baltic governments from the threat of Soviet invasion on the left,
and from the unwelcome German army on the right, which was allied to the old German Balt landed aristocracy in the new countries.

Hoover set forth his Baltic strategy in a memo to President
Wilson on May 9. He noted that the Baltic states were under
Bolshevik control except on part of the coast. Apparently, there
was no thought of food relief to the starving population under
Bolshevik control. There could be relief to the non-Bolshevik areas
of the coast, however, provided that the Allies place enough naval
forces on the coast and in the ports at Hoover's disposal "to protect
the relief of all the coastal towns"; furthermore, military supplies
should be furnished "to the established governments so as to enable
them to maintain order in the interior and to defend their
borders." Hoover concluded by hoping for a short period when
"the British and American naval authorities, who are familiar with
the situation, could appear, together with myself on the food side,
in the hope that some definite political relief policy could be arrived
at." And while the Communists were the major threat, Hoover noted that the German army continued to occupy Lithuania, "and
some instruction must be given them to cease interfering with the
development of the government there—for something must be
established to succeed the German occupation."[47]

The American government quickly responded by sending Admiral William S. Benson with a force of destroyers to the Baltic
states to assist Hoover's efforts. Hoover's requested British naval
force, under Admiral G. P. W. Hope, arrived at the end of June—
but too late for Hoover's military maneuvers in Latvia. Hoover had
little further trouble in Estonia and Lithuania, but Latvia was
another story.

In contrast to the Estonians and Lithuanians, who had beaten
back the Communist armies, the former with the aid of British
warships, the Latvian government of Karlis Ulmanis had been defeated in January by a combined Communist uprising and Soviet
invasion. The Communists thereby controlled most of Latvia, including the great port city of Riga. In March and early April,
Ulmanis managed a successful revolt against the Communists in
the coastal South Latvian city of Libau, at which point Hoover
promptly supplied the Ulmanis area with food. But in mid-April,
the Ulmanis regime in Libau was overturned by a mixed German
Balt-White Russian army headed by a German adventurer named
Baron von Stryck, quietly aided by the army of von der Goltz.

Hoover's favorite, Ulmanis, fled into exile, and Hoover's policy now faced a threat from the German right. Promptly, Hoover cut off food distribution in Libau and on April 20 sent a squadron of American destroyers to the Libau coast. Immediately responding to Hoover's pressure, von der Goltz issued a proclamation repudiating the von Stryck government, which promptly fled, leaving the field again to Ulmanis. Hoover immediately resumed the distribution of food.

But after May 9, Hoover still faced the problem of Riga and the remainder of Latvia. Unwilling to wait for the British forces, Hoover assumed personal responsibility for the situation. Since Admiral Benson was not strong enough to conquer Riga, Hoover asked von der Goltz to invade Riga; von der Goltz needed no further urging, and he was able, with the assistance of the remnant of the Latvian army, to occupy part of Riga by May 22. Hoover's food supplies followed promptly, assisted by one of Admiral Benson's destroyers.

No sooner had Riga been secured from the Communists, than von der Goltz's Baltic army instituted what Hoover concedes was a White Terror to replace the preceding Red Terror in the city. Hoover quickly ordered his aide, Colonel John Groome, to instruct the Balts to cease and desist immediately, for "the American people will not lend their support for an instant to any movement which would countenance such actions. . . ." The Baltic White Terror subsided and Ulmanis returned to Riga, and, as Hoover puts it, "with food behind him, set up a provisional government again." But, once more, war broke out in Riga between von der Goltz and the Balts on the one hand, and the Latvian government, assisted by an Estonian force, on the other. Hoover's aide, Colonel Groome, was able to arrange an end to the fighting, with a coalition government established under Ulmanis. Latvia was at last secured for the American policy.[48]

There are few figures in Hoover's *Memoirs* who receive more lavish praise than Karlis Ulmanis. Hoover repeatedly refers to him as a "unique figure," possessed of an outstanding "devotion to freedom." Similar to Paderewski, Ulmanis had been raised as a youth in the United States, where he had later taught economics. Hoover's admiration for the conservative peasant leader persisted for decades thereafter; as Hoover notes in his *Memoirs,* "twenty years later, at his invitation, I visited the prosperous Latvian Republic."[49] In the light of his continuing admiration for the "greatest leader in the Baltic States," Hoover's more detailed account in *An American Epic* seems curiously bland:

The greatest leader in the Baltic States—Ulmanis—at one time
had been voted out of his office as President by his unmanageable
Parliament. A few years prior to my visit [in March 1938] with the
aid of the Latvian Army, he had taken over the government and
transformed it into a Fascist state.[50]

The boundary lines of European nations as drawn by the Gaunt
Hand of Hunger. *Courtesy National Geographic Society.*

Herbert Hoover's attitude toward the Soviet Union was of a piece
with his other activities in Eastern and Central Europe. In opposition to Allied proposals for full-scale military intervention to crush
the Bolshevik regime, Hoover, in a memorandum to the president
on March 28, noted that the Communist "tyranny of the extreme
left" had succeeded, and in a sense was in response to the preced-

ing "tyranny of the extreme right." Full-scale American military intervention, he warned, in addition to involving years of police duty, would "in the nature of things make us a party to the Allies to re-establishing the reactionary classes" in Russia. What then to do? Certainly not recognize the tyranny of the "Bolshevik murderers," which act would stimulate "actionist radicalism in every country in Europe." Hoover then suggested a devious alternative to full-scale war on the one hand or recognition on the other, an alternative which he later termed a "faint hope." To meet the problem of widespread famine in Russia, Hoover proposed that some "neutral of international reputation for probity and ability" be found to suggest to Russia a supposedly "neutral" relief commission. But to carry out his purely "humanitarian task," the Bolsheviks would have to agree to "cease all militant action across certain defined boundaries," as well as—more significant stipulation!—"cease their subsidizing of disturbances abroad." Not the least of the virtues of the plan, for Hoover, was that, if agreed to by the Russians, "it might give a period of rest along the frontiers of Europe and would give some hope of stabilization."[51]

With the approval of Wilson, Hoover sought out his proposed eminent neutral, his old friend the Norwegian Arctic explorer, Fritjof Nansen. With great reluctance, and only because Hoover was able to enlist the Norwegian Prime Minister in helping put on the pressure, Nansen finally agreed to let himself be used as front man for Hoover in the enterprise. Hoover then drafted a Nansen letter to Wilson and the other Allied leaders, and then in turn drafted their reply. The exchange of letters spelled out more of the impudent conditions to be imposed on Russia by the Hoover scheme. In return for food to be supplied by the international neutral commission in a supposedly "wholly non-political" and "purely humanitarian" manner, Russia would have to: finance the entire enterprise; allow the Commission to supervise the entire transportation and distribution of food inside Russia; and, most important, unilaterally stop fighting the White forces in the civil war then raging within Russia. Not only would the Bolsheviks have to stop fighting; they would also have to cease transferring any troops or military equipment within the Soviet Union. The proposal made no mention, on the other hand, of the White armies ceasing hostilities, nor about ending Allied aid to the White forces. The Hoover-drafted Allied reply to Nansen concluded that "relief to Russia which did not mean a return to a state of peace would be futile, and impossible to consider."[52] Of course, similar conditions did not apply to the White armies and their areas held in Russia, which Hoover continued to supply throughout this period.[53]

Nansen transmitted the proposal to the Russians in early May; the Bolsheviks sensibly replied that they would under no circumstances cease fighting except by victory or by successful direct negotiations with the White forces. Such was the fate of the Nansen plan, which Hoover alleges at least bought time to allow the cooling off of Allied proposals for large-scale military intervention in Russia.

In his *Memoirs*, Hoover omits the inception of the Nansen plan at the beginning of March, by both himself and Vance McCormick, head of the War Trade Board. On March 4, Hoover and McCormick met in Paris with two leading Czarist émigrés, Boris Bakhmetev and Serge Sazonov; at the meeting, McCormick proposed a plan for economic relief of Russia "by joint Allied and neutral action, to be distributed under proper military protection." Furthermore, the Hoover picture of Nansen as a pure political innocent is belied by Nansen's calling on McCormick in mid-March with talk of becoming a front man for the Russian émigrés "to head an international movement to help Russia get arms and munitions and one hundred million dollars to down Bolshevism."[54] By March 26, Herbert Hoover, according to Wilson's chief aide Colonel House, in arriving at the Nansen plan, felt "that as soon as the fighting stops the Bolshevik army will disintegrate and the distribution of food to the people of Russia will make them less eager to continue their policy of agitation. . . ."[55]

Neither does Hoover mention in his recollections the fact that one day after Allied agreement to the Nansen proposal, already unworkably offensive to the Russians, Hoover insisted on issuing a vehement anti-Bolshevik manifesto "attacking the tyranny, cruelty, and incapacity of the Soviet regime." Colonel House was appalled that "just as soon . . . as we have it [the Nansen plan] signed by the president and the three prime ministers Hoover gives out a statement which would absolutely destroy any chance of its success." To dissuade Hoover, House had to invoke the sanction of President Wilson and his aides, who "were unanimous in the opinion that it was a childish thing to do."[56]

Herbert Hoover arrived back home from Europe on September 13, 1919. In later years, he liked to think of his relief work there as non-political and humanitarian, but in fact he engaged in a persistent and largely effective use of food as a political and diplomatic weapon, in the service of the Wilsonian ideal of imposing on starving and war-torn Europe a series of centrist regimes under the guidance of the United States, regimes that would be free of the right-wing taint of old-fashioned European monarchy and autocracy, and of the new and menacing left-wing taint of bolshevism.

NOTES

1   On the Wilsonian design, see N. Gordon Levin, Jr., *Woodrow Wilson and World Politics* (New York: Oxford University Press, 1968).

2   Herbert Hoover, *Memoirs: Years of Adventure, 1874–1920* (New York: Macmillan, 1951), vol. 1, esp. chaps. 31–48; Hoover, *The Ordeal of Woodrow Wilson* (New York: McGraw-Hill, 1958), esp. chaps. 9–11; and Hoover, *An American Epic* (Chicago: Regnery, 1960–61), vol. 2, sections 3–4; 3, *passim.*

3   Hoover, *Memoirs,* 1:217–18, 283, 286.

4   Hoover, *Memoirs,* 1:287–88.

5   Hoover, *Memoirs,* 1:289.

6   Hoover, *Memoirs,* 1:277.

7   Hoover, *Memoirs,* 1:290.

8   Hoover, *Ordeal of Woodrow Wilson,* p. 153.

9   Hoover, *Ordeal of Woodrow Wilson,* p. 156. Also see *ibid.,* pp. 151, 155, 157.

10   Hoover, *Memoirs,* 1:330–31. Also see *ibid.,* p. 329.

11   Hoover, *Memoirs,* 1:333. Also see Hoover, *An American Epic,* 2:313–16, 358–60.

12   Levin, *Woodrow Wilson,* p. 148. Also see Arno J. Mayer, *Politics and Diplomacy of Peacemaking: Containment and Counterrevolution at Versailles, 1918–1919* (New York: Knopf, 1967), pp. 272ff.

13   Hoover, *Memoirs,* 1:335, 347.

14   Cited in Mayer, *Politics and Diplomacy of Peacemaking,* p. 268.

15   Hoover, *An American Epic,* 2:322.

16   Hoover, *Ordeal of Woodrow Wilson,* pp. 164–65; Hoover, *Memoirs,* 1:341; Hoover, *An American Epic,* 3:85.

17   Hoover, *Memoirs,* 1:350; Hoover, *Ordeal of Woodrow Wilson,* p. 172; Hoover, *An American Epic,* 3:86.

18   Hoover, *Memoirs,* 1:349–50; Hoover, *An American Epic,* 3:87–88, 89–92.

19   Cited in Mayer, *Politics and Diplomacy of Peacemaking,* pp. 65–67.

20   In Mayer, *Politics and Diplomacy of Peacemaking,* p. 68.

21   Mayer, *Politics and Diplomacy of Peacemaking,* pp. 258–59, 261–62.

22   Hoover, *An American Epic,* 2:320–21.

23   Mayer, *Politics and Diplomacy of Peacemaking,* pp. 281–82.

24   Mayer, *Politics and Diplomacy of Peacemaking,* pp. 493–504.

25   *Arbeiter Zeitung,* March 23, 1919; cited in Mayer, *Politics and Diplomacy of Peacemaking,* p. 591. Also see *ibid.,* p. 721. In the same issue of the *Arbeiter Zeitung,* the government-led executive committee of the workers' councils of Austria echoed the same theme. Translated in Helmut Gruber, ed., *International Communism in the Era of Lenin* (Greenwich, Conn.: Fawcett, 1967), p. 197.

26   Mayer, *Politics and Diplomacy of Peacemaking,* p. 731.

27   Hoover, *An American Epic,* 3:120–21. Added to the Hoover warning was a similar statement of Colonel Thomas Cunningham, the chief British representative in Austria. Cunningham warned that any spread in "political unrest would lead to an interruption of all imports, including food." Cunningham's warnings were also posted on walls all over Vienna. See Alfred D. Low, "The First Austrian Republic and Soviet Hungary," *Journal of Central European Affairs* (July 1960), in Gruber, *International Communism,* p. 253n.

28   Hoover, *An American Epic,* 3:120–21; Hoover, *Memoirs,* 1:394.

29   The final confrontation, and the defeat of the Communists, came in mid-June, after which Austrian Foreign Minister Otto Bauer wrote to Bela Kun, reiterating that there could not be a Soviet Austria, since, *inter alia,* "The feeding of Vienna and of the industrial regions depends on imports from the Entente. The Entente, however, would stop them simply for the reason that it would look upon Bolshevik German Austria as not being a fair risk. The mere stoppage of food imports would result in dire starvation." Bauer to Kun, June 16, 1919. Cited in Low, "First Austrian Republic," in Gruber, *International Communism,* p. 264.

30   Hoover, *Ordeal of Woodrow Wilson,* pp. 134–35; Hoover, *An American Epic,* 3:123–26; Hoover, *Memoirs,* 1:398.

31   Hoover, *Ordeal of Woodrow Wilson,* p. 136.

32   Hoover, *An American Epic,* 3:358, 361.

33   Hoover, *An American Epic,* 3:362–63.

34   Hoover, *An American Epic,* 3:363–64.

35   Hoover to Wilson, June 9, 1919. Mayer, *Politics and Diplomacy of Peacemaking,* p. 828.

36   Minutes of the Daily Meeting of the Commissioners Plenipotentiary, July 1, 1919, in *Papers Relating to the Foreign Relations of the United States, the Paris Peace Conference 1919* (Washington, D.C.: GPO, 1945), 11:259–60.

37   Hoover, *An American Epic,* 3:364–65; Hoover, *Memoirs,* 1:400.

38   Hoover, *An American Epic,* 3:367.

39   Hoover, *An American Epic,* 3:370–71; Mayer, *Politics and Diplomacy of Peacemaking,* p. 850.

40   Hoover, *An American Epic,* 3:371–72; Mayer, *Poltics and Diplomacy of Peacemaking,* p. 850.

41   Hoover, *An American Epic,* 3:375.

42   Hoover, *An American Epic,* 3:374.

43   Mayer, *Politics and Diplomacy of Peacemaking,* pp. 851–52.

44   Hoover, *Memoirs,* 1:409.

45   Hoover, *An American Epic,* 3:66, 315.

46   For Hoover on his activities in relation to Poland, see Hoover, *An American Epic,* 3:62–68, 314–16; Hoover, *Memoirs,* 1:355–62.

47   Hoover, *An American Epic,* 3:43–44; Hoover, *Ordeal of Woodrow Wilson,* 127–29.

48   See Hoover, *An American Epic,* 3:46–52, 301–03; Hoover, *Memoirs,* 1:372–76; Hoover, *Ordeal of Woodrow Wilson,* pp. 131–34.

49   Hoover, *Memoirs,* 1:372n.

50   Hoover, *An American Epic,* 3:313.

51   Hoover, *Memoris,* 1:412–14; Hoover, *Ordeal of Woodrow Wilson,* pp. 117–19. The full text of the Hoover memorandum is in Mayer, *Politics and Diplomacy of Peacemaking,* pp. 24–27, and 474–78.

52   Hoover, *Memoirs,* 1:415–17; Hoover, *Ordeal of Woodrow Wilson,* pp. 120–22.

53   Hoover, *An American Epic,* 3:166–71.

54   Mayer, *Politics and Diplomacy of Peacemaking,* p. 473.

55   Mayer, *Politics and Diplomacy of Peacemaking,* p. 474.

56   Mayer, *Politics and Diplomacy of Peacemaking,* pp. 482–83.

EUGENE P. TRANI

Herbert Hoover and the
Russian Revolution, 1917–20

EDITOR'S INTRODUCTORY NOTE

Eugene Trani's characterization of Hoover's thinking about Russia as combining "great insight" with "extreme naiveté" could apply equally to many American leaders during the critical years 1917–20. Travel to a foreign country *may* be helpful in acquainting a person with customs, economic and social life, even the political institutions of the country visited. Yet, few travelers to prewar Russia, without knowledge of the language and correspondingly with limited opportunities to meet representative Russians, would likely come away with a keen appreciation of the potential for revolution or an appreciation of how Marxism would apply to the Russian environment. It is questionable whether Hoover's several visits to Russia prepared him intellectually for an understanding of the Bolshevik Revolution in 1917. His views of the Russian political crisis continuing throughout the Peace Conference of 1919 conformed to those expressed by many Wilsonians: that historically, Russia had suffered from tyrannical and despotic government; political upheaval was long overdue, and in the end the Russian state would construct a suitable democratic political structure; bolshevism was merely a transitory stage toward some Russian approximation of the democratic model; it would collapse inevitably due to its inner contradictions; hence, opposition to the Bolshevik leadership utilizing foreign military intervention would be both futile and counterproductive.

Hoover's observations had led him to expect some political upheaval in Russia. Sharp extremes between the aristocracy and the peasantry without the presence of a viable middle class did not portend a stable political climate. Mass starvation and fundamental economic needs left unmet provided fertile conditions for revolu-

Eugene P. Trani is professor of history and assistant vice-president for academic affairs at the University of Nebraska, Lincoln.

tion. In Hoover's view, continued and expanding economic dislocations elsewhere in Europe would extend the irrationalism of
bolshevism. Relief on a massive scale was needed not only for
humanitarian reasons but it would also serve the political purpose
of checking the spread of the corrosive ideology.

Perhaps no better illustration can be cited to demonstrate the
degree of control personally exercised by President Wilson during
the war than his response to the concerted pressure brought to
bear on the White House to send a relief mission headed by Hoover
to Russia during the summer of 1918. Trani takes pains to disclose
how virtually every influential adviser in the administration, including Secretary of State Robert Lansing, Edward House,
Bernard Baruch, and Louis Brandeis endorsed the proposal.
Hoover did not feel averse to it. Yet, for various reasons, Trani relates, Wilson vetoed the plan. Nevertheless, the thought lingered
that foreign economic intervention in Russia would afford an opportunity to halt the civil war, bring moderating influence to bear
on the Bolsheviks, and contain the expansion of this political
epidemic. It is possible that Hoover and others of like mind exaggerated the dangers of bolshevism in East-Central Europe
purposely in order to distribute larger quantities of American
agricultural commodities. The French suspected that the bogey of
bolshevism was being raised in order to lessen the economic
burdens for the defeated Central Powers. Historian John M.
Thompson has observed that "the fear of Bolshevism may . . . have
had less effect on the peacemaking than is sometimes thought. It
certainly prodded the statesmen at Paris to finish their task as
quickly as possible. . . . But it would be difficult to prove that
bolshevism affected the general structure of the Versailles settlement in major ways."[1] As Hoover assessed the situation, an expanding bolshevism would eventually pose a threat to American interests which would necessitate an American military response.
Meanwhile, Hoover advised against a resort to armed intervention
in Russia as a means for dealing with the Bolsheviks.

That Hoover actually served as President Wilson's principal adviser on Russia during the period prior to the signing of the Treaty
of Versailles is certainly suggested in this article. What is more important, I think, is that the issues of relief and rehabilitation were
intertwined in the American government's assessment of the
Russian question and the general appeal of bolshevism. Certainly
no political question at the Peace Conference exercised Herbert

Hoover's interest as much as his concern over the present and future status of Russia. Professor Trani's article shows the evolution of this interest.

1 John M. Thompson, *Russia, Bolshevism and the Versailles Peace* (Princeton: Princeton University Press, 1966), p. 395.

Herbert Hoover and the Russian Revolution, 1917–20

Herbert Hoover had a long and important relationship with Russia. As a young mining engineer at the turn of the century he had become fascinated with the resources, many of them unexploited, of the Far East. His tremendous energy and the almost boundless nature of his activity necessarily involved him in Russian concerns. His interest began with business trips that took him to Russia in pursuit of mining concessions before the First World War, extended to his observations about the Revolution of 1917 and the effect that event might have on the world, and involved his efforts to extend relief, particularly food, both inside and outside the country as the World War came to an end and the Russians turned their attention to a destructive civil war. Between 1921 and 1928, when Hoover served as secretary of commerce, his involvement continued. He headed the massive American response to Maxim Gorky's plea to aid the people of Soviet Russia, through the American Relief Administration, and also helped determine the extent of American business operations inside the Soviet Union. As president between 1929 and 1933, he continued the policy adopted by the Wilson administration in 1918 of refusing to extend recognition to the Soviet government, despite an enormous campaign to shift that policy. Even after 1933, Hoover maintained his interest in Russia and periodically made public statements on American relations with that country.

One of the most interesting periods during his half century of concern for Russian affairs came in the years between 1917 and 1920. The word that best characterizes his views between 1917 and 1920 is *consistency*. Notwithstanding all of the turmoil in Russia in that period, Hoover's views of Russia remained unchanged, and were based on two themes. The first was compassion for the Russian people. Hoover believed in the Russian people and did all he could to aid them. The second theme concerned his strong opposition to bolshevism. Yet he felt that the Western Allies could not succeed militarily in overthrowing bolshevism. He urged a moderate policy, waiting for bolshevism to fall because of what he felt were its own contradictions. His observations during these years were a combination of great insight and extreme naiveté.

His observations and actions regarding Russia between 1917 and 1920 resulted from events in those years, but also from personal experience in Russia. There is little evidence other than Hoover's *Memoirs* on his business trips to Russia before the World War, but these visits clearly affected the way he looked at the Russian Revolution. He first came into contact with Russians while a mining engineer in China at the turn of the century. There was a large Russian presence in China at that time and Hoover met and dealt with both Russian officials and businessmen. As general manager of the Chinese Engineering and Mining Company, he had to submit claims against countries that had sent troops into China at the time of the Boxer Rebellion and destroyed property belonging to that company. Destruction by "the Russians had been the worst, for they loaded several trains with machinery and supplies from the mines and ran them off the railway into Manchuria," part of which the Russian government controlled. Hoover had difficulty collecting the claims, as the Russian agent demanded a large commission, which Hoover refused. Eventually the claim was paid, and then, to his surprise, the military commander in Manchuria sold the machinery and stores back. These events gave Hoover a lot to think about.[1]

His initial negative reaction toward the Russian government was intensified during the years prior to 1914, when he made "numerous prolonged visits" to Russia. His *Memoirs* list that country as one he traveled in every year between 1909 and 1913.[2] He had gone because opportunities had opened for an "industrial doctor." The tsarist government was happy to see Americans come into Russia, for industry there was dominated by British and German entrepreneurs. Hoover could see that Russia was rich in resources, and in helping develop these resources he had intimate contacts with both private and government operations. He had large dealings with the Kyshtim estate in the Urals near Ekaterinburg, an enormous estate of about 1,500,000 acres, "comprising agricultural land, great forests, important copper deposits, an iron, steel and chemical industry, with a population of about 100,000 peasants and workers." He came to rescue the estate from years of waste and extravagance. He saw it as a microcosm of all Russia. At top, a Russian noble family. At bottom, 100,000 peasants and workers, with almost no one but priests and overseers in between. It seemed like a feudal setup, with everyone dependent on one family. Agricultural land on the estate was not good, with crops uncertain, but the forests and mining preserved a modest prosperity. Still it was all dependent on the attitude of the noble family, and Hoover's efforts to keep the family interested in the estate were much appreciated.

He also dealt with properties belonging to the tsar. Hoover's group was asked to take over some of the Cabinet Mines, personal property of the tsar. Having earlier read George Kennan's eye-opening sensation, *Siberia and the Exile System* (1891), which had exposed the treatment of political prisoners in these mines, Hoover knew the mines were valuable. Since Kennan's book had appeared, and partly because of it, there had been reforms at the mines and Hoover felt he could with good conscience help develop such mines, even though they were worked by convicts. He found many of the holdings to be rich beyond belief, remarking that one in the Altai Mountains, with deposits of copper, lead and zinc sulphides, and gold and silver, consisted of "probably the greatest and richest single body of ore known in the world." He was proud of the contrast between the mines Kennan had described and Hoover's operations, which were those of "engineers, systematically turning the mines into a decent industry with decently treated labor in wholesome communities."[3]

Nonetheless he knew there was trouble ahead for the Russian government. He was struck with the contrasts of the country. The extremes of wealth and poverty were obvious. So were the "hideous social and governmental" structures. He never forgot a sight he came upon one day at a railway station:

[A] long line of intelligent, decent people brutally chained together were marched aboard a freight car bound for Siberia. Some were the faces of despair itself, some of despondency itself, some of defiance itself. The whole scene was so revolting that I reacted to it in nightmares. Always there was a feeling among us that some day the country would blow up.

Some of his friends hoped Russian energies would be directed toward democracy. But, as he wrote, "centuries of poverty and repression do not express their explosions in law and peaceful transformation."[4]

With outbreak of the war in 1914, the trips to Russia stopped. When he took charge of the Belgian Relief, he resigned all his engineering connections and by 1917 had sold his personal holdings in Russian enterprises.[5] Still he continued to follow events in Russia and wondered if the explosion would come. He wondered what effect the war would have. He received word that many of the workers and officials of the mine concessions he had helped with were being drafted into the army. He heard that "transportation was disorganized" and told President Woodrow Wilson's adviser, Colonel Edward M. House, that Germans he was in contact with, through the Belgian Relief, "believed they had Russia on the way to disintegration." As 1917 came and the United States arrived at the edge of war, he wondered how some supporters of the war could argue that it was a war to save democracy and that America should enter the war, for he thought an Allied victory might "cement the Czarist regime upon the Russian people."[6]

His German contacts proved correct. In March 1917, he was in the midst of crossing the Atlantic on the Spanish vessel *Antonio Lopez* when a radio bulletin announced the Russian Revolution and the tsar's abdication. His reaction, given to his friend and traveling companion, the journalist Will Irwin, was:

> This revolution will be difficult to stabilize. There have been centuries of oppression. There is no large middle class. There is almost total illiteracy in the people. There is no general experience in government. Russia cannot maintain a wholly liberal republic yet. Revolutions always go further than their creators expect. And in its swing, this one is more likely to go to the left than to the right.[7]

His reaction combined happiness that an oppressive government had been overthrown with concern about excesses the revolution might unleash.

Throughout 1917 he watched events closely. He got some of his Russian friends in touch with the American ambassador, David R. Francis, thinking they might be able to help Francis. He asked, in one case, that Francis allow one Russian friend to use embassy cables "to send me a telegram from time to time on what he considers the vital issues in Russian politics, as I may be of help in these matters, and I am anxious to keep in touch with the Russian currents."[8] Once he took over as food administrator in May 1917, he received government telegrams concerning conditions.[9] He became alarmed about reports of food supplies and asked J. Ralph Pickell, who was going to Russia on business in June 1917, if he "would officially represent the new Food Administration in making investigations as to the food situation in Russia." Russia was, of course, of concern to the United States and Hoover felt he had to have "first-hand information in order to act with safety and propriety in the distribution of exports from this country."[10] Reports he received only alarmed him. He came to believe that one of the causes of the Bolshevik takeover in November 1917 was incompetence of the Russian food administration. "Every city was filled with mobs crying for food," he wrote. Although Russia had ample supplies of food, they were not well distributed and "the people in Moscow, St. Petersburg, and Rostov were starving and the Russian armies along the Front were hungry."[11] It was this situation, he believed, which brought the Bolsheviks to power.

His reaction to the Bolsheviks was both specific, in view of his experiences, and general. He looked with dismay and alarm as the Bolsheviks encouraged workers to take over plants, expropriated private property, dismissed management, and dramatically increased wages. He knew that untrained workers could not supply the technical and administrative skills an industrially developing Russia needed. He was later to find out what this process meant to the Kyshtim estate.[12] On a more general level he was concerned with the international policies followed by the Bolsheviks. Withdrawal of Russia from the war, the hostile attitude toward the Allies, the treaty with Germany which allowed the Germans to move troops to the Western front, all concerned Hoover and other members of the American government. He worried about Americans in Russia and wrote Ambassador Francis expressing concern for the ambassador's "safety in this melee."[13] But he was busy with the war and found it increasingly difficult, as did all Americans, to understand events in Russia in late 1917 and the first half of 1918.

As the American government, especially President Wilson, tried to make sense out of what was happening in Russia and create a policy in regard to that country, there was a good deal of Allied pressure for American intervention. This pressure, which began almost immediately after the Bolsheviks came to power, increased during the first half of 1918. The Allies called for a joint Japanese-American presence in Siberia. The Allies presented many arguments, diplomatically and through the Supreme War Council in Paris, but these represented an attempt to replace the Bolsheviks with a government that would resume the Russian war against the Germans. Wilson fought these proposals, and got Hoover's support. The president had sought as many opinions as possible and, knowing of Hoover's experience, Wilson had asked the food administrator's views. Hoover opposed any move of Japanese troops into Siberia, because of Russian racial hatred for the Japanese, a belief that "if the Japanese moved in they would never get out," and a feeling that such intervention would "consolidate many Russian elements behind Lenin and Trotsky." He was convinced the Japanese would "demand Eastern Siberia as a reward" for going into Russia and he opposed this.[14] Hoover's advice supported the president's views, but the problem would not go away. Pressure from the British ambassador in Washington, Lord Reading, and Sir William Wiseman, the special British diplomatic agent to the United States, as well as that which came through the American military representative to the Supreme War Council, General Tasker Bliss, became difficult to resist. Wilson's position on Siberian intervention, which he saw as only one part of the Russian question, weakened when the Allied campaign for action in Siberia gained important American advocates.[15]

It was in June 1918 that this issue was reaching a crisis and Hoover briefly came to the center. While Secretary of State Robert Lansing and also House opposed military intervention in Siberia, they came to conclude that the United States had to do something in Siberia. On June 13 both wrote the president urging that Hoover head a Russian Relief Commission.[16]

The proposal came, apparently, from Gordon Auchincloss, House's son-in-law, working at that time as a special assistant to the secretary of state. The idea of sending a relief commission to Russia had gained wide support by early June. The name of John Mott, general secretary of the International Committee of the Y.M.C.A., had been suggested but Auchincloss telephoned House on the night of June 12 and suggested Hoover. Since Hoover knew Russia, had had interests there, and was one of the best organizers the country had produced, he seemed an ideal choice. The idea appealed strongly to House.[17] They decided to approach Hoover and see if he had any interest. House told Auchincloss to stress the plan and also personal benefits for Hoover, who "had been so entirely associated with food problems, that for his own sake, it would be a good thing to show the world that he was capable of just as good work in other directions."[18] Hoover and Auchincloss discussed the Russian situation and Auchincloss was impressed with Hoover's "sane view." Hoover said he was "willing to do anything that the Colonel wanted him to do and that the organization of the Food Administration was in such shape that he could turn it over to another to run for him."[19] Hoover's reaction to the plan, according to House, was enthusiastic, thinking it "the best solution of the Russian problem."[20]

The next step was to get as much support as possible behind the suggestion, before going to the president. Proclaiming the plan, "The Commission for the Relief of Russia," Auchincloss saw Lansing and the secretary thought the idea a good one, and agreed that Auchincloss should draw up a letter to the president for his signature. Auchincloss wrote the letter, checking it out with House and Frank L. Polk, the counselor of the State Department, and Lansing signed it "without changing a word." Auchincloss discussed the plan with Wiseman, who indicated approval, and Vance McCormick, head of the War Trade Board, who thought highly of it. With this backstage maneuvering completed, the president received two letters, both dated June 13.[21]

The letter Lansing signed was detailed. It pointed out that Great Britain, France, Italy, and Japan, as well as the Russian people were awaiting a constructive American plan "for meeting the present chaotic conditions in Russia."[22] This could be done by sending relief to Russia along the same lines as the "Commission for the Relief of Belgium," paid for, at least initially, with money from the president's War Fund. Lansing noted that such a plan would give "tangible evidence" the United States planned to stand by the Russian people. He said there was nobody better qualified to head such a commission than Hoover, whose appointment "would be widely acclaimed as another evidence of the determination of the United States to assist the Russian people towards the establishment of an orderly Government independent of Germany." The secretary believed the commission would, at least temporarily, dispose of the proposal for armed intervention, which would depend on Hoover's observations on the scene. House had Auchincloss send a note to Mrs. Wilson, indicating House's support of the project.[23] House decided to write Wilson directly.[24] He hoped the president thought well of the plan. He argued that Hoover could be replaced in the Food Administration and could not be opposed, because of his reputation, by any government in Russia, friendly or unfriendly. House stressed Hoover's ability as an organizer, his knowledge of Russia, his reputation, and argued that "his appointment will, for a moment, settle the Russian question as far as it can be settled by you at present."

Hoover informed the president he would serve anywhere, but expressed doubt, so he later wrote, about combining the plan with military intervention. To send an army, he noted, "to attack the Bolshevists' Eastern Front while extending kindness on their Western Front was not quite logical. In any event, our ideas of industrial organization would scarcely fit into the philosophy of Messrs. Lenin and Trotsky, even if they did not reject the plan utterly as an Allied Trojan horse."[25]

The next move was up to Wilson and the president seemed in no hurry, notwithstanding increasing pressure in Hoover's behalf, and the fact that (according to Auchincloss) Hoover "would very much like to be appointed to handle the situation." House and Hoover by June 17 had worked out the best procedure in the event Wilson asked Hoover to go. House thought Hoover should have control of any Russian mission, even if it included military components.[26] House got Reading, the British ambassador, to concur and even suggested arguments Reading might use in trying to convince the president.[27]

By late June, Wilson had decided against Hoover's going to Russia, though he did not rule out an economic mission, and Hoover heard nothing more about it. In a discussion with McCormick, the president said he was not disposed to appoint Hoover, "stating that Hoover's temperament was not fitted for this work and also that he did not like to put Russia in the same class as Belgium."[28] Despite support for Hoover from Supreme Court Justice Louis Brandeis, War Industries Board Administrator Bernard Baruch, and Minister to China Paul Reinsch, Wilson stuck to his position. There were other reasons he did not appoint Hoover. To Baruch's statement that by sending Hoover, the Russians would realize that "you are sending someone to help, not to conquer," the president answered that he could not "without dislocating some of the most important things we are handling spare him from his present functions."[29] Another of the president's objections became clear when Wilson raised Hoover's "ownership of Siberian mines, thus introducing a capitalistic element."[30] Hoover's name was removed, a decision for which Hoover later expressed relief.[31] It seems clear that he was interested in going, but seeing how the Russian situation turned out he realized it was fortunate Wilson did not send him.

Wilson decided against any economic mission. In July 1918, he reluctantly agreed to dispatch American troops to North Russia and Siberia and hoped his concessions to the Allies had put an end

to plans for intervention. He saw little need for an economic commission, and may have thought the sending of such a commission
more interventionist than the dispatch of limited American troops
with instructions to avoid involvement in internal Russian affairs.[32]
Hoover, as a result, remained in the United States.

The months between July 1918 and March 1919, when Hoover
emerged as the dominant figure in American-Russian affairs, gave
him a good deal of time to come to some ideas about bolshevism
and Soviet Russia. He became convinced that bolshevism
flourished where starvation existed. To him, bolshevism and
starvation went hand in hand. It was perhaps a simplistic explanation but one, given Hoover's background, that was natural. As he
watched the Bolsheviks solidify their control in European Russia
and withstand the onslaught of the anti-Bolshevik movements, all
he read seemed to prove his analysis right. He became alarmed
about the spread of bolshevism beyond Russia and worried about
the newly "liberated peoples" of Austria, Serbia, Bulgaria, and
Turkey. He wrote the president in November about feeding these
people, urging that Allied military forces aid the United States
Food Administration. He realized it would be expensive but "it is
not necessary for me to mention how fundamental it appears to me
that this is, if we are to preserve these countries from Bolshevism
and rank anarchy."[33]

By late October, shortly before the Armistice, Hoover was in
Paris. In December, he was named director general of relief for the
Supreme War Council. The Paris Peace Conference was to begin its
sessions in January, and they would run for weeks and months, until signature of the treaty with Germany in June. Was there a
chance that Hoover could help solve the Russian difficulties during
this grand meeting of most of the major statesmen of the world? A
century had passed since the conference of Vienna, and it seemed
as if once again the powers of the universe would be coming
together to reorder life everywhere. If contrary to 1814–15, Russia
was not represented, the Russian problem nonetheless was present,
and it was possible that Hoover could do something constructive.

But by that time Germany had become a prime concern. Hoover
urged the president to get the Allies to help feed the German people "not only out of humanity but out of its fundamental necessity
to prevent anarchy." The four associated governments had to take
a stand on Germany. If the Bolsheviks came to control in any section of Germany it would bring a "break down in commercial distribution and in the control and distribution of existing food." Peo-

ple would be susceptible to Bolshevik slogans. Hoover worried about separatist movements in the German states. Such movements had to be stopped, he told the president, for parts of the country might develop food surpluses and by embargoes create "food debacles in other centres." Supplies had to remain evenly distributed, and the Allies had to do all they could to assure this. If the Allies stated they would not send food to any area of Germany controlled by Bolsheviks, he thought, "it would at once strengthen the whole situation in Germany and probably entirely eliminate the incipient Bolshevism in progress, and make possible the hope of saving their food situation."[34] And he influenced the president, who unsuccessfully urged the Allies to relax the blockade against Germany. Wilson shortly cabled Congress supporting an appropriation of $100,000,000 for "which Mr. Hoover has asked for the administration of food relief."[35] Wilson, picking up Hoover's ideas, proclaimed food relief the key to the whole European situation, and indeed "to the solutions of peace." Bolshevism was advancing westward, had almost overwhelmed Poland, and was poisoning Germany. It could only be stopped by food. American money, the president stated, would not be spent for food in Germany, "because Germany can buy its food, but it will be spent for financing the movement of food to our real friends in Poland and to the people of the liberated units of the Austro-Hungarian empire and to our associates in the Balkans." There could be no peace, the president concluded, unless "the tide of anarchism" was stemmed. Congress responded, allocating funds for food relief.

Perhaps the most comprehensive and mature statement by Hoover on bolshevism at the time of the Paris Peace Conference appeared in a letter in late March to the president, in response to Wilson's request for Hoover's opinion of the Soviet problem.[36] He based his "views as to the American relation to Bolshevism and its manifestations" on his own experience and the independent sources he had had all over Europe. He began by noting that "as a result of Bolshevik economic conceptions, the people of Russia are dying of hunger and disease at the rate of some hundreds of thousands monthly in a country that formerly supplied food to a large part of the world." It was necessary to examine bolshevism closely. He felt he understood why the revolution had come to Russia and why it was spreading and noted that "this swinging of the social pendulum from the tyranny of the extreme right to the tyranny of the extreme left is based on a foundation of real social grievance." Russia and other countries in Eastern and Central

Europe had been ruled for generations by reactionaries, and common people in those areas had suffered greatly. With the war and then the Armistice, famine spread, which "further emphasized the gulf between the lower and upper classes. The poor were starved and driven mad in the presence of extravagence and waste." Bolshevism, he pointed out, had been limited to areas of former reactionary tyranny and was a course that represented "the not unnatural violence of a mass of ignorant humanity, who themselves have learned in grief of tyranny and violence over generations." Americans, accustomed to liberty and comfort, had to sympathize with these people and their "blind gropings for better social conditions." He was sure that the pendulum would swing back to some moderate position.

In the meantime, while sympathetic to conditions that brought bolshevism, he believed Americans should recognize "the utter foolishness" of its economic tenets. American processes of production and distribution, which stimulated individual initiative and stressed equality of opportunity, were far superior. The Bolsheviks believed they could perfect such human qualities as "avarice, ambition, altruism, intelligence, ignorance and education, of which the human animal is today composed," by destroying the capitalist processes of production and distribution. The Bolsheviks, he noted, were a minority wherever they were in control and in fact constituted "a tyranny that is the negation of democracy." Bolsheviks had to resort to terror to maintain control and had "to a greater degree relied upon criminal instinct" than autocracy ever did. But the Bolsheviks were able to weave the "cry of the helpless and the downtrodden" into their doctrines and had become popular.

What of the future? Bolshevik propaganda, Hoover believed, would stir people only in ratio to the numbers "of the suffering and ignorant and criminal." Where the gulf between upper and middle classes on one hand and the lower classes on the other was the largest, "and where the lower classes have been kept in ignorance and distress, this propaganda will be fatal and do violence to normal democratic development." He had no immediate fear for the United States. But there was one other possibility that had to be studied and that was whether "the Bolshevik centers now stirred by great emotional hopes will not undertake large military crusades in an attempt to impose their doctrine on other defenseless people." If this happened the United States had to be ready to fight. If it did not, Americans should not become involved in "what may be a ten year military entanglement in Europe." He doubted if outside "forces entering upon such an enterprise can do other than infinite harm, for any great wave of emotion must ferment and spread under repression." Such activities, if carried out, would be difficult for Americans, for they would be involved in "years of police duty," and "make us a party to reestablishing the reactionary classes in their economic domination over the lower classes." Such activities were against the national spirit and Hoover doubted Americans would want to become such "a mandatory with a vengeance." He worried that in such action American soldiers would not be able to "resist infection with Bolshevik ideas." He urged Wilson to avoid getting involved in any European plans for military intervention, for "our views and principles are at variance with the European Allies" and "we find ourselves subordinated and even committed to policies against our convictions."

Out of this analysis came three recommendations. Hoover told Wilson he opposed recognition of Soviet Russia, for such might stimulate "actionist radicalism in every country in Europe," and would transgress every American ideal. Next, he urged the creation of a Relief Commission, headed by "some Neutral of international reputation." This Commission should work with Allied governments in the "humane work of saving life" in Russia. If the Commission could get assurances that the Bolsheviks would "cease all militant action across certain defined boundaries and cease their subsidizing of disturbances abroad," and that there would be equitable distribution of the supplies, the United States and the Allies should support the relief. He assured the president that "this plan does not involve any recognition or relationship by the Allies of the Bolshevik murderers now in control any more than England recognized Germany in its deals with the Belgian Relief." Such a proposal, he argued, would test whether bolshevism "is a militant force engrossed upon world domination." It would give the frontiers of Europe some period of quiet, which might bring stabilization. It might even present the Russian people an opportunity to "themselves swing back to moderation and themselves bankrupt these ideas." Finally, he asked the president to reassert "spiritual leadership of democracy," by pointing to weaknesses of bolshevism and other tyrannies and stressing the progress of democracy.

Hoover's best-known and most important work regarding Russia at the Peace Conference was the so-called Hoover-Nansen Relief Plan, the name given to the plan for feeding Russia. It represented his reaction to the Allied deliberations over Russia, which he felt was "the Banquo's ghost sitting at every Council table."[37] There was no unity among the Allied and Associated powers over Russia. Approaches to solving the Russian problem went all the way from negotiation to an Allied invasion. During the conference the situation remained in flux. The civil war in Russia was reaching its climax as the Soviets tried to hold European Russia and expand into Poland, the Baltic States, and Siberia. The Soviets found themselves fighting anti-Bolshevik armies led by Kolchak in Siberia, Denikin and Wrangel in South Russia, and Yudenich in the Baltic area. Turmoil made many proposals obsolete by the time they were acted on. Differences of the positions of the Allies on Russia defeated the Prinkipo Proposal, the Bullitt Mission, and Winston Churchill's demand for an invasion of Russia.

Hoover watched in distress as the Allies squabbled over Russia. He was particularly disturbed over Churchill's proposal; not only was it apparent that the financial and military burden would fall on the United States, but "restoration of the old regime seemed likely to be the result of White Russian and Western European Allied collaboration." It was out of this situation that he "concluded that, in view of the desperate food situation in Petrograd, Moscow, and the other large Communist cities, there might be a remote chance to stop fighting everywhere and at the same time to save millions from starvation."[38]

Proposals for Russian relief, of course, were not new and had been urged by others at Paris. Vance McCormick thought about joint Allied and neutral action with "proper military protection," and even talked to Fridtjof Nansen in mid-March. These proposals were more in the nature of anti-Bolshevik crusades for economic and military relief.[39] By late March the Peace Conference looked seriously at relief as an alternative to proposals William C. Bullitt brought back from Russia. Already, Wilson had decided against dispatching any more American troops and in fact began to make plans to withdraw those already in that country. Still, there was a need to do something and at the suggestion of subordinates he asked House to find out if Hoover thought relief possible. Hoover thought it was, though he believed the chances for success rested on the plan proposed. Hoover realized that some dealings with the Soviets were necessary and, provided the Bolsheviks were willing to stop trying to spread revolution, he would do all he could to help in relief of the Russian people. He believed that "as soon as the fighting stops the Bolshevik army will disintegrate and the distribution of food to the people of Russia will make them less eager to continue their policy of agitation."[40]

Thus he outlined his proposal to send Nansen to Russia, as part of his observations on Bolshevik Russia to the president. He had come to know Nansen when the Norwegian had visited the United States seeking food for his country during the war. Nansen, like most Norwegians, had resented the British blockade and was sympathetic to the suffering in Russia. While he did not like the Bolsheviks and was not eager to assume the burden, Nansen understood the problem and agreed to do it if the United States could help get him started "by furnishing initial ships, buying the food," and getting him an expert staff.[41] The president reacted favorably. The plan, Hoover believed, appealed to the president, because it would "keep the Allied militarists in Paris busy debating for some time, and also because, if it succeeded, it would be of great value in saving human life and bringing stability to Europe."[42]

Hoover began to try to organize the relief program. He talked with House and Auchincloss about details and tried to round up support among the Allies and neutrals. He spoke to Robert Cecil about getting Lloyd George's support, and talked to Karl H. Branting, a distinguished Swede.[43] By April 3 plans were moving ahead enough that he drafted letters from Nansen to Allied leaders. In the letter to Wilson, Nansen noted problems in Russia and formally proposed an organization based "upon the lines of the Belgian Relief Commission." It would entail no recognition of existing authorities in Russia, and Nansen's letter wondered "under what conditions you would approve such an enterprise and whether such Commission could look for actual support in finance, shipping and food and medical supplies from the United States Government."[44] A response approving the proposal was prepared for the president. The letter, which Wilson hoped the other Allied leaders would sign, agreed that such a plan was needed, but pointed out that there were many difficulties. If all hostilities ceased, "within definitive lines in the territory of Russia," Wilson was sure Nansen's plan "could be successfully carried into effect, and we should be prepared to give it our full support." The president wrote Lloyd George asking if the prime minister approved.[45]

Meanwhile, activities behind the scene were fast and furious. The British were leary of the plan. Cecil was concerned about Nansen's letter and doubted the wisdom of sending food into Russia "unless we can devise some means of re-establishing her economically and politically." The Britisher counseled his own government to refuse the plan unless limits of Russian combatant frontiers were determined, careful estimates of the cost to Britain were made, and consideration given "as to propaganda."[46] The British position became clear to Hoover as he talked to Cecil along with French and Italian representatives to an *ad hoc* committee set up to advise the Council of Four on the relief plan. Hoover, who represented the United States, reported to the president an agreement in principle but told Wilson the financial aspects of the relief had to be settled, with the Russians paying "from their own resources." Another problem had to do with shipping. He urged Wilson to make sure that the United States and Britain as well as the other countries assumed their burdens and hoped the president would get Lloyd George's approval for a British portion of the shipping. Finally, after Wilson's draft reply had been revised in light of British comments, Lloyd George agreed to sign the letter, as did Orlando, the Italian premier.[47]

The French proved more difficult. The most anti-Bolshevik of the major powers, they were concerned about any program that might keep the Soviet government in power. House talked to Clemenceau and apparently got the French premier's approval, but the letter drafted by Wilson remained unsigned. House again went to Clemenceau, pointing out that Wilson, Lloyd George, and Orlando signed, and Clemenceau said: "I will sign it."[48] He may have agreed to sign, but the proposal was strongly opposed by Stephen Pichon, the French foreign minister.[49]

The Allies responded to Nansen and on April 17 the Norwegian was ready to send the response to the Soviet government. Nansen's communication to Lenin proposed that the commission serve without remuneration, though "expenditures in the purchase and transportation of supplies must be met by the Soviet Government." Hoover had tried to arrange for either the French or British to send the message, but both refused, as did the Dutch. Finally it went through Norwegian auspices, sent from Berlin.[50]

Hoover was stung by the public and private criticism which the proposal evoked. He felt the need to give some public justification, which would perhaps gain public support and head off much conservative criticism. Hoover prepared a statement on bolshevism for the press, which paralleled his third recommendation to President Wilson.[51] It was a denunciation of bolshevism and pointed out that the Nansen plan demanded "complete justice in distribution" and a halt to all "militant action" by the Bolsheviks. Hoover's proposed statement pointed out that the Nansen plan was humanitarian—people were dying of starvation—and hoped an end to the fighting would give the new democracies "a breathing spell to build up some stability." Since bolshevism, in Hoover's mind, was founded on famine, the statement noted that such a plan might help bolshevism die more quickly. It concluded that the plan meant "no intention of recognizing the men whose fingers are even today dripping with the blood of hundreds of innocent people of Odessa."[52]

The reaction to the proposed statement was not favorable. House was disturbed and thought it the "most foolish thing" he had known Hoover to propose. He believed such a statement would destroy any chance for the plan's success and even wondered "whether this action is because of his inordinate desire for publicity." He got Hoover to agree to quash the statement, but when criticism of the plan continued Hoover decided to go ahead, even if he had to make the statement in his own name. Hoover thought it necessary for the Allies to "define our stand on Bolshevism," and told House he had revised the statement, making "certain alterations in the text which relieves everyone else of responsibility." He thought the statement essential, for "unless we disarm the parlor operators we will have to answer for a stimulus to this clap trap over the next twelve months." The revisions did not change House's mind and he told Hoover the president and the other commissioners were unanimously against its release.[53] According to House, the president hoped Hoover "would not make any statement at the moment because it would be impossible for him to disassociate himself either from our government or the governments of the Allies." But Hoover was not to be stopped and sent a copy of the revised statement to the president. The statement noted three considerations: no recognition of the Bolsheviks by the Allies; complete justice of distribution; and need for a Bolshevik pledge not to try to expand. Wilson responded readily that Hoover was free to give it out to the press.[54] And Hoover did.

Events both at Paris and in Russia were working against the Hoover-Nansen plan. McCormick was perhaps representative of those who opposed it. He noted that the proposal would be "hard on Kolchak as he is winning now." McCormick tried to point this out to the president but found it "almost impossible to have satisfactory talk with the President on this matter on account of other pressing peace terms now concluding." McCormick suggested that the Russian ambassador to Washington, Boris Bakhmeteff, cable Kolchak to make relief available to the Soviets. He thought "it would have good political effect in Russia and outside just at the time of Nansen's relief offer." A little later he even advised Nansen to withdraw his offer and make a new one, "in view of the apparent success of Kolchak."[55] McCormick was not alone in doubts about the plan. Other Americans at Paris opposed it, as did members of the British, Italian, and especially the French delegations. Non-Bolshevik Russians opposed the plan and on May 4 the Russian Political Conference, the group representing them at Paris, took a formal position against it.[56]

The death knell for the Hoover-Nansen plan came from the Soviets. In a long reply, made on May 7 but not received in Paris until May 15, the Soviet Commissar for Foreign Affairs Georgi Chicherin accepted the proposed relief but refused to stop the fighting until the Bolsheviks had expelled the invaders from Russia.[57]

Hoover believed there was room for negotiation and pointed out to the president that while the Soviets did not accept the conditions laid down by the Allied leaders, they did "propose that Doctor Nansen should go ahead with his food work and that on the political side they should open up peace negotiations direct with the Allied and Associated Governments." Nansen thought the response hopeful and planned to open discussions with Soviet representatives. But the more common attitude was that uttered by Auchincloss, that the Soviet response was "in substance a rejection of the proposition and a reiteration of their offer to a Peace Conference."[58]

Further consideration of Chicherin's reply by the *ad hoc* committee of the Council of Four did not change anything. Hoover soon cabled the committee's reaction to Nansen:

> Please inform Nansen that until the whole matter has been given further consideration by the Governments here we consider it extremely inadvisable to arrange any meeting with Bolshevik representatives.[59]

The committee submitted a memorandum on Russian policy to the Council of Four, seemingly drafted by Hoover. It pointed out that there were only two courses open to the Allies in view of the Soviet response: either decide to defeat the Soviets by aiding the anti-Bolshevik Russians; or proclaim and enforce an armistice inside Russia. In case the first alternative were selected, the Nansen plan had to be thrown out. If the second were adopted, aid could be extended to all Russians who accepted the armistice. The memo noted that either alternative had a chance for success but "what is not defensible is a combination of the two." When the Council of Four

considered Chicherin's response along with this memo on May 20,
the Hoover-Nansen plan died. Aid to Russians inside Soviet Russia
became a proposal of the past. The French felt most strongly about
the issue and Clemenceau told the Council of Four that "Dr.
Nansen had suggested a humanitarian course, but Lenin was clearly trying to draw it into a political course."[60] While Wilson and
Lloyd George did not go that far, they were not prepared to fight
for it. The plan "might have served as a first step toward some kind
of uneasy accommodation between the Allies and the Soviet regime, with a consequent narrowing of the gulf of bitterness that was
steadily forcing Soviet Russia and the West apart." But it was dead.
In fact it was the last peaceful attempt to settle the Russian problem
until the anti-Bolshevik Russians were defeated, for the Allies soon
moved to partial recognition of Kolchak's Siberian government.[61]

The only Russian relief Hoover got involved in was aid to
Russians in certain portions of Russia not controlled by the
Bolsheviks. In both northwest Russia and in south Russia he found
himself sending supplies, and when General Yudenich made his
approach to Petrograd, Hoover prepared to relieve inhabitants of
that city. But Yudenich's army crumbled. In neither area was the
effort large, and Hoover insisted that his organization's supplies be
used for civilians, not military forces opposing the Bolsheviks.[62]

Another concern to Hoover during the Peace Conference was
the protection from bolshevism of the newly emerging countries,
especially those carved out of Russian territory. Here Hoover ex-
erted a good deal of influence. In January he wrote of the need to
help such countries to prevent the "renewed rise to Bolshevism,"
and went down a list country by country, pointing out the needs.[63]

Hoover supervised the massive assistance that Poland received
from the Allies during 1919. He became concerned in the spring of
1919 when there were reports that the new Polish government was
persecuting Jews. A great deal of agitation sprang up over the issue
in the United States, and Hoover feared the aid to Poland might be
stopped. He urged an investigation and a commission eventually
reported much exaggeration.[64] He went to Poland in the summer
of 1919 to show the American commitment to that country, which
became more important when the Bolsheviks emerged victorious
from the Russian Civil War. With Finland much the same happened. He arranged for Finland to receive supplies and also wrote
the president, calling for full independence of Finland. Urged by
Hoover, the Allies recognized the independence of Finland on May

3. He helped Wilson overcome his principle of not violating Russian territorial integrity. Wilson commented to Lansing:

> I am pretty clear in my view that the case of Finland stands by itself. It never was in any true sense an integral part of Russia. It has been a most uneasy and unwilling partner, and I think that action in regard to the recognition of the Finnish government would not commit us or embarrass us with regard to the recognition of any other part of the former Russian empire that might be separately set up.[65]

Hoover was active in support of the Baltic peoples of Latvia, Lithuania, and Estonia in their struggle for independence. Hoover wanted assistance and urged the president to act. Hoover's policy was clear: aid these people with supplies, and the spread of bolshevism would be stopped.[66]

Hoover had strong feelings about the influence of bolshevism in other parts of Europe and became influential in Allied policy toward the revolutionary government in Hungary. While the particulars were different, the theme was constant. He viewed bolshevism with alarm, believed it flourished side by side with poverty and starvation, and thought the way to prevent its spread, and even bring on its overthrow, was to extend aid to peoples of Europe who were grappling with it.[67]

At the time of the armistice in November 1918, there were one-and-a-half million Russian prisoners in Germany. As director general of relief, Hoover came to feel that something had to be done for these men. The blockade of Germany, which remained until July 12, 1919, plus events such as the Bolshevik withdrawal from the war, the civil war in Russia, and the defeat of Germany, made their situation very bad and according to one account "only the timely intervention of Herbert Hoover saved the survivors from destruction."[68] The armistice between Germany and the Allies made no provisions for these prisoners and the responsibility for their return was left to Germany. With the chaos in Germany and Eastern Europe in late 1918 and early 1919, their situation was growing worse.

Hoover watched the plight of these men with a real sadness. On Christmas Day 1918, he had informed the State Department:

> It is my view that the most suffering in Europe today is that of the Russian prisoners in Germany and Austria and en route home.

They are dying wholesale from neglect. This is a matter of charity which Government therefore cannot handle. It would seem to me a proper work for the American Red Cross and I understand that Commissioner here has put up to them the question as to whether their funds are available for that purpose.[69]

But, as in other concerns, his hope ran into difficulties. The Red Cross concluded it could not fund such an operation. Marshal Foch, Allied commander-in-chief, asked that the Supreme War Council allow him to establish an "Executive Committee" in Berlin to control the feeding and repatriation of these men. Foch apparently thought of these men as the basis, along with Polish troops, of an army to protect Poland and attack the Bolsheviks. The Council approved Foch's suggestion on January 12, 1919, and in a convention, signed with Germany four days later to prolong the Armistice, the Allied governments reserved "the right to arrange for the repatriation of Russian prisoners of war to any region which they may consider most suitable."[70] Foch stopped all repatriation.

When it became apparent that Germany could not feed the prisoners, Hoover determined to see what he could do. While details for the payment of supplies were being worked out, conditions of the prisoners were growing worse. He wrote the president on February 6 asking if the American government could aid in furnishing supplies to the prisoners "to prevent them from going back to Russia in the middle of the winter and joining in the Bolshevik army." "Is it not," he asked, "the proper duty of the American army to furnish supplies for the American contribution to this end?" He asked the same question of Secretary of War Newton D. Baker later that month. Baker's response was that he could not "use any funds legally to supply food for such purpose."[71] Finally Hoover got the French to agree to pay for some supplies, advanced by the American quartermaster, but delays continued. Eventually French and American stocks of food were used to supply the prisoners, and then the problem became their repatriation.

By summer the number of prisoners had dwindled to 200,000, as many began to walk home and others died. Hoover remained interested. In mid-July he sent a memorandum to Henry White, for submission to the Supreme Economic Council. The memo noted that the British Red Cross, one of the major suppliers of food for the prisoners, would soon cease operations, and alternatives had to be planned. Were the prisoners to be repatriated at once? How? If not, what was to be done? He emphasized "that the relief agencies under co-ordination through the Supreme Economic Council have

now practically exhausted their resources and cannot take part in
this matter, so that other arrangements must be set up at the
earliest possible moment."[72] Eventually, in the spring of 1920,
Soviet and German representatives worked out an agreement for
exchange, and in cooperation with the League of Nations and the
International Committee of the Red Cross the exchange was completed by 1922.

What of Hoover's part in this issue? He had kept the issue alive at
the Paris Conference and supplied relief. Relief deliveries to the
prisoners accomplished under Hoover's direction during the
armistice period amounted to about $4,000,000.[73] In addition to
the Russian prisoners, Hoover took cognizance of the German and
Austro-Hungarian prisoners in Russia and worked on their behalf.
While not giving direct aid, he helped get the Allies to assist in the
return of these men to their homes.[74]

All these activities at Paris involving Russia proved to be a searing
experience. Hoover remained convinced, so he told Wilson, that
the Bolshevik government would fall. He recommended that the
Allies send a commission, which, "if placed upon an economic and
not a political basis, could if conducted with wisdom, keep itself free
from conflicting political currents and allow a rational development
of self-government in Russia." Starvation and unemployment had
to be overcome, and such a commission, if headed by someone with
authority, could do it. It was a naïve proposal and the president
answered that it was impossible "for an Inter-Allied body to give
such aid without getting mixed up in politics." Wilson noted that
"the Russian people must solve their own problems without outside
interference and that Europe had made a great mistake when they
[sic] attempted to interfere in the French Revolution." While it
would be hard on the present Russian generation, "in the long run
it means less distress for Russia." The president's observations did
not satisfy Hoover, who thought Europe would continue to be
dominated by revolutions, starvation, and chaos.[75]

Hoover's activities and his ideas about Russia at the Paris Peace
Conference were a curious combination. He had as much personal
experience with Russia as any of the major figures at the conference. He at times showed great insight into Russian affairs and
at other times seemed naïve. He understood the roots of bolshevism and its power better than most statesmen. He had seen
prewar Russia and knew firsthand the oppression that brought
about the Revolution. He realized that the country might move
from one extreme to the other and knew military intervention

could never succeed. He believed bolshevism was not something limited to Russia and unless conditions were cleared it might spread to the rest of Europe. In all these observations he showed insight. But he clung to an idea of equating bolshevism with starvation and perhaps more than anyone else at Paris was responsible for the belief that full stomachs would eliminate bolshevism in Russia, as well as preventing its spread. All of this meant that the Allies waited for the Bolsheviks to be overthrown, one way or another, and did not really grapple with the Russian problem.

In the end, one can say that he was consistent and influential at Paris. While not an advocate of a hard-line policy, he stood as an opponent of the soft line. Out of such a position no realistic policy was possible.[76]

Events in the last half of 1919 did little to change his mind. Upon return to the United States in September, he watched as the Allies divided over dealings with the Soviet Union. By early 1920 he was protesting the lack of any American policy toward the Soviet government. He thought about events in the Soviet Union and decided there were two points to be considered: the Soviet government which was "the most primitive form of democracy" and bolshevism as a social theory. The Bolsheviks had "captured the control of Russia because they had the political acumen to seize upon a governmental structure within the experience and vision of this great mass of ignorant people."[77] The socialist basis of bolshevism brought, according to Hoover, a breakdown in production, distribution, transportation, and currency. He did not believe socialism could work in the area of economics, and the Bolsheviks remained in power "through a terrorism to which the French Revolution was mere child's play." They brought instability, especially regarding ownership of land, and would be forced to back away from nationalization of the land. Kolchak and Denikin were no better, for the peasants understood that their victory would have meant "return of the land-owner and the destruction of the peasants' holdings." Between the two sides, the peasants would probably continue "to adhere to the Bolshevik Government." The mistake of the Allies, he believed, was in giving aid to the anti-Bolshevik Russians without demanding reform. The Allies should have insured a "guarantee of the land to the peasants" and things would have been different. He supported the British plan to remove the blockade of the Soviet Union and "allow them to open up commercial relations with the rest of the world and to show in its real colors the utter hollowness of their pleas to the peasants." He did not know if this would do any good but remained opposed to military intervention: "ideas cannot be overwhelmed by military force." The mission for America, he thought, was perhaps to save Poland and prevent "a Bolshevik branch office in Vienna." He urged all the aid that was possible to be sent to Poland.[78]

In July 1921 Maxim Gorky appealed for aid in halting the "stupendous famine among Russian people in the Ukraine and the valley of the Volga."[79] Hoover, now secretary of commerce, was favorably disposed and was supported by President Warren G. Harding and Secretary of State Charles Evans Hughes, though there was some opposition in the cabinet and among the American people. Harding indicated he had given his "fullest approval of the action on the part of the American Relief Administration in initiating an effort to mitigate the famine in Russia, particularly to save the lives of children."[80] Hoover's response to Gorky was positive. The relief was funded by money from many sources. About $78,000,000 was expended, of which about $10,000,000 came from Russian gold. Of the rest, about $28,000,000 were American government monies and the remainder raised from public charity. Chicherin spoke of

> the grandiose, disinterested aid rendered by the American people through the ARA, the self-sacrificing activity of the personnel of the ARA, and splendid organization of its entire work who have left an indelible impression upon our people.[81]

This episode did not change Hoover's opinion of the Soviet government. As secretary of commerce he opposed recognition, and even pointed out in 1921 that there was a connection between recognition and economic philosophy. Trade between the Soviet Union and the United States was more a political matter than economic, according to Hoover. Hughes and Harding shared the secretary of commerce's views. While Hoover became more tolerant of trade during the 1920s, his stand on recognition did not change, and continued during his presidency.[82]

There was a consistency in Hoover's view of events in Russia between 1917 and 1920. He retained his compassion for the Russian people, but simply never accepted the fact that socialism, more particularly bolshevism, could work. Part of this belief came out of his personal experiences, part out of belief in capitalism which stood at the center of his philosophy of life. Hoover's confusion was the confusion of the times. Still, the vast majority of Americans understood much less about events in Russia than

Hoover. Hoover's own blinders prevented him from understanding even more than he did and perhaps counseling a different policy.

NOTES

1 Herbert Hoover, *The Memoirs of Herbert Hoover*, vol. 1, *Years of Adventure, 1874–1920* (New York: Macmillan, 1952), p. 58. A general treatment of Hoover's relationship with Russia is Manfred Bauer's, "Herbert Hoovers Verhältnis zu Sowjet-Russland von der Pariser Friedenskonferenz (1919) bis zum Ende seiner Präsidentschaft (1933)," (Ph.D. diss., University of Munich, 1954), but as the title indicates this covers the period 1919 to 1933 and is based on published sources.

2 Hoover, *Years of Adventure, 1874–1920*, pp. 99, 102.

3 *Ibid.*, p. 108. A very critical treatment of Hoover's business interests in Russia is James J. O'Brien, *Hoover's Millions and How He Made Them* (New York: O'Brien, 1932), which was apparently brought out to help defeat Hoover in the 1932 election.

4 Hoover, *Years of Adventure, 1874–1920*, pp. 102–09.

5 *Ibid.*, pp. 108–09. The Soviets dispute Hoover's contention that he sold all his interests in Russian enterprises before the Revolution and contend that his behavior regarding Russia after 1917 was based on a hope that he would regain these interests. The *Malaia Sovetskaia Ientsiklopediia* (Small Soviet Encyclopedia), 3d ed., 3 vols. (Moscow: 1958), 1:218.

6 Hoover, *Years of Adventure, 1874–1920*, pp. 139–40, 218.

7 *Ibid.*, p. 221.

8 Herbert Hoover to David R. Francis, April 19, 1917, Xerox from David Francis Papers, Missouri Historical Society, now at the Herbert Hoover Presidential Library.

9 See, for example, William Phillips to Hoover, June 6, 1917, 763.72114/2713, containing Francis to Secretary of State, May 30, 1917, Record Group 59, State Department Records, National Archives.

10 Hoover to Francis, June 22, 1917, Xerox from Francis Papers, Hoover Presidential Library.

11 Hoover, *Years of Adventure, 1874–1920*, pp. 248–49.

12 *Ibid.*, pp. 105–06.

13 Hoover to Francis, March 6, 1918, Xerox from Francis Papers, Hoover Presidential Library.

14 Hoover, *Years of Adventure, 1874–1920*, pp. 265–66.

15 See Eugene Trani, "Woodrow Wilson and the Decision to Intervene in Russia: A Reconsideration," *Journal of Modern History*, 48 (September 1976), pp. 440–61.

16 Robert Lansing to Woodrow Wilson, June 13, 1918, and Edward House to Wilson, June 13, 1918, Woodrow Wilson Papers, Library of Congress, Washington. It should be noted that it was in June 1918 that Raymond Robins came back from the Soviet Union preaching against intervention of any kind. Robins saw Hoover, in addition to other American officials like Secretary of State Lansing and Secretary of War Newton Baker, but the forces for some kind of intervention were already at work. See Raymond Robins to Bessie Beatty, June 27, 1918, Xerox from Raymond Robins Papers, State Historical Society of Wisconsin, now at the Hoover Presidential Library.

17 Edward House Diary, June 13, 1918, Edward House Papers, Yale University.

18 House Diary, June 13, 1918, House Papers, Yale University.

19 Gordon Auchincloss Diary, June 13, 1918, Gordon Auchincloss Papers, Yale University.

20 House Diary, June 13, 1918, House Papers, Yale University.

21 Auchincloss Diary, June 13, 1918, Auchincloss Papers, Yale University; and Lansing to Wilson and House to Wilson, both June 13, 1918, Wilson Papers, Library of Congress. For a discussion of the British reaction to Hoover's possible service in Russia, see Richard Ullman, *Intervention and the War* (Princeton: Princeton University Press, 1961), the first volume of his *Anglo-Soviet Relations, 1917–1921*.

22 Lansing to Wilson, June 13, 1918, Wilson Papers, Library of Congress.

23 Auchincloss Diary, June 13, 1918, Auchincloss Papers, and House Diary, June 13, 1918, House Papers, Yale University.

24 House to Wilson, June 13, 1918, Wilson Papers, Library of Congress.

25 Hoover, *Years of Adventure, 1874–1920,* p. 266.

26 House Diary, June 17, 1918, House Papers, and Auchincloss Diary, June 18, 1918, Auchincloss Papers, Yale University.

27 House Diary, June 21, 1918, House Papers, Yale University.

28 Auchincloss Diary, June 29, 1918, Auchincloss Papers, and Auchincloss to Frank Polk, June 29, 1918, Frank Polk Papers, Yale University.

29 Auchincloss Diary, July 1, 1918, Auchincloss Papers, Yale University; and Bernard Baruch to Wilson, July 13, 1918, Wilson to Baruch, July 15, 1918, and Paul Reinsch to Wilson, August 31, 1918, Wilson Papers, Library of Congress.

30 William Phillips Notebooks, July 23, 1918, William Phillips Papers, Harvard University.

31   Herbert Hoover, *An American Epic*, vol. 2, *Famine in Forty-Five Nations: Organization Behind the Front, 1914–1923* (Chicago: Regnery, 1960), pp. 133–35.

32   Eugene Trani, "Woodrow Wilson and the Decision to Intervene in Russia," pp. 440–61.

33   Hoover to Wilson, November 9, 1918, Hoover-Wilson Correspondence, Hoover's Pre-Commerce Papers, Hoover Presidential Library.

34   Hoover to Wilson, December 20, 1918, Hoover-Wilson Correspondence, Pre-Commerce Papers, Hoover Presidential Library.

35   Wilson to Joseph Tumulty, January 11, 1919, Wilson Papers, Library of Congress. The complicated problem of feeding Germany is told in John Thompson, *Russia, Bolshevism, and the Versailles Peace* (Princeton: Princeton University Press, 1966).

36   Hoover to Wilson, March 28, 1919, Wilson Papers, Library of Congress. See also Herbert Hoover, *The Ordeal of Woodrow Wilson* (New York: McGraw-Hill, 1959), p. 117.

37   Hoover, *Years of Adventure, 1874–1920*, p. 411. The most complete treatment of the Russian problem at the Paris Conference is John Thompson, *Russia, Bolshevism, and the Versailles Peace*. Other accounts of interest are N. Gordon Levin, Jr., *Woodrow Wilson and World Politics: America's Response to War and Revolution* (New York: Oxford University Press, 1968); Arno J. Mayer, *Politics and Diplomacy of Peacemaking: Containment and Counterrevolution at Versailles, 1918–1919* (New York: Knopf, 1967); Richard Ullman, *Britain and the Russian Civil War* (Princeton: Princeton University Press, 1968), the second volume of his *Anglo-Soviet Relations, 1917–1921;* and Louis Fischer, *The Soviets in World Affairs*, 2 vols. (London: Jonathan Cape, 1930).

38   Hoover, *Years of Adventure, 1874–1920*, p. 412.

39   Vance McCormick Diary, March 4 and 18, 1918, Vance McCormick Papers, Yale University. John Thompson, in his *Russia, Bolshevism, and the Versailles Peace,* credits McCormick with being the father of the plan.

40   Auchincloss Diary, March 27, 1919, Auchincloss Papers, and House Diary, March 27, 1919, House Papers, Yale University.

41   Hoover, *Years of Adventure, 1874–1920*, pp. 414–15.

42   *Ibid.*, pp. 412–15; Hoover, *The Ordeal of Woodrow Wilson*, p. 119.

43   House Diary, March 29, 1919, House Papers, and Auchincloss Diary, March 29, 1919, Auchincloss Papers, Yale University; Robert Cecil Diary, March 29, 1919, Robert Cecil Papers, British Museum; Robert Cecil to David Lloyd George, March 29, 1919, David Lloyd George Papers, Beaverbrook Library, London.

44   Fridtjof Nansen to Wilson, April 3, 1919, Wilson Papers, Library of Congress.

45   House Diary, April 6, 1919, House Diary, Yale University; Wilson to Nansen, April 9, 1919, Wilson Papers, Library of Congress; and Wilson to Lloyd George, April 8, 1919, Lloyd George Papers, Beaverbrook Library.

46   Cecil to Lloyd George, April 8, 1919, Lloyd George Papers, Beaverbrook Library.

47   Hoover to Wilson, April 9, 1919, and Hoover to Wilson, April 9, 1919, Wilson Papers, Library of Congress.

48   House Diary, April 14, 15, and 16, 1919, House Papers, and Auchincloss Diary, April 16, 1919, Auchincloss Papers, Yale University.

49   Pinchon Statement, April 16, 1919, Russian Relief File, Pre-Commerce Papers, Hoover Presidential Library.

50   Allied Leaders to Nansen, April 17, 1919, and Nansen to Lenin, April 17, 1919, Russian Relief File, Pre-Commerce Papers, Hoover Presidential Library; Hoover, *The Ordeal of Woodrow Wilson,* p. 123; Hoover, *Years of Adventure, 1874–1920,* pp. 417–18. George Kennan, in his *Russia and the West under Lenin and Stalin* (Boston: Little, Brown, 1960), is very harsh on the proposal sent to the Soviet government. He writes, on page 141 of his book: "Was there ever, one wonders, any greater nonsense than this curious document, bearing the signatures of Orlando, Lloyd George, Wilson, and Clemenceau?" Arno Mayer believes that "political rather than humanitarian purposes were at the heart of the Nansen Plan," and says that Hoover and Wilson both viewed Russian bolshevism as "a condition to be cured rather than a conspiracy to be destroyed." Arno Mayer, *Politics and Diplomacy of Peacemaking: Containment and Counterrevolution at Versailles, 1918–1919,* pp. 24–27.

51   Hoover Statement, April 18, 1919, Russian Relief File, Pre-Commerce Papers, Hoover Presidential Library.

52   Notwithstanding this public criticism of what happened in Odessa, Hoover told Auchincloss that "the Bolshevik outrages in Odessa were frightful, but that the Russian refugees, who had been slaughtered there, deserved their fate, because they had been dissipating and living in a profligate manner, while the poor people of Odessa had been on a ration of two ounces of food a day." See Auchincloss Diary, April 23, 1919, Auchincloss Papers, Yale University.

53   House Diary, April 19, 1919, and Hoover to House, April 19, 1919, and House to Hoover, April 20, 1919, House Papers, Yale University.

54   Wilson to Hoover, April 23, 1919, with enclosure of Hoover's Statement, Hoover-Wilson Correspondence, Pre-Commerce Papers, Hoover Presidential Library.

55   McCormick Diary, April 21, April 26, and May 7, 1919, McCormick Papers, Yale University.

56   Statement by the Russian Political Conference, May 4, 1919, enclosed in B. Bakhmeteff to Secretary of State, May 7, 1919, 861.48/42, *Papers Relating to the*

Foreign Relations of the United States, 1919: Russia (Washington: GPO, 1937), pp. 109–10. See also John Thompson, *Russia, Bolshevism, and the Versailles Peace,* pp. 260–62.

57   Chicherin to Nansen, May 14, 1919, Russian Relief File, Pre-Commerce Papers, Hoover Presidential Library.

58   Hoover to Wilson, May 16, 1919, Wilson Papers, Library of Congress; Auchincloss Diary, May 15, 1919, Auchincloss Papers, Yale University; and Swenson to Hoover, May 16, 1919, Russian Relief File, Pre-Commerce Papers, Hoover Presidential Library.

59   Hoover to Swenson, May 16, 1919, Russian Relief File, Pre-Commerce Papers, Hoover Presidential Library.

60   Notes of Meeting of the Council of Four, May 20, 1919, 180.03401/20, Record Group 256, State Department Records, National Archives. The memorandum, dated May 16, 1919, is published in *Papers Relating to the Foreign Relations of the United States, 1919: Russia,* pp. 116–17.

61   John Thompson, *Russia, Bolshevism, and the Versailles Peace,* pp. 266–67.

62   Hoover Statement, May 29, 1919, Russian Relief File, Pre-Commerce Papers, Hoover Presidential Library. There is a good deal of documentation on Hoover and the relief in Northwest Russia in *Papers Relating to the Foreign Relations of the United States, 1919: Russia,* especially, pp. 693–700.

63   Hoover to Food Administration, Washington, January 6, 1919, Wilson Papers, Library of Congress.

64   Hoover to Wilson, June 2, 1919, and Wilson to Hoover, June 3, 1919, Wilson Papers, Library of Congress; Hoover, *Years of Adventure, 1874–1920,* pp. 355–62.

65   Hoover to Wilson, April 1919, and Wilson to Robert Lansing, May 13, 1919, Wilson Papers, Library of Congress; Hoover, *Years of Adventure, 1874–1920,* pp. 363–68.

66   Hoover to Wilson, May 9, 1919, and Wilson to Hoover, May 21, 1919, Wilson Papers, Library of Congress; Hoover to Wilson, June 21, 1919, Hoover-Wilson Correspondence, Pre-Commerce Papers, Hoover Presidential Library; Hoover, *Years of Adventure, 1874–1920,* pp. 368–78; Hoover, *The Ordeal of Woodrow Wilson,* pp. 126–34; and John Thompson, *Russia, Bolshevism, and the Versailles Peace,* pp. 340–45.

67   For accounts of Hoover's activities regarding Hungary, see Hoover, *The Ordeal of Woodrow Wilson* and *Years of Adventure, 1874–1920;* John Thompson, *Russia, Bolshevism, and the Versailles Peace;* Arno J. Mayer, *Politics and Diplomacy of Peacemaking: Containment and Counterrevolution at Versailles, 1918–1919;* N. Gordon Levin, Jr., *Woodrow Wilson and World Politics: America's Response to War and Revolution;* and Alfred D. Low, *The Soviet Hungarian Republic and the Paris Peace Conference* (Philadelphia: American Philosophical Society, 1963). William Appleman Williams, in his *American-Russian Relations, 1781–1947* (New York: Rinehart, 1952), p. 152, is particularly harsh on Hoover for his Hungarian activities, writing that Hoover "engineered the non-violent overthrow of Bela Kun."

68   Edward F. Willis, *Herbert Hoover and the Russian Prisoners of World War I: A Study in Diplomacy and Relief, 1918–1919* (Stanford: Stanford University Press, 1951), p. 6. See also Hoover, *An American Epic*, vol. 3, *Famine in Forty-Five Nations: The Battle on the Front Line, 1914–1923*, pp. 283–88.

69   Hoover to Acting Secretary of State, December 25, 1918, as cited in Edward Willis, *Herbert Hoover and the Russian Prisoners of World War I*, p. 22.

70   Edward Willis, *Herbert Hoover and the Russian Prisoners of World War I*, p. 25.

71   Hoover to Wilson, February 6, 1919, Wilson Papers, Library of Congress; Hoover to Newton Baker, February 28, 1919, and Baker to Hoover, March 3, 1919, Newton Baker Papers, Library of Congress.

72   Hoover to Henry White, July 16, 1919, with enclosure "Feeding of Russian Prisoners in Germany." Memorandum by Hoover, July 16, 1919, Henry White Papers, Library of Congress.

73   Edward Willis, *Herbert Hoover and the Russian Prisoners of World War I*, p. 54.

74   Hoover, *Famine in Forty-Five Nations: The Battle on the Front Line, 1914–1923*, pp. 286–88.

75   Hoover to Wilson, June 21, 1919, 861.00/786, Record Group 256, State Department Records, National Archives; McCormick Diary, June 23, 1919, McCormick Papers, Yale University; House to Wilson, July 30, 1919, Wilson Papers, Library of Congress.

76   N. Gordon Levin, in his *Woodrow Wilson and World Politics: America's Response to War and Revolution*, p. 191, writes, with perhaps some exaggeration, that "in the last analysis, this Hoover-directed program of anti-Bolshevik food relief, with its emphasis on the breaking down of nationalistic barriers to trade and economic recovery, was a classic expression of the more general proto-Marshall Plan tendency of Wilson and his advisers to use America's expansionist economic power in the postwar period to establish international liberal-capitalist stability in the face of threats to world order from irrational nationalism on the Right and from revolutionary-socialism on the Left." Arno Mayer goes even further by suggesting that much of Hoover's interest in relief in general was because "Hoover dreaded the collapse of American farm and commodity prices which, in turn, could set off a general economic crisis." See Arno Mayer, *Politics and Diplomacy of Peacemaking: Containment and Counterrevolution at Versailles, 1918–1919*, p. 272.

77   Hoover Memorandum, January 24, 1920, Russian Policy File, Pre-Commerce Papers, Hoover Presidential Library.

78   *Ibid.;* and Hoover to Norman H. Davis, September 27, 1930, 86148/1930, Record Group 59, State Department Records, National Archives. Hoover remained convinced of these beliefs and soon wrote a book, *American Individualism* (Garden City, New York: Doubleday Page, 1922), in which he appealed to Americans to uphold the fundamentals of their life and stand against communism and totalitarianism.

79   Hoover, *The Memoirs of Herbert Hoover*, vol. 2, *The Cabinet and the Presidency, 1920–1933* (New York: Macmillan, 1952), pp. 23–26; and Hoover, *Famine in Forty-Five Nations: The Battle on the Front Line, 1914–1923*, pp. 423–521.

80   Hoover, *Famine in Forty-Five Nations: The Battle on the Front Line, 1914–1923*, p. 446.

81   *Ibid.*, p. 512. Peter G. Filene, in his *Americans and the Soviet Experiment, 1917–1933* (Cambridge: Harvard University Press, 1967), p. 78, contends that Hoover hoped that the ARA's relief would mean "the introduction of American investment and technology. In Hoover's opinion, then, the ARA would succeed where Allied armies had failed in rescuing Russia from the Soviets " This seems harsh for Hoover had long displayed compassion for the Russian people and while he was no friend of the Bolsheviks, he saw the Russian people in trouble. The Soviets later became much more critical of Hoover and the ARA. William Benton, in "The Great Soviet Encyclopedia," *Yale Review*, 47 (Summer 1958), pp. 552–63, shows how the treatment of Hoover's activities changed in the various editions of this reference work. The Archives of the ARA are at the Hoover Institution at Stanford, California. The fullest accounts of Hoover's involvement with the Russian relief are Benjamin M. Weissman, *Herbert Hoover and Famine Relief to Soviet Russia, 1921–1923* (Stanford, California: Hoover Institution Press, 1974); and the same author, "Herbert Hoover's 'Treaty' with Soviet Russia, August 20, 1921," *Slavic Review*, 28 (June 1969), pp. 276-88.

82   For accounts of Hoover's involvement in Russian-American relations in the 1920s, see Edward Bennett, *Recognition of Russia: An American Foreign Policy Dilemma* (Waltham, Mass.: Blaisdell, 1970); Peter G. Filene, *Americans and the Soviet Experiment, 1917–1933;* Joan Hoff Wilson, *American Business and Foreign Policy, 1920–1933* (Lexington: University Press of Kentucky, 1971), and *Ideology and Economics: U.S. Relations with the Soviet Union, 1918–1933* (Columbia: University of Missouri Press, 1974); and Eugene Trani and David Wilson, *The Presidency of Warren G. Harding* (Lawrence: Regents Press of Kansas, 1977).

ROBERT H. VAN METER, JR.

Herbert Hoover and the
Economic Reconstruction of Europe, 1918–21

EDITOR'S INTRODUCTORY NOTE

Even a cursory examination of the relevant statistics reveals the extent to which Europe had dominated American foreign trade, imports, and exports, prior to the First World War. European nations had accounted for 74.61% (dollar value) of total U.S. exports in 1900, diminishing to 59.98% in 1913 but still remaining a strong market for American commodities. In the same years, Europe provided appoximately 50% of America's imports (dollar value). Among European states, the United Kingdom led and Germany was not a distant second in providing markets and also chief sources of imports for the United States. When these statistics are refined further, it becomes apparent that the United Kingdom was not keeping pace as the volume of American world trade nearly doubled during the years 1900–13. In 1900, the U.K. accounted for 38.3% of total American exports; by 1913 this percentage had shrunk to 24.21%. The U.K.'s share in America's imports also dipped, but slightly, from 18.82% to 16.33%. What becomes important in this statistically reflected trend and was no doubt weighed heavily in the postwar calculations of Wilson, Hoover, and others interested in the patterns of postwar international trade, is that the German figures showing purchases of American goods and services 1900–13 displayed remarkable stability and did not decline relative to mounting total American exports and imports. In 1900 Germany had accounted for 13.31% of total U.S. exports, and in 1913 it had bought 13.46%. In 1900, Germany had provided 11.41% of all U.S. imports; in 1913, the figure was 10.42%.[1] Figures of this sort provided impressive evidence that the reconstruction of the German economy was essential to the economic prosperity of all Europe and also to that of the United States.

Robert H. Van Meter, Jr., is academic adviser, University Without Walls, Skidmore College, Saratoga Springs, New York.

Postwar economic reconstruction for Europe, with strong participation by Germany, therefore appeared to be an essential ingredient for a prosperous world and an American capitalist order.

In the next article, Robert Van Meter finds in Hoover the catalyst generating the continuity between the Wilson era and the Republican era of the 1920s. If this continuity was not reflected in ethical behavior and social values, there nevertheless seems much to commend this interpretation with reference to foreign economic policy. Few Americans, Democratic or Republican, would have disputed the following proposition: "A stable, peaceful accessible world market place was at once essential to American prosperity and conducive to the world's economic progress." Access to foreign markets, an important proviso found in Wilson's Fourteen Points and later incorporated into the international mandate system, was for Hoover a prime requisite to a peaceful and prosperous world. Every form of statism, whether of the militarist, Bolshevik or reactionary, imperialist variations, was viewed by Hoover to be contrary to America's and the world's best interests.

According to Van Meter's analysis, leaders of the Wilson administration during the winter of 1918–19 came to perceive economic reconstruction in Europe as having a high priority even though preceding the Armistice woefully little concern had been manifest toward the subject by American leaders. Van Meter sees Hoover's heightened concern for European reconstruction not only as an imperative to any peaceful world order but also to America's economic prosperity. He relates this concern to four broad elements: ethnic self-determination as a principle for locating national boundaries was not compatible to the many economic needs of European states; the establishment of a League of Nations might have made a substantial contribution to European reconstruction but for the absence of the United States, which clearly limited the organization's strength for so vast an undertaking. Thus we are left with Van Meter's third and fourth elements, namely, a program of emergency relief for which Hoover was chiefly responsible, and long term economic assistance.

Near the end of this article, Van Meter summarizes the highlights of Hoover's significant position paper of July 3, 1919. In this analysis, Hoover explained Europe's economic woes in terms of the sharply declining gross national products experienced in the postwar months. When related to the decline in international trade, his economic prognosis did not allow for much optimism. Still, as Van Meter rightly observes, Hoover resisted any suggestion that the system of capitalism had failed in Europe. He persevered in thinking that only modest reforms would cure the existing economic ills. He recognized that there would be insufficient private capital in the United States available to extend as loans and investments, so he favored supplementary financing through special U.S. government agencies. Strangely, the Wilson administration rejected this plan because Treasury leaders were not favorably disposed toward the notion of the American government's getting into the finance business. Van Meter also makes the significant observation that by the summer of 1919, Hoover's credibility with the Treasury Department in Washington was eroding because his data was being disputed by the officials. Whether or not correct in his analysis and his suggested action, Hoover as secretary of commerce continued his central concern with the problems of European postwar reconstruction.

1   The raw statistical data used in this paragraph are found in *Historical Statistics of the United States Colonial Times to 1957* (Washington: GPO, 1960), pp. 550–53. Percentages were computed by the editor for presentation here.

Herbert Hoover and the Economic Reconstruction of Europe, 1918–21

"The rehabilitation of Europe is immediately and primarily a European task," wrote Herbert Hoover in January 1920, "but it is of tremendous concern to America and for that matter the entire world." "If America and the other countries of the world are to prosper," he continued, "if civilization is to go forward rather than backward, Europe must get on her feet."[1]

Recently returned from a gruelling ten months in Europe as director general of relief and economic adviser to the American Peace Commission, Hoover in this statement pointed up what had been and was to be a major continuing preoccupation through almost twenty years of public service. At the same time he revealed three key assumptions which informed his outlook on the problem. First, Hoover was convinced that European recovery was vital to American and world prosperity. Second, he believed that the major part of the effort had to come—indeed could only come—from Europe. Finally, he accepted the proposition that the United States could and should lead Europe to take those steps necessary to insure her own recovery. These three assumptions appear repeatedly as one examines Hoover's words and actions during the years 1918–21. In fact one can say that the problem of how the United States could get Europe to help itself became one of the major challenges of Hoover's public career—providing an important thread connecting his service under Woodrow Wilson with his subsequent years as secretary of commerce and president.

The intent of this paper is not to offer a comprehensive review of Hoover's early effort to promote European recovery. Rather, it is to examine his activities and his thinking during the period 1918–21, with two objects in view: first, to place Hoover's own contribution to the formation and implementation of America's policy toward European recovery within the larger contours of that policy as it was hammered out by the Wilson administration during 1918 and 1919; and second, to suggest the essential continuity in American foreign policy between Wilson's great crusade and the Republican era of the 1920s. As an essential preliminary it is necessary to begin by looking briefly at Hoover's outlook on the world.

II

As Hoover moved to grapple with the problem of European economic reconstruction in the months after the Armistice, he acted from assumptions similar to those which informed President Woodrow Wilson's thinking on American policy toward Europe.[2] Like Wilson, Hoover believed in the constructive potential of a reformed and progressively managed corporate capitalist system. The overriding economic problem for America and the world, Hoover pointed out in 1919, was "the better division of the products of industry and the steady development of higher productivity."[3] To encourage efficiency and maximum productivity, Hoover had by 1919 concluded that a modicum of governmental intervention was necessary to discourage vicious speculation, insure an equitable division of the fruits of production, and generally to protect the producers, i.e., workers and small entrepreneurs, from the "misery which the ruthlessness of individualism has imposed upon a minority."[4] The precise nature of such intervention and the overall structure for the political economy appear but hazily in 1919. It is possible, however, to see in Hoover's thinking signs pointing toward that associational or cooperative capitalism which, by 1921, had become Hoover's answer to the challenge which industrialization and the large corporation posed for America's nineteenth-century liberal heritage.[5]

Closely related to Hoover's commitment to reformed corporate capitalism was the belief, shared with Wilson, that a stable, peaceful, accessible world market place was at once essential to American prosperity and conducive to the world's economic progress. "We must maintain our foreign markets if our working people are to be employed . . . ," Hoover wrote in 1917.[6] The following year, in response to an inquiry from the secretary of state, Hoover outlined existing restrictions on foreign mining activities in the British Empire, expressed concern at the impact which such restrictions had on American business, and urged international recognition of the right to trade.[7] By championing such policies Hoover believed the United States could lead the world toward a new era of prosperity. In recounting his voyage to Europe in November 1918 to take charge of relief, Hoover recalled talking long into the night of reforms which would abolish want in the world through the application of "the methods of increased productivity learned in the war. . . ."[8]

As a logical corollary of this belief in the importance of a world market place which was at once stable, peaceful, and open, Hoover, like Wilson, believed that American foreign policy should oppose those international forces and movements which tended to breed instability, war, or economic restrictions. By the same token Hoover supported Wilson's effort to restructure the world in such a way as to promote an international climate characterized by peace, orderly change, and an "open door" for international trade and investment. For Hoover, as for Wilson, the enemies of the "open door" world were, on the one hand, autocracy with its handmaidens of militarism, old style imperialism and reactionary capitalism and, on the other hand, revolutionary socialism.

Hoover's deep seated hostility to autocracy and militarism lay rooted not only in moral revulsion but in the conviction that the ways of the autocrat and the militarist were inimical to the efficient production and distribution of goods and services. Hoover's account of the trials and tribulations of the Committee for the Relief of Belgium is, among other things, a powerful indictment of war and a testament to the economic obtuseness of those whose profession was arms.[9] Like Wilson, Hoover believed the kaiser's Germany was the stronghold of autocracy and, at one point, he told the president that the United States had "been fighting autocracy and militarism" in going to war against the Central Powers.[10]

Hoover also realized that strong autocratic and militaristic tendencies existed in the major Allied countries. These reactionary tendencies, fortified by the legacy of hate and bitterness which four years of war had left among the peoples of Europe, posed a threat to the realization of Wilson's new world order of which Hoover was acutely aware.[11] Excessive territorial and economic demands on the Central Powers, the continued blockade of Central Europe after the Armistice, and attempts to preserve and extend western colonialism in the underdeveloped world—all attested to the strength of reactionary influences within the Allied camp.

The reactionary side of Allied policy also appeared in efforts to link the political and economic power of the state to the furtherance of narrowly nationalistic objectives. Such neomercantilist tactics threatened American markets and access to raw materials. Equally important, to Hoover as to Wilson, they represented a wrongheaded and dangerous approach to international economic relations.[12] In the international sphere no less than in the domestic, excessive statism would stifle productivity and distort distribution patterns so as to restrain economic growth and obstruct the optimum allocation of goods. Beyond that, Wilson and members of the administration believed that the adoption of such tactics by Germany in the years prior to 1914, and the competitive reaction of other European powers, had contributed greatly to the outbreak of war. Avoidance of neo-mercantilist practices, with their potential for the military escalation of economic conflict, thus became a key condition of international peace and stability. The resulting prosperity would, it was hoped, be widely diffused. It also seems clear, however, that Hoover had little doubt that, provided the major industrial powers could outlaw statist and restrictive economic practices, American efficiency would yield the United States a generous if not the dominant share of the world economic pie.

If the forces of autocracy posed a danger to the realization of Wilson's vision from within the Allied camp, an equally potent external danger (with a potential for internal disruption as well) lay in revolutionary socialism. Following the October Revolution, Wilson and his associates viewed bolshevism with ever-growing concern, and Hoover himself, in an often quoted comment, recalled that "Communist Russia was a specter which wandered into the Peace Conference almost daily."[13]

Perhaps the most sophisticated and articulate spokesman for Wilsonian anti-bolshevism and one of its most zealous agents, Hoover analysed bolshevism in terms of three propositions.[14] First, he believed that generations of reactionary tyranny in Eastern and Central Europe had created a legacy of real social grievances which, aggravated by the experiences of the war, provided the potential basis for Bolshevik support. By the same token, in places where such conditions were absent (e.g., the United States) bolshevism posed no threat. Second, Hoover held that food not force should constitute America's response to bolshevism. Unless the threat took a distinctly military form aimed directly at the West—an unlikely eventuality in Hoover's view—force would only aggravate the underlying social problems. By contrast economic relief, particularly food, would serve to alleviate the underlying distress while at the same time providing an opportunity to test Bolshevik intentions with regard to military expansion. In the third place, Hoover grounded his opposition to bolshevism on the unshakable conviction that the system was not economically viable. "It is not necessary for any American to debate the utter foolishness of these economic tenets," he asserted.[15] With Europe's material survival in grave doubt due to destruction of property and disruption of the productive processes, there simply was no margin for social and economic experimentation, particularly when such experimentation was bound to fail, thereby further aggravating the shortage of goods and creating in turn more political instability. In summary, Hoover believed that a reformed American capitalism operating in a world cleansed of the twin enemies of stability, militaristic imperialism and revolutionary socialism, could lead the world toward an optimization of wealth and welfare.

To these four central elements of the Wilsonian faith there should be added a fifth and crucial point of agreement between Hoover and the president. Specifically, Hoover by 1917, if not before, had come to support the concept of an American led crusade to eradicate autocracy and militarism and to erect a new and hopefully more stable and prosperous order in its stead. Through 1915 and 1916 Hoover repeatedly warned Wilson and Colonel Edward M. House of hostility within the Allied camp to the sort of peace for which the president was striving.[16] By 1917, however, he had concluded that America could develop sufficient leverage to overcome the opposition from this quarter. Early in that year with the country poised on the brink of war, Hoover prepared a memo for Colonel House stating that the United States should seek to mobilize a large military force in order to influence the character of the peace settlement. "As our terms of peace will probably run counter to most of the European proposals," Hoover wrote, "our weight in the accomplishment of our ideal will be greatly in proportion to the strength which we can throw in the scales."[17]

Subsequently, although he came to have important differences with Wilson on timing and tactics, Hoover remained committed to the central Wilsonian proposition that America, as the "one great moral reserve in the world," should deploy its power so as to promote a reformed international order.[18] It was within the framework of these attitudes and assumptions that Hoover approached the problem of European economic recovery during the winter of 1918–19.

III

As they confronted the myriad problems of peacemaking, the Wilson administration came to see the economic reconstruction of Europe as a function of four principal elements: (1) a peace settlement that left the nations of Europe economically and politically viable; (2) the establishment of a League of Nations; (3) emergency relief, particularly foodstuffs, for certain countries; and (4) a measure of long term economic assistance in the shape of credits for raw materials, machinery, and currency stabilization.[19] From the outset of the Peace Conference Hoover became the key figure in organizing and distributing emergency relief. Subsequently he devoted much time and thought to the longer term problems of reconstruction. By contrast, with regard to the first two elements, the overall peace settlement and the League, Hoover's role was neither central nor decisive. As one of Wilson's senior economic advisers he commented from time to time on various aspects of the settlement and the League but he did not share major responsibility. Hoover did, however, perceive American policy toward the reconstruction of Europe as a product of the four elements operating interdependently. For this reason, and because his efforts to deal with emergency relief and with long term reconstruction repeatedly confronted him with the inter-relationships between these elements, it is well to look briefly at Hoover's views on the peace settlement and on the function of the League of Nations.

Central to any peace settlement lay the question of Germany. Like other members of the American peace delegation, Hoover went to Europe in late 1918 committed to the idea of a peace which would reintegrate a democratized, demilitarized, and economically viable, though weakened, Germany into the political and economic fabric of Europe. A politically tranquil Germany, at work and at peace with her neighbors, would exert a powerful influence toward stability and the return of prosperity to the continent. By the same token, failure to realize these conditions in Germany would render precarious all efforts to promote recovery. Through the difficulties which he encountered in arranging food shipments to Germany, particularly the long drawn out haggling over the blockade, Hoover, along with other American advisers, came to appreciate the extent to which French military fears and British commercial ones conflicted with American objectives.[20] These same fears left a strong imprint on the Treaty of Versailles.

When the full text of the German Treaty became available, Hoover concluded that the Treaty imposed a settlement which was economically unworkable and politically dangerous. The heavy initial reparations payments which deprived Germany of working capital, the indeterminate level of reparations which undermined initiative, the loss of her merchant marine, and the fact that territorial changes left Germany with little over half of her prewar supplies of coal, while her population was reduced by only a third, constituted the most glaring economic defects. Hoover did not believe that the existing German goverment would accept the treaty in the form in which it was originally presented, unless it was forced to do so by further military action or a reimposition of the blockade. However, even if they did sign the Treaty without modification, the long term political repercussions of territorial dismemberment, when added to the impact of a shackled economy, would create a dangerously combustible mixture which could easily explode, leading Germany to reaction or bolshevism. Whatever the eventuality, the objective of a stable Europe based on a democratic Germany would be lost unless the Treaty were substantially modified.[21]

Hoover, whose concerns were shared by other members of the American delegation, urged Wilson to insist on revisions before signing the Treaty. He even suggested to Wilson that revision was worth risking a breakup of the Conference. But in the face of the president's personal stake in the Treaty, the continued intransigence of the Allies, and an overriding fear that a prolonged delay or breakup of the Conference would throw Europe into chaos, Hoover's pleading got nowhere.[22]

In subsequent months Hoover remained publicly loyal to the work of the American delegation, but he deeply resented what he believed to be short-sighted and grasping policies advanced by reactionary elements within the Allied delegations. A truncated German economy and an Austrian state which was not self-sufficient, economic disorganization and disunity in the successor states, and a widespread tendency to resort to arms added up to a Central Europe on the verge of a general economic breakdown.

This state of affairs, Hoover believed, was the legacy of reactionary folly as it had manifested itself in the blockade and the peace settlement with Germany, Austria, and Hungary.[23] Correcting the results of these excesses became for Hoover a major precondition for any lasting progress on reconstruction, and he remained convinced that the primary responsibility in these matters lay with Europe— especially the victorious Allies. Only if one appreciates these circumstances and remembers the bitterness and suspicion which Hoover carried away from the Peace Conference, can one understand the intensity with which Hoover urged European self-help in his efforts to promote reconstruction. Although he placed primary responsibility on European nations to correct the peace settlement, Hoover believed that the United States could greatly assist in these efforts by participating in the League of Nations.

Within the Wilsonian framework, the League of Nations was designed to serve three principal functions. It was, first of all, to be a permanent forum for the adjudication of international disputes. The existence of such machinery, its continuous use, and the body of laws and precedents generated would, it was hoped, help avoid future wars among the major industrial powers.[24] The resultant international climate of peace and stability would also serve the growing American interest in world trade, a point which Wilson understood though he preferred the idiom of morality and service to the cause of democracy.[25] Secondly, the League was designed to monitor and sustain the peace settlement, a function which entailed not only the adjustment of conflicts arising from the various treaties but also, if the occasion demanded, the use of economic or military power to enforce compliance. Finally, the League was seen as an agency for developing new ground rules to govern access to the underdeveloped world and to promote the gradual dismantling of the old style formal colonialism.[26]

Gordon Levin has recently emphasized the extent to which Wilson looked to the League to rectify the inequities and shortcomings of the peace settlement.[27] This attitude was, if anything, even stronger in Hoover's thinking and caused Hoover to draw a sharp distinction between the punitive enforcement character of the League and its function as a "court of appeal for the remedy of wrongs in the treaty." Intensely aware of the political dynamite being stored in the peace settlement, Hoover in April became fearful that the United States, through its identification with various inter-Allied commissions, would become merely one of the victors enforcing a victors' peace. This would probably mean repeated calls for military assistance to enforce the Treaty. Equally important, Hoover feared, it would tend to subvert the independence of the League and thereby destroy its potential usefulness as a court of appeal.[28]

As he became ever more aware of the shortcomings and inequities of the Treaty, the logic of Hoover's position, and his belief that the United States was "the great moral reserve in the world today," led him to cling tenaciously to the idea of American membership in the League even as he insisted that the role of policing a victors' peace must be avoided. Thus he supported ratification with the Lodge reservations, adhered steadfastly to this position throughout the campaign of 1920, and abandoned the League only reluctantly in April 1921.[29]

Conceived as a crucial prop for world stability, the League's stabilizing function was seen to be particularly necessary with regard to Europe, a point which Hoover emphasized in urging Wilson to accept the Lodge reservations. Not only would the League assist in rectifying the inequities of the peace settlement, but only when the machinery of the League covenant had been put into "constructive operation" would Americans develop the confidence in Europe's future which was an essential prerequisite for "credit facilities" and "commercial machinery" to enable private American capital to assist in reconstruction.[30]

Although he thoroughly understood the relationship between the League, the peace settlement, and economic reconstruction, it was the problems of relief and the mobilization of long-term American capital that mainly occupied Hoover's attention during the period in question. Therefore, it is to an examination of Hoover's record on these questions to which we should now turn.

IV

For Hoover the American food relief program was never simply a matter of extending charity to people in need. As early as October 1918 Hoover and Wilson began discussing the deployment of American food relief to Europe during the post-Armistice months.[31] Logistically this represented a continuation of Hoover's wartime role in maintaining food supplies for occupied Belgium and for the Western Allies. From the beginning, however, both Hoover and Wilson consciously sought to use American food to achieve a series of inter-related and overlapping political and economic objectives aimed at promoting Wilson's peace settlement. The most basic of these was to place a material and psychological floor under Central and Eastern Europe. The point was well stated in a Hoover press release on the feeding of Germany: "there are seventy millions of people who must either produce or die . . . their production is essential to the world's future and . . . they cannot produce unless they are fed."[32] The restoration of German productivity was, in turn, deemed vital for the maintenance of "order and stable government" and for the avoidance of "anarchy." [33]

In Central Europe, during the winter of 1918–19, anarchy became synonymous with bolshevism and opposition to bolshevism became, in fact, the principal criterion for the selective distribution of American food supplies to Austria, Germany, and Hungary. In German-Austria, where, in November 1918, there were reports of incipient bolshevism, American promises of food and coal were linked to an insistence that the newly-formed bourgeois liberal government maintain order and prevent social revolution. On the basis of Hoover's estimates that Vienna would be without food in ten days, shipments were rushed in.[34] Later, in March, Hoover wrote Wilson: "We have a clear proof of the value of feeding in the maintenance of order in the case of German-Austria where any action of the Bolshevik element is, on statement of their own leaders, being withheld until the next harvest, because of their dependence on us for their daily supply of food."[35] Subsequently, when Hoover learned of planned May Day actions by radical groups in Vienna, he had placards put up with a statement pointing out that social unrest could lead to a cut off of food. "No disturbance took place," Hoover later recalled.[36] In Hungary, the threat of a food cut off (substantially implemented in one case) helped to topple the Bolshevik government of Bela Kun in July, and in August forestalled a Hapsburg comeback.[37]

In Germany the situation, though less immediately pressing, was potentially much more dangerous, and was aggravated by Allied insistence on maintaining the blockade until mid-March. In his repeated objections to the Allied blockade policy, Hoover made it clear that he conceived of American food relief in political terms. Receipt of food in adequate quantities could, at one and the same time, engender confidence in the effectiveness of the new government of Friederich Ebert and, by alleviating the threat of famine, lessen the political appeal of bolshevism.[38]

Common to the situations in Austria, Germany, and Hungary, as well as those in Czeckoslovakia and Yugoslavia where the United States also dispensed its food for political ends, was the absence of an external Bolshevik military threat. In these situations Hoover used American food to undercut radical and reactionary elements and to lend support to Wilsonian type bourgeois liberal regimes. By contrast, in northeastern Europe, the Baltic countries, and Poland, where the exigencies of the Russian Civil War and the intervention made actual or threatened Bolshevik military advances a continuing problem, American food distribution became in varying degrees linked with the counter-revolutionary military effort. As a result, Wilson's hope that he could avoid reaction while checking bolshevism was at best imperfectly realized, and American food, although in a fundamental sense still aimed at promoting productivity and stability, became an important economic underpinning for the "cordon-sanitaire."[39]

Hoover also developed an elaborate scheme for food distribution inside Russia. It too was aimed at countering Bolshevik influence and strengthening the hand of bourgeois elements in that divided country. The scheme was never implemented, however, and it was quickly submerged in the complex and shifting cross currents of Allied anti-Soviet diplomacy.[40]

To maintain efficient distribution of food, Hoover found it necessary to assume a variety of ancillary responsibilities. In order to thread his way through the long-standing ethnic antagonisms of Eastern Europe, which were compounded by the creation of new states, Hoover from the first insisted on developing his own distribution organization down to the local level, together with his own independent sources of information. This machinery also helped avoid waste and prevented jockeying by the other Allies from subverting Wilson's larger political objectives.[41] In addition, the Allied leadership granted Hoover extensive powers over railroad operations in Central and Eastern Europe, coupled with essentially autonomous control over large quantities of locomotives and rolling stock.[42]

Hoover's work in organizing food relief and the extensive railroad and communication network which he controlled in Eastern Europe made him a logical choice to unravel the tangled problem of distributing coal to that region. In April serious shortages were reported imminent, due to reduced production and to the fact that actions by the newly created political entities had disrupted long-standing trade patterns. Given broad authority to deal with the situation, Hoover drew on qualified technical and professional men serving with the American Expeditionary Forces to set up an organization to oversee both distribution and, in some cases, production from the coal fields of Teschen, Upper Silesia, and other parts of Eastern Europe.[43]

Success in the emergency management of food, railroads, and coal led to arrangements under which several of the new governments of Central and Eastern Europe retained, as technical advisers, men from the relief, railway, and coal organizations. The Polish government, for example, acting at Hoover's urging and on his recommendation, established such a mission in July 1919, and a total of nine American experts (in railways, coal, food, oil and gas, and general transportation) served the Polish government for varying periods between 1919 and 1922. Similar missions were established in Czechoslovakia, Yugoslavia, and Austria. All were financed by funds which had accrued to the credit of the American Relief Administration.[44] Finally, Colonel James A. Logan, who had served as chief of staff for Hoover's relief organization, remained in Paris to coordinate the activities of the various European Technical Adviser Missions. Through this machinery, Hoover was able to translate into more permanent form his early efforts to counter the adverse economic effects of political fragmentation in Eastern Europe.[45]

Hoover's emergency relief program, although focused directly on Germany and the so-called "back bloc" countries of Eastern Europe, was conceived also as part of a broad deployment of American economic power aimed at the Western Allies. From this perspective there were several overlapping objectives. In the first place, the Wilson administration wished to block British and French attempts to use wartime inter-Allied economic agencies to commandeer American resources for statist schemes aimed at Allied hegemony in shipping, commerce, and raw materials. In withholding American support from such schemes, and, where necessary, countering them, Wilson and his associates were seeking to protect the American economic stake in the world. They were also trying to retain full control over American resources so that these could be used later as a lever to secure Allied adherence to American peace plans.

American fears of a commercial "war after the war" had been greatly stimulated by the reports from the Allied Economic Conference held in Paris in June 1916 and were rarely absent thereafter.[46] During the summer of 1918, these fears became intense in some quarters of the administration as the Allies, responding to their own not unwarranted concern with America's growing economic power, jockeyed for postwar commercial advantages. "There is a spirit rampant of getting ready for trade after the war," reported one American official in Europe, "and no opportunity is neglected to improve industrial position."[47] Hoover was aware of these developments and critical of statist and restrictive tendencies in Allied policy. But it was Edward N. Hurley and his associates at the United States Shipping Board who mounted the most vigorous and alarming critique of Allied policy, thereby initiating a major debate on the shape of the postwar international economy, which lasted up to the time that Wilson departed for Europe.[48]

Hurley and his supporters believed that America should resist these efforts and that such an approach to be effective would entail a sizeable dose of statism—in other words the United States had, in a sense, to fight fire with fire. Among other proposals, Hurley recommended a government supported raw material monopoly and a policy of calculated indecision (designed to keep the British off balance) regarding the disposition to be made of the U.S. Shipping Board's merchant fleet. In defending such policies, Hurley emphasized not the gain in competitive advantage by the United States, but rather the leverage which would be afforded in securing Wilson's new international order.[49]

The principal opposition to Hurley's views came from Secretary of Commerce William C. Redfield. Redfield generally agreed with Hurley on the kind of spirit which he hoped would inform the postwar international marketplace. But, the secretary of commerce expressed alarm at the idea of a "national attempt to become a benevolent monopolist." Deploring what he saw as a "sort of commercial apoplexy in the air respecting 'after the war' conditions," Redfield discounted, as greatly exaggerated, the American fears of Britain's postwar commercial behavior, and he argued that the United States would only poison the atmosphere further by adopting the kind of restrictive practices with which Germany had been identified in the prewar years.[50]

As Wilson's position emerged it reflected elements of both Redfield's and Hurley's, but the president came down closer to Hurley than he did to his secretary of commerce. The government raw material monopoly was not pursued and, in his annual message to Congress in December, Wilson spoke out against a statist approach to domestic reconstruction. In addition, Wilson pointedly cautioned Hurley against statements about U.S. postwar policy which might aggravate British suspicions. Notwithstanding British impressions to the contrary, the president wrote, "We do not intend to seek any unfair advantage of any kind or to shoulder anybody out, but [seek] merely to give the widest possible currency to our own goods. . . ." Unlike Redfield, however, Wilson found much cause for concern in reports that British officials were actively pursuing a policy of commercial aggrandizement under the guise of the war effort. Consequently, although he disclaimed any intention of embarking on a commercial war against the British, the president was drawn to Hurley's belief that American resources should be closely held so as to serve the nation's larger political and economic objectives.[51]

The upshot was that the administration moved defensively to insist that American food, credit, and shipping remain under American control. This would insure that they were not used indiscriminately to underwrite Allied commercial expansion and at the same time place them at the president's disposal for bargaining at the Peace Conference. Hoover became the chief spokesman for this new thrust to American policy, and his negotiations during November and December to block British plans for pooling relief supplies represented the cutting edge of a broad administration effort aimed at reasserting American economic independence, and using that position to induce Allied adherence to American peace objectives.[52]

Judged against these expectations, Wilson's policy was a failure. Control was, to be sure, effectively maintained and American resources were generally used only for approved national objectives. However, the impact of this leverage on Allied behavior at the Peace Conference appears to have been minimal. Except in the case of the naval building program, which Wilson was able to use with some effect against the British, the evidence suggests that no significant changes in Allied peace proposals were the result of American economic leverage.[53]

The specific reasons for this failure varied in the case of credit, shipping, and food, but they boiled down to two considerations. First, the needs of the Allies for American resources proved to be less pressing once peace was at hand. Second, with the American economy tooled up to support the war effort and with two million soldiers and sailors deployed in Europe (entailing a heavy American demand for franc and sterling exchange), the United States found itself strongly dependent on the continuity of economic relations with the Western Allies.[54] Since Hoover's relief program had been the principal vehicle through which Wilson had chosen to assert America's economic independence, it was fitting, if more than a little ironic, that American efforts to implement the relief program should reveal early and dramatically the vulnerability of the American economy to European pressures.

On New Year's Eve 1918, Allied officials responsible for food purchasing, shipping, and blockade matters, meeting on short notice and without notifying their American counterparts, abruptly cancelled all outstanding orders (some confirmed as late as the previous day) for American beef, pork, grain, and dairy products. At the same meeting, Allied officials also reversed an earlier decision to relax restrictions on food imports into Germany. Commitments to American farmers and packers designed to stimulate increased wartime production for Allied needs had generated a gigantic surplus of pork products, many of them cut specifically to British tastes. Because of limited cold storage facilities, the cancellation order threatened a massive logistical crisis and widespread economic distress involving not only American farmers and packers but hundreds of banks and credit institutions throughout the Midwest.[55] Intensifying the sense of crisis, fears of domestic depression spread in late January, as copper producers and other industries found themselves confronting drastically reduced postwar markets.[56]

Although badly jolted, Hoover reacted immediately with characteristic energy. Consultations with American officials in both the United States and Europe confirmed that storage could be found for non-perishables—wheat, flour, and sugar—but revealed that a serious problem existed with meat products, especially pork. Vigorously supported by Wilson and assisted by various government agencies, Hoover's organization withstood the Allied onslaught. Counterpressures on France and Italy soon resulted in a restoration of orders by those nations. Increased purchases by the War Department and Belgian Relief Agency took up some of the slack and, backed by the United States Navy, Hoover's ships simply ignored the Allied blockade in order to deliver large quantities of food already in transit to Baltic and northern neutral countries. The remaining supplies were stockpiled at Allied and neutral ports. Finally in March, amid reports of famine and a rising Bolshevik tide which threatened Germany and the Balkans and did engulf Hungary, the Allies agreed to relax the blockade. The tightness of Hoover's position through these weeks was greatly aggravated because, in order to maintain increased production, he had committed the United States government to peg pork prices until the end of March 1919.[57]

How is one to explain Allied policy in this episode? In his accounts of the pork episode written in later years, Hoover attributed the cancellation to an excess of zeal on the part of second echelon British bureaucrats who desired, at one and the same time, to break the price of foodstuffs, which they judged too high, and to shift British purchasing to cheaper Latin American and Australian markets.[58] While this was doubtless true as far as it went, it seems probable that the British were playing for higher stakes.

A look at the timing of the British move is revealing. The food cancellation intruded itself in the middle of the fight which Hoover and Wilson were having to insure exclusive American management of relief. On the same day as the cancellation, the Treasury Department, bent on tightening its control of American credit and asserting in its own way Wilson's policy of American economic independence, formally turned down a British request for a $500 million credit to cover expected purchases of American cotton, oil, foodstuffs, and other commodites. Citing domestic pressure and a lack of authority, the Treasury politely suggested that the British take their business to private American bankers, an idea hardly calculated to soothe prevailing fears of commercial decline and an impending eclipse of London's financial supremacy.[59] Similarly unsettling to the British at this time was the fear, carefully nurtured by Wilson's policy of calculated indecision, that the United States government would retain control of America's recently constructed merchant fleet and, by operating it at a loss, make serious inroads into England's commercial position.[60]

Whether it was planned or not, the British cancellation order had the effect of blunting the impact of America's economic unilateralism. Responding to pressures from Hoover and Wilson, Treasury officials finally loosened up on loans to the Allies.[61] During the same period, consultation between Hoover and Sir Robert Cecil led to the creation of a new inter-Allied economic agency, the Supreme Economic Council. In no sense did this body subvert the principle of American control, although this was attempted periodically. It did, however, soften its practical impact by providing a forum more conducive to joint consultation and coordination than had the previously established Supreme Council of Supply and Relief.[62] In the matter of shipping, Wilson continued to maintain his silence on America's postwar plans. But the potential threat diminished when the British discovered that they were able to move vigorously back into their old trade routes and at the same time allocate roughly three times as much tonnage as the Americans to moving Hoover's relief supplies.[63]

Hoover's management of emergency relief operations effectively asserted and sustained Wilson's policy of independent control of American resources. But the results of this effort were mixed. To be sure, American resources were made to serve Wilson's political and economic objectives in Central and Eastern Europe and opportunities for the Allies to employ them for narrowly nationalistic ends were circumscribed. At the same time, however, Hoover's organization became the target for British economic reprisals. The vicissitudes which, as a consequence, beset Hoover's food operations revealed the extent of American dependence on Europe and help explain why America's vast economic power, when applied against the Allies, yielded only modest gains.

Intensive and continuous exposure to the problems of emergency relief led Hoover to reflect on the long-term requirements of European reconstruction. His conclusions, set forth in a series of statements and memoranda drawn up during the summer of 1919, provide a remarkably complete and comprehensive catalog of the attitudes and ideas on this question which Hoover carried with him into the Commerce Department in 1921. Equally important, Hoover's views serve to place in sharper focus the other policy options advanced during 1918 and 1919, including the course which Wilson finally adopted. Conversely, it is within the context of the evolving American policy on long-term reconstruction that one can best appreciate Hoover's views.

V

American policy toward European reconstruction took shape in several stages beginning in the fall of 1918. Prior to Wilson's departure for Europe in December, responsible officials, especially those in the Treasury Department, had concluded that Europe's long-term material needs from the United States (as opposed to emergency relief) should be financed through private channels. This decision was arrived at within the framework of the general debate on foreign economic policy already discussed, and was consistent with both a non-statist orientation and with the idea that American resources remain under American control. In addition to its larger political implications, such a policy would yield certain tangible economic advantages. Private financing of European reconstruction would mean not only orders for American goods, which in any case would have followed government financing, but would also result in commissions for American bankers and an acceleration of the rise of New York as the world's great financial center, widely touted as a desirable and inevitable result of the war.[64]

Consistent with this decision to rely on private financing, members of the American Peace Commission did not carry with them any detailed plans for economic reconstruction. In fact, it was not until May 1919 that they produced anything which might be called an overall plan for European recovery. In these months American policy on long-term reconstruction was guided not only by the commitment to private financing, but also by the belief that the critical variables in reconstruction were a viable peace settlement and an effective international agency for resolving disputes and providing stability. "It is perfectly true," Norman Davis recalled in 1922, "that we did not offer any detailed plans for the economic revival of Europe, but we stood for sound economic principles and fought for the adoption of political and economic settlements, which if adopted, would have made detailed solutions practically academic, but without which no plan would work."[65]

In May 1919 Wilson's economic advisers in effect reopened the question of long-term reconstruction policy and, during the succeeding four months, the possibility of governmental financing and control re-emerged. What primarily induced the American delegation to re-examine its initial decision on this question was a growing realization that the peace settlement simply would not work; that it would, among other things, seriously curtail the German economy and through this the economy of Europe as a whole.

Fears that the Treaty would prove unworkable economically had been present throughout. Members of the American delegation repeatedly experienced doubts on this score as the Treaty was hammered out section by section. These concerns were accentuated by reports that widespread economic distress prevailed in Central Europe despite food deliveries.[66] But it was the publication, on May 7, 1919, of the full text of the German Treaty which brought these accumulating doubts sharply into focus. Hoover recalled vividly the impact this event had upon him. A servant awakened him at four o'clock in the morning to deliver the printed draft treaty. Despite his previous knowledge of many of the provisions, the perusal of the entire document at one sitting shocked him, driving home the belief "that peace for the long run could not be built on these foundations . . . [that] the Treaty contained the seeds of another war . . . [and] that the economic provisions alone would pull down the whole continent and, in the end injure the United States." In his agitated state of mind he rose at early daylight and took a walk through the deserted Paris streets, only to encounter General Jan Smuts and British Treasury Advisor John Maynard Keynes, like himself "greatly disturbed."[67]

As Hoover's story suggests, members of the British delegation were also driven by fears regarding the economic viability of the Treaty. Two weeks earlier in fact, on April 23, 1919, the British had presented a comprehensive reconstruction plan drawn up by Keynes. Although initially receptive to the British overture, Wilson's advisers found, after careful examination, that the burden of financing the scheme would fall on the United States Treasury. This was quite out of the question and, in a letter to Lloyd George, Wilson angrily rejected the British plan.[68] "How can your experts or ours," he wrote the prime minister, "be expected to work out a new plan to furnish working capital to Germany when we deliberately start by taking all of Germany's present capital?"[69]

Although they rejected the Keynes plan, American officials did not abandon the subject of long-term reconstruction. In the weeks following the publication of the German Treaty, they gave the subject much time and thought.[70] It was in this context that Hoover, during the spring and summer of 1919, pulled together his own thinking on the question. Most comprehensively expounded in a long memorandum of July 3, 1919, Hoover's ideas also found expression in letters, congressional testimony, private conversations, and statements to the press. During much of this period Hoover, as the only senior adviser remaining in Europe after Wilson's return to America, was also struggling to surmount the desperate shortage of coal, smoothing the conversion of the American Relief Administration to a private agency, and representing the United States on the Supreme Economic Council.

Basic to Hoover's analysis of Europe's long-term needs lay the assumption that wartime destruction of tools and manpower represented only a small part of the problem.[71] Rather, he believed Europe was suffering from an accumulation of non-material factors which he characterized as massively "demoralized productivity." As a result, fifteen million families were receiving some kind of unemployment allowance and exports had been reduced to the point where the roughly 20% of Europe's population which normally depended on imports was in an extremely precarious position. The causes of this state of affairs were varied and complex. War and postwar political jockeying with the attendant instability of the newly created governments; slowdowns and stoppages by workers, growing out of "the proper and insistent demand of labor for higher standards of living"; a general relaxation of effort after wartime exertions; restricted flows of raw materials caused by the blockade, shipping shortages, and credit uncertainties; all these were in some measure responsible for the demoralization. Aggravating the whole situation were class and group antagonisms and a certain propensity to extravagance, itself a reflex from wartime austerity. Compared with these institutional, social, and political factors, the destruction of tools and manpower accounted for but a small part of the problem.[72]

Since the roots of the crisis lay so largely in non-material considerations, so too did the solution. Hoover believed that "the imutable human qualities of selfishness, self-interest, altruism, intelligence and education" must be activated. Admitting the very real grievances of millions of Europeans growing out of the legacy of war and economic oppression, Hoover still insisted that the answer lay not in changes in the economic system. "Tampering with the delicate and highly developed organization of production and distribution" would do no good. Men must be given tools, raw materials and safety and then go back to work. Economic experimentation, he believed, had consistently resulted in decreased production and "there is no margin of surplus productivity in Europe to risk revolutionary experimentation." To this central prescription, Hoover then added a small list of practices and policies which Europe should avoid—price controls, currency inflation, military establishments and blockades, and the "discriminatory control of ships, railways, waterways, coal and iron."

Within the framework of this analysis the role assigned American capital was paradoxical. Actual physical destruction, Hoover believed, was relatively small. At the same time, Europe's monthly deficiencies were running so high that any sustained attempt to make them up from the United States would quickly exhaust the limited surplus of productivity available in the Western Hemisphere. In the process, since Europe would have no exports with which to remit, Continental credit would be destroyed and Europe would become an economic vassal of the Western Hemisphere. This, in turn, would lead once more to war. These eventualities were repugnant to Hoover and for him they pointed to a policy of strictly limiting the allocation of surplus American productivity. Paradoxically, however, while minimizing Europe's material needs and America's ability to meet them, Hoover argued that the United States should deploy its resources so as to overcome the formidable non-material obstacles to Europe's recovery. This meant that America's limited material contribution must be made to yield substantial leverage in Europe's internal affairs.

To achieve the requisite leverage, Hoover concluded that American capital, once mobilized, had to be coordinated. Such coordination would insure that the available American capital went to those countries and those projects where it was most needed and could produce the best results. Equally important, central control of American capital exports would place the United States in a position to demand that recipient countries put their political and economic houses in order. Since the crux of the production problem lay in the attitudes and policies of the European countries themselves, such housecleaning was essential to insure recovery. By the same token, even larger amounts of American capital would yield negligible results unless the necessary conditions prevailed inside Europe. Understandably, in view of his experience administering food relief, Hoover was sanguine about the efficacy of such tactics. Thus he observed to the press in June 1919:

> We should have consolidated organized control of the assistance we give in such a way that it should be used only if economy in imports is maintained and if the definite rehabilitation of industry is undertaken . . .—if the people return to work, if orderly government is preserved, fighting is stopped, disarmament is undertaken, and there is no discrimination against the United States in favor of other countries.[73]

Clear in his mind on what had to be done, the next question for Hoover became that of means.

Faced with the need to coordinate the flow of American capital to Europe, Hoover turned to the idea of a governmental role in long-term reconstruction. He reasoned that, in order to assure the requisite volume of American credit, the government would have to step in. Some direct government assistance would be required for food and, to the extent of $500 million, to rehabilitate and stabilize currencies in Central and Eastern Europe. Beyond that, Hoover estimated that Europe would need, on credit, roughly $3 billion worth of American cotton, copper, and other commodities over a twelve-month period. Some of these shipments could be financed through private channels. In other cases, particularly goods destined for Germany and Eastern Europe, the government would have to assume part of the risk. By a judicious use of the War Finance Corporation to guarantee the commercial paper generated by these shipments, Hoover believed that he could mobilize private American capital and, what was more important, tap the initiative and energy of American businessmen for the task of European reconstruction.

With a government role required in any case to mobilize the necessary capital, a basis would exist for instituting the necessary controls. Thus the WFC, working with "some sort of an economic committee in the United States representing the different departments of the government and such other persons as [the president] might select," could provide central coordination.[74] This would insure distribution according to economically rational priorities and enforce adherence to certain institutional and political conditions.[75]

There were, in Hoover's view, three major conditions: (1) a fixed reparation schedule which both the Germans and potential outside creditors believed Germany could meet; (2) disarmament (which presupposed peace) by the Allies and especially by the nations of Central and Eastern Europe; and (3) restoration of economic unity to Central and Eastern Europe through territorial adjustments and the elimination of politically inspired trade barriers.[76] With these conditions substantially achieved, capital invested in Europe would be much more likely to effect recovery. It would also be easier to attract additional capital if that became necessary.

In sum, Hoover hoped to enlist the initiative and energy of thousands of American merchants, bankers, and manufacturers who would operate on a strictly commercial basis. Such activity would take place within the context of a massive coordinated national program. This would insure the optimum allocation of American resources to the problem of European reconstruction and enable the United States to effect necessary changes in Europe's internal affairs.

When American policy on long-term reconstruction finally crystallized in August 1919, Hoover's ideas received short shrift. This occurred despite his wealth of experience and information on Europe's economic problems and his importance in shaping relief policy. Hoover's personal estrangement from Wilson and the fact that he was in Paris not Washington during the summer doubtless weakened his position. In retrospect, it seems to have been particularly crucial that Hoover was unable to present his view in person to the top officials of the Treasury. Plagued by fears of inflation and a growing concern about government spending, and bent on reasserting its ascendancy in this area of policymaking, Treasury officials in Washington, led by Assistant Secretary Russell C. Leffingwell, firmly reiterated the original administration emphasis on private financing in the face of mounting domestic and foreign pressure for some form of governmental assistance.[77]

Particularly disturbing to the Treasury at that time was a scheme hatched by Morgan partner Henry P. Davison, and supported inside the administration by Secretary Redfield. This scheme would have placed the prestige of the government behind a powerful consortium of private bankers to enable them to raise reconstruction loans from the American public.[78] The kind of coordination proposed by Hoover was of a different sort. Its aim was not primarily to relieve bondholders' fears but, rather, to insure judicious use of American resources and to engender an attitude of self-help on Europe's part. The Treasury felt, however, that any such grand scheme would tend to dampen initiative and encourage people to expect assistance from the government which it was not prepared to give. Although the Treasury emphatically approved of most of the conditions which Hoover sought to enforce, it was willing to leave it to private bankers in individual transactions to make the demands.

The impact of Hoover's recommendations was also weakened by an erosion of confidence in his judgment. As early as May, various high officials had begun to question Hoover's estimates and predictions. By the summer of 1919, he had, so far as some officials were concerned, cried "wolf" too often. Writing to Leffingwell from Paris in August, Governor Benjamin Strong of the Federal Reserve Bank of New York forwarded a memorandum of Hoover's on reconstruction and then went on to challenge the latter's estimate that Europe would need roughly $3 billion worth of American commodities on credit. After interrogating Hoover in some detail about his figures and making independent observations, Strong decided that Hoover had overstated Europe's requirements by a factor of three. The governor readily conceded that Hoover had done "a magnificent piece of work" and "more than anyone else [had] saved this part of the world from a breakdown immediately after the armistice." But he found Hoover inclined to develop "a state of mind particularly under resistance, which might be dangerous to the development of sound plans." "When it comes to cold blooded, deliberate judgment of what Europe needs," Strong concluded, "I think he expressed in over strong terms an impression which he gathers from a great mass of statistical material gathered from sources which in many cases are quite unreliable." In view of the combination of factors which led to the rejection of his proposals, it was perhaps fitting that Hoover's return to the United States, where he immediately retired to private life, followed by only two days Wilson's decision to endorse the Treasury's approach to European reconstruction.[80]

In trying to assess the significance of Hoover's ideas on long-term reconstruction, it is possible for one to argue that the adoption of Hoover's proposals in the summer of 1919 would have rapidly increased European productivity. By thus avoiding the debilitating social and political effects of protracted stagnation and by placing Western prosperity on a solid basis, so the argument runs, later economic disturbances and attendant political crisis would have been prevented. Such an argument requires a careful analysis of European productivity figures for the early 1920s. It also presupposes that the United States was willing at that time to make substantial economic commitments and some political ones to remake Europe and that the continental nations, encouraged and guided by American pressure, were psychologically prepared in 1919 to arrange a viable settlement with Germany and with each other. A thorough analysis of these questions would lead well beyond the scope of the present paper. Rather than trying to pursue them here, I will limit myself to commenting on certain other implications of Hoover's approach, and to tracing briefly the successive proposal which Hoover made over the next two years for dealing with the problem of European recovery. This will serve to underline the essential continuity in Hoover's thinking between 1919 and the Commerce years, and will suggest broad similarities between the policy established by Wilson and that pursued during the 1920s.

VI

Throughout the period under review, Hoover assumed that European recovery and its integration into a functioning world economy was vital to American prosperity. He further believed that it was primarily Europe's own folly which prevented this. Within the context of these two propositions, the central question for Hoover came to be how the United States could induce Europe to take those steps essential to insure her own reconstruction and with it America's prosperity. This had, of course, been Wilson's problem and, although Hoover deplored the use of military means (which he came to see as self-defeating) he did not give up the larger objective when he accepted the invitation to join Harding's cabinet. Neither did he at first abandon his efforts to secure American participation in the League. It was only after a month's effort, spent in lobbying anti-League senators with Secretary of State Charles Evans Hughes, had convinced him that ratification was hopeless that he abandoned the League Treaty.[81] But he did not give up his belief in the importance to the United States of European recovery.

As a logical consequence of this position, the shaping of American foreign policy became for Hoover, to a large degree, an attempt to fashion a suitable lever for influencing European affairs. Even with the League Treaty approved, additional means would still have been required to persuade Europe to order its house to American specifications. With the Senate's rejection of the Treaty, such means became even more essential. Not surprisingly, Hoover repeatedly sought ways in which American economic power might be effectively deployed. Begun during the fall of 1918, this search never really ended, a fact which tends to blur the distinction between Hoover's public and private roles and provides a central thread connecting his work at the Peace Conference with his later career as secretary of commerce in President Warren Harding's cabinet.

Within weeks after he had laid down his official responsibilities, Hoover was again forced to confront the recovery problem. Summoned to consultations at the State Department in December by reports of another food crisis in Austria and other parts of Eastern Europe, Hoover, who had argued at the Conference for a union between German-Austria and Germany, used the occasion to emphasize the link between the existing crises and the shortsightedness of the Allied peace terms.[82] This one last time, he testified to the House Ways and Means Committee, the United States should assist. But, he continued, "if a political situation is to be maintained in Austria that makes Austria a perpetual mendicant . . . those who consider they benefit should pay the bill." In March, Congress responded by authorizing the United States Grain Corporation to sell on credit five million barrels of surplus flour to Austria and other needy countries. Sizeable quantities of breadstuffs were subsequently shipped, but this effort was not made to yield any substantial leverage for the United States.[83]

In addition to the public measures described above, some relief to Austria and other East European countries was maintained on a basis of private charity. Before leaving Europe, Hoover had arranged to convert the American Relief Administration into a private organization and it continued to help. Some assistance was also provided through a special plan for consolidating immigrant remittances to Poland which Hoover set up through the Guaranty Trust Company.[84] But these agencies operated on a modest scale and, like the shipments of American breadstuffs, yielded little effective leverage to the United States. Consequently, Hoover continued to entertain ideas of some broad comprehensive approach to reconstruction.

During 1920, Hoover lent his support to two initiatives looking toward some sort of comprehensive reconstruction plan. In January, he joined Paul Warburg and a number of prominent Americans and Europeans in endorsing a memorial requesting the United States and other governments to consider a comprehensive approach to reconstruction. The Treasury, wary of any comprehensive scheme, sensed a backhanded attempt by Europe to reduce inter-Allied debts and rejected the proposal.[85]

Later, Hoover played a prominent role in launching the massive and ultimately stillborn Foreign Trade Financing Corporation. Chartered under the Edge Act at $100 million, the FTFC was expected to serve as a vehicle for mobilizing the capital of bankers, merchants, manufacturers, and farmers for investment overseas.[86] In Hoover's mind, it would, while avoiding statism, capitalize on the advantages of private initiative and provide the kind of centralized management of American capital necessary to insure efficient usage and the fulfillment of the various conditions which Hoover believed so important to the success of European recovery. In his speech to the FTFC kick-off meeting in Chicago in December 1920, Hoover reiterated two of the essential conditions, disarmament and balanced budgets, and linked them with a call for "economic statesmanship." He thus left little doubt that he expected the FTFC managers to push for arms reductions and balanced budgets at the same time that they negotiated their loans to Europe.[87]

After he became secretary of commerce, Hoover initially continued to plug the FTFC approach. In April 1921, he publicly chided Wall Street bankers for their unwillingness to take a long view of their interests and provide support. The results of this effort were disappointing.[88] By that time, however, Hoover and other members of President Harding's administration were engaged in a frenzied effort to combat the depression of 1920–21 by developing ways for the government to relieve the strain which quantities of unsold agricultural surpluses had placed on the banking system. At first Hoover hoped that, through liberal use of the War Finance Corporation, many of the surpluses could be sold on credit to Europe. In his haste to make such credit available, the idea of insisting on conditions was temporarily laid aside.[89] But by the summer of 1921 it became apparent to Hoover that any sizeable increases in sales to Europe had to await the stabilization of exchange rates and the requisite underlying internal reforms—especially disarmament.[90]

Seeking ways to effect such internal reforms, Hoover turned once again to the question of securing leverage from American economic power. During the next two and a half years, he explored the possibility of a central bank consortium led by Governor Strong,[91] proposed to President Harding a comprehensive settlement linking an American stabilization loan of $500 million to reductions in land armaments and reparations,[92] and engaged in a continuing effort to persuade major American bankers to insist (as a condition for loans) that Europe disarm, settle reparations on an economically sound basis, and generally put its fiscal house in order.[93] The financial reconstruction of Austria in 1922 and 1923 was one of the fruits of these efforts, the work of the Dawes Commission another.

In striving to implement that part of Wilson's vision represented by the reconstruction of Europe, Hoover found himself in a position familiar to many American policymakers before and since. Having defined certain changes in other societies as vital to American prosperity, Hoover was confronted with the task of bringing these changes about. The use of military means between 1917 and 1919 had not only failed but, in view of the situation in Russia and Eastern Europe, proved counterproductive. Such means were, in any case, morally repugnant and in flat contradiction to Hoover's emphasis on increased productivity through stability, security, and individual initiative. Final rejection of the League Treaty in 1921 ruled out formal political participation in Europe. Turning naturally to economic means, Hoover was faced with a further constraint, his inability because of conviction and prevailing attitudes to conscript the taxpayers' money for policy ends abroad. He was thus forced to rely largely on his ability to persuade European statesmen and to harness the activities of American businessmen and bankers to the larger ends of policy.

The halting and limited achievement of the measures deemed essential to reconstruction is, in part at least, attributable to the nature of the tools with which American policy makers were forced to work. It did not, as is evident from Hoover's thinking on the subject, stem from any failure to understand the nature and the magnitude of the problem. Rather than dwell on the limitations of these tools and the incompleteness of the achievement of reconstruction during the 1920s, another thought seems particularly pertinent today. In recent years Americans have seen vast sums of the taxpayers' money and enormous military power, both overt and covert, deployed in repeated and impatient efforts to effect changes in other people's societies. Measured against this record,

Hoover's patience and ingenuity and the rigor with which he accepted the limits which public opinion and his own outlook placed on the means at hand merit respect, even from those who would define American interests differently.

NOTES

For their comments and suggestions the author thanks: Ellis Hawley, University of Iowa; Robert Cuff, York University, Toronto; Michael Hogan, Miami University of Ohio; Fred Adams, Drake University; and Melvyn Leffler, Vanderbilt University.

1   Herbert Hoover, "Memorandum on the Economic Situation," *Annals of the American Academy of Political and Social Science*, 87 (January 1920), 106.

2   On Wilson's foreign economic policies and the link between these and his ideology, see William Diamond, *The Economic Thought of Woodrow Wilson* (Baltimore: Johns Hopkins University Press, 1943), pp. 162–92; Martin J. Sklar, "Woodrow Wilson and the Political Economy of Modern United States Liberalism," *Studies on the Left*, 1 (1960), 17–47; William A. Williams, *Tragedy of American Diplomacy*, 2d ed. (New York: Dell, 1962), pp. 53–102; N. Gordon Levin, *Woodrow Wilson and World Politics* (New York: Oxford University Press, 1968), pp. 1–28, 123–53, 169–80. Still of great value on Wilson and the Conference is Ray Stannard Baker, *Woodrow Wilson and World Settlement*, 3 vols. (Garden City, N.Y.: Doubleday, Page, 1922–23). The similarities between Hoover's outlook and Wilson's are discussed in the works by Williams and Levin cited above and in Arno Mayer, *Politics and Diplomacy of Peacemaking* (New York: Knopf, 1969), pp. 21, 24–27, 266–83, 474–87. Best of all on this point is Herbert Hoover, *The Ordeal of Woodrow Wilson* (New York: McGraw-Hill, 1958). The essential continuity of Wilson's foreign policy with that of succeeding Republican administrations is emphasized in Williams's *Tragedy,* pp. 104–59, and Carl Parrini, *Heir to Empire: United States Economic Diplomacy, 1916–1923* (Pittsburgh: University of Pittsburgh Press, 1969).

3   American Institute of Mining Engineers, *Bulletin,* no. 154 (October 1919), 1–8. An extremely useful survey of Hoover's early thinking on political economy is contained in two unpublished papers prepared by Robert E. Treacey for a graduate seminar at the University of Wisconsin. "Herbert Hoover in the World War: The U.S. Food Administrator" (November 1960) and "Herbert Hoover to 1920" (May 1961).

4   A.I.M.E. *Bulletin,* no. 154 (October 1919), 7; See also Hoover to Wilson, September 11, 1918, enclosed in Whitmarsh to Hoover, January 29, 1919, Woodrow Wilson Papers, Library of Congress, Series 5B, Box 12, cited hereafter as Wilson Mss.

5   On Hoover's political economy, see Herbert Hoover, *American Individualism* (Garden City, N.Y.: Doubleday, 1922); William A. Williams, *Contours of American History* (New York: New Viewpoints, 1961), pp. 425–38, and "What this Country Needs," *New York Review of Books,* November 5, 1970, pp. 7–11; Ellis W. Hawley,

"Herbert Hoover and American Corporatism, 1929–1933," unpublished paper, 1972, furnished courtesy of the author; Murray Rothbard, "Herbert Hoover and the Myth of Laissez Faire," Ronald Radosh and Murray Rothbard, eds., *A New History of Leviathan* (New York: Dutton, 1972), pp. 111–45.

6   Herbert Hoover, "Food, An International Problem," United States Food Administration Bulletin, no. 6 (Washington, 1917), 31; quoted in Treacy, "Hoover in the World War," 10.

7   Hoover to Lansing, May 10, 1918, Record Group 40, National Archives, Records of the Department of Commerce, Secretary's Correspondence, file 77270. . Material from this Record group hereafter cited as RG 40 NA File —.

8   Herbert Hoover, *An American Epic,* 4 vols. (Chicago: Regnery, 1961), 2:261–62.

9   Hoover, *American Epic,* 1:21–24, 50, 119–60, 171–78, 198–214. Hoover implied that much of his success in dealing with the Germans was due to the fact that his liaison with the German army was handled through German businessmen who had been called into the army for the duration. See also Vernon Kellogg, *Headquarters Nights* (Boston: Atlantic Monthly Press, 1917).

10   Hoover to Wilson, June 4, 1919, in Hoover, *Ordeal,* p. 245.

11   Herbert Hoover, *The Memoirs of Herbert Hoover,* 3 vols. (New York: Macmillan, 1952), 1, pp. 214–25; Hoover, *Ordeal,* pp. 2–9, 151–78.

12   Leland Summers to Baruch, August 9, 1918, Senate Special Committee to Investigate the Munitions Industry, 73rd and 74th Congresses, *Hearings Pursuant to S. Res. 206, 73rd Congress,* 39 parts (Washington: GPO, 1934–1937), pt. 30, pp. 9727–729, hereafter cited as *Munitions Hearings;* Hoover to Lansing, May 10, 1918, RG 40 NA File 77270; The Wilson administration's attitude toward neomercantilist and restrictive arrangements is discussed in Parrini, *Heir to Empire,* pp. 1–71; Robert H. Van Meter, Jr., "The United States and European Recovery, 1918–1923: A Study of Public Policy and Private Finance" (Ph.D. diss., University of Wisconsin, 1971), pp. 1–29; Michael J. Hogan, "The United States and the Problem of International Economic Control: American Attitudes Toward European Reconstruction, 1918–1920," *Pacific Historical Review,* 44 (1975), 84–103.

13   Hoover, *Ordeal,* pp. 115–16.

14   Probably the fullest exposition of Hoover's views on bolshevism during this period is contained in a memorandum he submitted to Wilson on March 28, 1919, Wilson Mss. Ser. 5B, Box 24. The memo is reprinted in Mayer, *Peacemaking,* pp. 474–78. See also Hoover, "Memorandum on the Economic Situation of Europe," July 3, 1919, in United States Department of State, *Papers Relating to the Foreign Relations of the United States, Paris Peace Conference, 1919,* 13 vols. (Washington, D.C.: GPO, 1942–47), 10:465–66. This series hereafter cited as *FR* (PPC), —.

15   Hoover to Wilson, March 28, 1919, Mayer, *Peacemaking,* p. 475.

16   Hoover, *Memoirs,* 1:214–15; Hoover, *Ordeal,* pp. 2–5.

17   Hoover to House, February 13, 1917, in Hoover, *Ordeal*, pp. 5–6. House forwarded the memo to Wilson, who was impressed. See also Charles Seymour, ed., *Intimate Papers of Colonel House*, 4 vols. (Boston: Houghton Mifflin, 1926), 2:419.

18   Quotation from Hoover to Wilson, April 11, 1919, Wilson Mss. Ser. 5B, Box 217. See also Hoover to Wilson, October 24, 1918, Hoover, *American Epic*, 2:251–54.

19   House Committee on Ways and Means (66th Congress, 2 Sessions), *Hearings on Relief of European Populations* (Washington: GPO, 1920), pp. 57–66. Hoover's comments to the press on the European situation, *New York Times*, June 10, 1919, p. 14; Norman Davis to Ray Stannard Baker, July 26, 1922, Norman Davis Papers, Library of Congress, Box 3; Norman Davis's Address to Annual Meeting Laurel Hill Association, Stockbridge, Mass., September 5, 1919, also in Norman Davis Papers, hereafter cited as Davis Mss.

20   Minutes of Meeting of the Supreme Economic Council, April 23, 1919, *FR* (PPC), 10:211; Hoover, *Ordeal*, pp. 151–78; Baruch to Wilson, March 29, 1919, Wilson Mss. Ser. 5B, Box 24; G.F.C. (Close) to Wilson, April 7, 1919, *Ibid.*, Box 26; Hoover to Wilson, April 21, 1919, *Ibid.*; Box 30, Norman Davis to Albert Rathbone, April 16, 1919, Record Group 39, Washington National Records Center, Treasury Department, Bureau of Accounts, World War I (63A–659) File: Peace Commission. Material from this Record group hereafter cited as RG 39 WNRC; Davis to Rathbone, Record Group 39 National Archives, Treasury, Bureau of Accounts, Country Files, File: France, hereafter cited as RG 39 NA.

21   Hoover, *Ordeal*, pp. 233–52; Hoover, *Memoirs*, 1:464–66.

22   Baruch to Wilson, March 29, 1919, Wilson Mss. Ser. 5B, Box 24; Hoover, *Ordeal*, pp. 243–49; Baker, *Wilson and World Settlement*, 3:500–03; Phillip M. Burnett, *Reparations at the Paris Peace Conference from the Standpoint of the American Delegation*, 2 vols. (New York: Columbia University Press, 1940), 2:101–18. Relevant here is the fact that men such as Baruch and McCormick had come to distrust Hoover's estimates and predictions, see Baruch Diary (Paris Peace Conference), entry June 14, 1919, p. 72, Bernard M. Baruch Papers, Princeton University, and Vance McCormick Diary, entry for May 23, 1919, Library of Congress.

23   Hoover's testimony, September 2, 1919, House Select Committee on Expenditures in the War Department (66th Congress, 2nd Session) Subcommittee No. 3, *Hearings on Foreign Expenditures*, ser. 4, v. 1, 547–48, 556–60; Hoover to A. B. Ruddock, June 20, 1920, Record Group 59, National Archives, Records of the Department of State, Decimal File 863.48/1086, records from this group hereafter cited as RG 59 NA—; Hoover's remarks at meeting of American Mission, July 25, 1919, *FR* (PPC), 11:347–49.

24   A perceptive discussion of the League which carefully distinguishes its role as a policeman for the Treaty from that as a permanent forum can be found in Roland Stromberg, *Collective Security and American Foreign Policy* (New York: Praeger, 1963), pp. 22–45. See also Levin, *Wilson*, pp. 161–85.

25   Norman Davis in his diary recorded Wilson as saying that for America, membership in the League was not a moral question but a matter of enlightened selfish-

ness. According to Davis, Wilson argued that the American failure to join "had re-
tarded the prosperity and stability of the World on which our own welfare is so dependent." Davis Diary, entry March 10, 1921, Davis Mss. Box 16a.

26   For Wilsonian thinking with regard to the League and the underdeveloped
world, see Secretary of the Navy Daniels to Wilson, December 3, 1918, with enclosed
memoranda, Wilson Mss. Ser. 5B, Box 1; Black Book No. 2, Intelligence Section
Recommendations to Wilson on Colonial Questions, February 13, 1919, *Ibid.*, Box
16; Levin, *Wilson,* pp. 236–51; Baruch to Wilson, December 3, 1918, Wilson Mss.
Ser. 5B, Box 1.

27   Levin, *Wilson,* pp. 161–82.

28   Hoover to Wilson, April 11, 1919, Wilson Mss. Ser. 5B, Box 27; Hoover to
Wilson, June 4, 1919, Hoover to Lansing, June 5, 1919, Hoover, *Ordeal,* pp. 245–48.

29   Quotation from Hoover to Wilson, April 11, 1919, Wilson Mss. Ser. 5B, Box 27.
For Hoover's position on the League, from his return to the United States in September 1919 until April 1921, see Hoover, *Ordeal,* pp. 279–93; Hoover, *Memoirs,*
2:36–37, and references cited in fn. 81 *infra.*

30   Hoover to Wilson, November 19, 1919, in Hoover, *Ordeal,* p. 283; on the importance of the League in Wilsonian plans for the economic reconstruction of
Europe, see Norman Davis, "Address at the Annual Meeting Laurel Hill Association," September 5, 1919, Davis Mss; "The Secretary of Commerce: The League and
the Restoration," July 25, 1919, RG 40 NA File: 79161; R. C. Leffingwell to Glass,
August 13, 1919, RG 39 WNRC File: Reconstruction – Europe.

31   E. David Cronon, ed., *The Cabinet Diaries of Josephus Daniels* (Lincoln: University
of Nebraska Press, 1963), pp. 342, 347; Hoover, *American Epic,* 2:251–60.

32   "Why we are Feeding Germany," March 21, 1919; Hoover, *Ordeal,* p. 172.

33   *Ibid.*

34   Lansing to House, November 16, 1918, RG 59 NA 863.48/125a; Hoover,
American Epic, 2:278–79; Mayer, *Peacemaking,* pp. 264, 280.

35   Hoover to Wilson, March 31, 1919, Wilson Mss. Ser. 5B, Box 24.

36   Hoover, *Ordeal,* pp. 140–41.

37   On Hoover and American policy toward Hungary, see *FR* (PPC), 11, 312–22;
345–51; Hoover, *Ordeal,* pp. 134–40; William A. Williams, *American-Russian Relations, 1781–1947* (New York: Rinehart, 1952), pp. 172–73.

38   Wilson to Tumulty, January 10, 1919, Wilson Mss. Ser. 5B, Box 7; Hoover to
Wilson, December 20, 1918, Wilson Mss. Ser. 5B; Hoover to Wilson, April 21, 1919,
Ibid., Box 30; Hoover, *Ordeal,* pp. 151–78; Mayer, *Peacemaking,* pp. 263–83; E.
Dresel, Report on Conditions in Germany, January 10, 1919, Wilson Mss. Ser. 5B,
Box 8; Gerhard to American Mission, February 2, 1919, *Ibid.,* Box 13.

39   This is evident from the discussion in Hoover, *Ordeal*, pp. 123–34, but the point is developed in Warren Adams Dixon, "Revolution, Reconstruction and Peace, Herbert Hoover and European Food Relief, 1918–1919" (Master's thesis, University of Wisconsin, 1964), pp. 44–50, 114–16. Dixon's analysis is extremely able and makes the additional point that in German-Austria Hoover's organization singled out the workers and the petit-bourgeoisie of Vienna for priority receipt of food in the belief that these groups were most politically volatile. On the Polish situation, see the testimony of Secretary of War Newton D. Baker, January 15, 1920, House Committee on Ways and Means (66th Congress, 2nd Session) *Hearings Relief of European Populations* (Washington: GPO, 1920), pp. 105–07.

40   Mayer, *Peacemaking*, pp. 450–87; John M. Thompson, *Russia, Bolshevism and the Versailles Peace* (Princeton: Princeton University Press, 1966), pp. 222–67.

41   Statement on Food Relief, December 13, 1918, Wilson Mss. Ser. 5B, Box 2; Hoover, *Ordeal*, pp. 86–102, 113–14; Vance McCormick Diary entries, March 17, 1919, March 19, 1919, April 28, 1919, pp. 54–55, 77.

42   Hoover, *Ordeal*, pp. 104–08; Suda L. Bane and Ralph Lutz, *Organization of American Relief in Europe, 1918–1919* (Stanford: Stanford University Press, 1943), pp. 434–40. Later, faced with similar disorganization and obstructions in Danube shipping, Hoover was able to partially rectify the situation along a comparable line. See Hoover, *American Epic*, 2:423–26.

43   Hoover, *American Epic*, 2:429–36; Bane and Lutz, *Organization of Relief*, pp. 381–84, 453–61, 610–11, 686–717; *Fr* (PPC), 11:256–62, 345–51, 621–23.

44   Alvin B. Barber, *Report of the European Technical Advisers Mission to Poland, 1919–1923* (New York: N.P., 1923), pp. 3–7; Bane and Lutz, *Organization of Relief*, pp. 610–11, 685.

45   Bane and Lutz, *Organization of Relief*, pp. 684–85. The appointment of these experts who had no official connection with the American government reflected Hoover's preference for avoiding government-to-government arrangements and his belief in the efficacy of economic means for overcoming political antagonisms. Logan subsequently served with the United States unofficial delegation to the Reparations Commission and in that post became an important adviser on reconstruction policy to Secretary Hughes and to the Dawes Commission.

46   On the whole question of the American response to Allied neo-mercantilist tendencies, see Parrini, *Heir to Empire*, pp. 1–71; Van Meter, "United States and European Recovery," pp. 1–25; Hogan, "United States and International Economic Control."

47   Leland Summers to Baruch, September 13, 1918, *Munitions Hearings*, pt. 29, 9414–418.

48   Hoover to Lansing, May 10, 1918, RG 40 NA File: 77270; Summers to Baruch, August, 9, 1918, *Munitions Hearings*, pt. 30, 9727–729.

49   Hurley to Baruch, May 21, 1918, and L. H. Woolsey to Lansing, May 25, 1918, RG 40 NA File: 77270. An illuminating discussion of Hurley's thinking and Shipping Board policies is in Jeffrey J. Safford, "Edward N. Hurley and American Ship-

ping Policy: An Elaboration On Wilsonian Diplomacy, 1918–1919," *Historian*, 35 (August 1973), 568–86.

50 Quotations from Redfield to Hurley, May 28, 1918, RG 40 NA File: 77270. See also Redfield to Wilson, May 29, 1918, RG 40 NA File: 77270; Redfield to Wilson, November 11, 1918, Wilson Mss. Ser. 4B, File: 3; Redfield to Taussig, November 16, 1918, RG 40 NA File: 77977.

51 Wilson to Hurley, August 29, 1918, Ray Stannard Baker, *Woodrow Wilson Life and Letters*, vol. 8 (Armistice) (New York: Doubleday, Page, 1939), pp. 365–66; Wilson to Lansing, August 29, 1918, *Ibid.*, pp. 364–65; Wilson to Redfield, November 12, 1918, Wilson Mss, Ser. 3, v. 55, 227–28; *Congressional Record*, v. 56, 10886–888, 11490; *Ibid.*, v. 57, 6–7; Safford, "Hurley," 571–79. Safford sees a greater competitive element in Wilson's position than is indicated in my interpretation.

52 Negotiations with the British on food relief can be traced in Hoover, *American Epic*, 2:247–90; Hoover, *Memoirs*, 1:278–99. Also see Cotton to Hoover, October 30, 1918; Hoover to Cotton, November 8, 1918, *FR* (1918, Suppl. 1), 1: 615–17. On credit, see Crosby to McAdoo, November 13, 1918, *FR* (PPC), 11: 533–35; McAdoo to Crosby, November 21, 1918; Baker, *Wilson and World Settlement*, 3:319–22; Davis to Rathbone, December 1, 1918, RG 59 NA 800.51/248. On shipping, see Safford, "Hurley," 573–79. These developments are dealt with in Parrini, *Heir to Empire*, pp. 1–71, and Hogan, "United States and International Economic Control."

53 Harold and Margaret Sprout, *Toward A New Order of Sea Power: American Naval Policy and the World Scene, 1918–1922*, 2d ed. (Princeton: Princeton University Press, 1946), pp. 62–72.

54 Especially revealing are McAdoo to Wilson, October 26, 1918, with enclosure in William G. McAdoo Papers, Library of Congress Box 525; Crosby to McAdoo, October 25, 1918, RG 59 NA 851.51/101; Crosby to Glass, December 31, 1918, RG 59 NA 851.51/110; Glass to Wilson, April 5, 1919, Wilson Mss. Ser. 5B, Box 26; Testimony of R. C. Leffingwell and Albert Rathbone, February 4 & 5, 1936, *Munitions Hearings*, pt. 29, 8983, 9050–51, 9190, 9120–21. The United States military forces in Europe were hostages requiring the continued furnishing of dollar credits, given the unwillingness of the Treasury to destroy Allied credit by calling British and French demand obligations.

55 Hoover, *American Epic*, 2:304–17; Hoover, *Memoirs*, 1:229–36; Hoover to Wilson, January 8, 1919, Baker, *Wilson and World Settlement*, 2:323–28; Hoover to Rickard, January 8, 1919, Wilson Mss. Ser. 5 B, Box 7. Gary Dean Best, "Food Relief as Price Support, Hoover and American Pork, January–March, 1919," *Agricultural History*, 45 (April 1971), 79–84, has a useful recent summary of these developments. However, in his effort to emphasize the seriousness of the domestic economic implications (something which Hoover never denied), Best tends to minimize the real fear with which bolshevism was viewed. Such fears were repeatedly expressed before the cancellation of December 31, 1918. Best estimates that pork production above domestic consumption was running at 400 million pounds per month during this period.

56 The files of the secretary of the treasury and the secretary of commerce both show top men in Washington feared a depression in late January and early February

1919. "America's internal affairs are drifting toward the rocks of industrial depression and unemployment," Leffingwell to Glass, February 3, 1919, Record Group 56 National Archives, Treasury Department, Secretary's Correspondence, File: Secretary Glass. Robert Himmelberg has explored some of the implications of this fear in "Business Anti-trust Policy and the Industrial Board of the Department of Commerce 1919," *Business History Review,* 42 (1968), 1–23.

57   Hoover, *Ordeal,* pp. 155–76; Hoover, *American Epic,* 2:300. Best, "Food Relief," 79–80, describes the mechanics of Hoover's price supports.

58   Hoover to Food Administration, January 4, 1919, *FR* (PPC), 2:789; Hoover to Rickard, January 8, 1919, Wilson Mss. Ser. 5B, Box 7; Hoover, *American Epic,* 2:316–17.

59   Rathbone to Lever, December 31, 1918, Senate Committee on the Judiciary (67th Congress, 2nd Session) *Loans to Foreign Governments,* Resumé prepared by Don M. Hunt, Senate Document 86 (Washington: GPO, 1921), pp. 23–24, hereafter cited as *Loans to Foreign Governments.* Baker suggested a connection between the loan refusal and the cancellation of pork orders; see *Wilson and World Settlement,* 2:322–23, 337–39.

60   Safford, "Hurley," 574–80; Hurley to Wilson, December 23, 1918, Wilson Mss. Ser. 5B, Box 4.

61   Davis to Glass, January 7, 1919; Baker, *Wilson and World Settlement,* 2:338; Wilson to Glass, January 9, 1919, Wilson Mss. Ser. 5B, Box 7; Glass to Davis, January 9, 1919, *Ibid.;* Glass to Davis, January 20, 1919, *Loans to Foreign Governments,* p. 35; Davis to Rathbone, February 15, 1919, RG 59 NA 851.51/116; Davis to Rathbone, February 22, 1919, RG 59 NA 851.51/118; Rathbone to Davis, March 6, 1919, Russell C. Leffingwell Papers, Library of Congress, v. 24, 475; Davis to Glass, March 6, 1919, RG 59 NA 851.51/123 1/2; Glass to Davis, April 2, 1919, Rathbone to Blackett, April 14, 1919, *Loans to Foreign Governments,* pp. 48–51; Davis to Wilson, April 4, 1919, Wilson Mss. Ser. 5B, Box 25. Glass worried about the impact of high priced food on both the domestic economy and the export trade and did not like to use loans to the Allies as indirect food subsidies. Tentative arrangements for renewed American lending to England were made on March 6, 1919, about the time the British shifted their position on the blockade. By then, of course, the pork had been diverted to other recipients.

62   Hoover, *American Epic,* 2:295–96. The Supply and Relief Council appears to have been little more than a rubber stamp and communication conduit for Hoover's decisions.

63   Safford, "Hurley," 584–85; Memo of Conversation on World Shipping Position, January 14, 1919, RG 40 NA File: 78369; Hoover, *American Epic,* 2:398; Hoover, *Ordeal,* pp. 102–04. The British even earned Hoover's praise for their cooperation in allocating shipping to move relief supplies.

64   See especially McAdoo to Crosby, November 21, 1918, McAdoo to House, December 11, 1918, *FR* (PPC), 2:535–38; Wilson, Annual Message to Congress, December 2, 1918, *Congressional Record,* 57:5–8.

65   Davis to Ray Stannard Baker, July 26, 1922, Davis Mss. Box 3.

66   Hoover to Wilson, April 21, 1919, Wilson Mss. Ser. 5B, Box 30; Baruch Diary, (PPC), entry May 6, 1919, p. 28, Baruch Mss.; Minutes of Meeting Raw Material Section Supreme Economic Council, April 16, 1919, Record Group 256 National Archives, Records of the American Commission to Negotiate the Peace, FW 180.05301/6; Vance McCormick Diary, entries April 4, 1919, April 28, 1919, pp. 64, 77.

67   Hoover, *Ordeal,* pp. 233–34.

68   Baker, *Wilson and World Settlement,* 3:344–46; Leffingwell to Davis, April 28, 1919, Davis Mss. Box 16a.

69   Wilson to Lloyd George, May 5, 1919, in Baker, *Wilson and World Settlement,* 3:344–46; see also Vance McCormick Diary, entries April 24, 1919, April 25, 1919, pp. 74, 75.

70   Baker, *Wilson and World Settlement,* 3:347–62; Baruch Diary entries for May 6, 10, 11, 16, 1919, pp. 28, 31, 32, 34, 35, Baruch Mss.; Vance McCormick Diary, entries May 11, 13, 19, and June 10, 1919, pp. 84–85, 88, 100; Paul P. Abrahams, "American Bankers and the Economic Tactics of Peace: 1919," *Journal of American History,* 56 (December 1969), 572–83.

71   This analysis is based primarily on Hoover, "Memorandum on the European Economic Situation," July 3, 1919, *FR* (PPC), 10:462–69, supplemented by Hoover to Norman Davis, May 16, 1919, Davis Mss. Box 16a; Hoover to Wilson, June 4, 1919; Hoover to Lansing, June 5, 1919; and Hoover Press Release, July 28, 1919; Hoover, *Ordeal,* pp. 245–49, 267–69; Hoover to Wilson, June 27, 1919; Hoover, *American Epic,* 3:220–22; Hoover comments to the press, *New York Times,* June 10, 1919, p. 14; Minutes of Meeting of American Peace Commissioners, July 25, 1919, *FR* (PPC), 11:348–49. Unless otherwise noted, quotations are from Memorandum of July 3, 1919.

72   Hoover saw the coal situation as a sort of microcosm of Europe's economic problems and here he found the actual physical destruction relatively minor as compared to the impact of "the human factor of the limitation of effort." See Hoover, "Memorandum . . . ," July 3, 1919, *FR* (PPC), 10: 463.

73   *New York Times,* June 10, 1919, p. 14.

74   Hoover to Wilson, June 27, 1919, Hoover, *American Epic,* 3:220–22. The Fifth (or Victory) Liberty Loan Act of March 3, 1919, expanded the powers of the War Finance Corporation by authorizing them, for a period of six months after the end of the war, to lend up to a total of one billion dollars to American exporters of domestic products and to banks financing these exports. On this, see *Annual Report of the Secretary of the Treasury,* November 20, 1920 (Washington: GPO, 1920), pp. 147–48.

75   Minutes of Meeting American Peace Commissioners, July 25, 1919, *FR* (PPC), 11: 348–49; Hoover to Davis, May 16, 1919, Davis Mss. Box 16a; Hoover testimony, September 2, 1919, *Hearings on Foreign Expenditures,* pp. 548, 555–60.

76   *New York Times,* June 10, 1919, p. 14; Hoover to Wilson, June 4, 1919, and Hoover to Lansing, June 5, 1919, in Hoover, *Ordeal,* pp. 245–49; Minutes of Meeting American Peace Commissioners, July 25, 1919, *FR* (PPC), 11: 348–49. Though he tended to see Russia as a separate situation, Hoover occasionally during 1919–21 spoke of the political and economic reintegration of Russia as a vital condition of reconstruction. By 1921 Hoover had apparently concluded that measures to effect reconstruction must be premised, for the short run, on the continued isolation of Russia. See, e.g., *New York Times,* December 13, 1920, pp. 1, 2.

77   See especially Leffingwell to Glass, September 8, 1919, and Glass to Rudolph Foster, September 11, 1919, RG 39 WNRC, Treasury, Bureau of Accts. WWI, File: Reconstruction–Europe. These developments are treated extensively in Van Meter, "United States and European Recovery," 114–57, and in Abrams, "American Bankers."

78   Fred I. Kent to Leffingwell, August 1, 1919, with Leffingwell's comment, RG 39 WNRC Treasury, Bureau of Accts., WWI File: Reconstruction – Europe; Redfield to Wilson, July 23, 1919, Wilson Mss. Ser. 4, File 3; Leffingwell to Glass, August 9, 1919, appended to Meyer to Leffingwell, August 6, 1919, RG 56 NA File: WFC.

79   Strong to Leffingwell, July 31, and August 17, 1919, *Munitions Hearings,* pt. 30, 9572–9579; Baruch and McCormick had earlier come to doubt Hoover's estimates and predictions. See note 22.

80   Glass to Wilson, September 11, 1919, RG 39 WNRC, Treasury, Bureau of Accts., WWI File: Reconstruction – Europe; Hoover, *Ordeal,* p. 269.

81   Hoover to Wilson, November 19, 1919, in Hoover, *Ordeal,* pp. 282–83; *New York Times,* October 10, 1920, p. 1; October 15, 1920, p. 1; December 13, 1920, pp. 1, 2; Hoover to Hughes, April 5, 1921, with memorandum enclosed entitled "Economic Aspects of the Treaty," Hoover to Hughes, April 6, 1921, Herbert Hoover Papers, Commerce Papers, Personal File: Hughes, Herbert Hoover Presidential Library, West Branch, Iowa; Hoover, *Memoirs,* 2:36–37; Merlo J. Pusey, *Charles Evans Hughes,* 2 vols. (New York: Macmillan, 1951), 2:431–39.

82   Memorandum of Conference on Economic Situation in Austria (no date but internal evidence indicates November or December 1919), RG 59 NA 863.50/64 1/2; Davis to Rathbone, December 9, 1919, Davis Mss. Box 48; Davis to Rathbone, January 23, 1920 (containing message from Hoover to J. A. Logan) Leffingwell Mss. v. 40:41–42.

83   Quotation from Hoover testimony, January 12, 1920, *Hearings Relief of European Populations,* p. 69. See also House Committee on Ways and Means, 67th Congress, 2nd Session, *Report No. 830 to Accompany S. J. Res 160 Release on Lien and Extension of Time on Austrian Loan* (Washington: GPO, 1922), pp. 1–3. Norman Davis to Albert Rathbone, March 31, 1920, *FR* (1920), 1:275; Colby to American Commissioner in Vienna April 10, 1920, RG 59 NA 863.48/143a; Hoover, *Memoirs,* 2:22–23.

84   Hoover, *American Epic,* 3:243–61; Hoover, *Ordeal,* pp. 111–14. Hoover continued to have an important voice in ARA policy and appears to have viewed it in the same way as the technical missions, that is, as a device through which the United

States could promote stability in Eastern Europe without assuming a formal political role. See Hoover to Rickard, July 13, 1920, Davis Mss. Box 27. The consolidation of remittances helped protect immigrants from fraud and gave the Polish government control over badly needed foreign exchange. See *Commercial and Financial Chronicle,* March 5, 1921, p. 885; Hoover to Hughes, May 27, 1921, *FR* (1921), 2:695; E. D. Durand to Herter, October 19, 1921, Hoover Mss. Commerce, 1-1-76 File: Eastern Europe, E. D. Durand.

85   Carter Glass to Homer L. Ferguson, January 28, 1920, in *Annual Report of the Secretary of the Treasury,* November 20, 1920 (Washington: GPO, 1920), pp. 80-84; *FR* (PPC), 10:686-93.

86   Richard N. Owens, "The Hundred Million Dollar Foreign Financing Corporation," *Journal of Political Economy,* 20 (1922), 346; *Chronicle,* December 18, 1920, p. 2378.

87   Hoover's remarks to FTFC meeting, December 10, 1920, *New York Times,* December 11, 1920, p. 3; Hoover, *Memoirs,* 2:13-14.

88   Hoover speech to Merchants Association of New York, January 19, 1921, *Chronicle,* January 29, 1921, pp. 421-22; *Chronicle,* March 26, 1921, p. 1207; *Federal Reserve Bulletin,* 7 (April 1921), pp. 378-80. In June, Paul Warburg wrote Hoover: "About the Foreign Trade Financing Corporation I take it that you are fully advised. The patient is still alive, but his pulse is getting weaker every hour." Warburg to Hoover, June 29, 1921, Hoover Mss. Commerce, File: Warburg, Paul.

89   See especially, Transcript of Meetings held in Washington, April 4, 1921, in the offices of Eugene Meyer, Record Group 154 National Archives, Records of the War Finance Corporation, File: Export General, Box 253/1/1; Harding to Hoover, May 17, 1921, Warren G. Harding Papers, Ohio Historical Society, Columbus, Ohio, Box 5, Fldr. 3-1; and, Hoover to Don Livingston, March 19, and April 4, 1921, Hoover Mss. – Personal, File: Livingston, Don; Hoover to Meyer, June 8, 1921, and Meyer to Hoover, June 3 and 9, 1921, Hoover Mss. –Commerce, File: WFC.

90   Hoover to Capper, April 23, 1921, Hoover Mss. – Commerce, File: Sen. Capper; Hoover to Don Livingston, July 27, 1921, Hoover Mss. – Personal, File: Livingston, Don; Hoover testimony on Norris Bill, June 25, 1921, Senate Committee on Agriculture and Forestry (67th Congress, 1st Session) *Hearings Farmers Export Financing Corporation,* S. 1915 (Washington: GPO, 1921), pp. 67-85.

91   Hoover to Strong, August 30, 1921; Lester V. Chandler, *Benjamin Strong Central Banker* (Washington, D.C.: Brookings Institution, 1958), pp. 253-54.

92   Hoover to Harding, January 4, 1922, Harding Mss. Box 5, Fldr. 3-2.

93   Hoover to Hughes, April 29, 1922, RG 59 NA 800.51/316; Memorandum dated April 22, 1922, signed by C. A. Herter summarizing conversation between Hughes and Hoover, Hoover Mss. 1-1/549. After 1922 Hoover also explored ways of using war debts to secure leverage in European affairs.

CARL PARRINI

Hoover and International Economics

EDITOR'S INTRODUCTORY NOTE

Herbert Hoover could hardly be classified as a neophyte in the world of economics when the First World War called him to public service. For nearly twenty years, his extensive business affairs had brought him into regular and even intimate contact with the processes of international trade and finance. His responsibilities as mining engineer and consultant had allowed him unusual opportunities to observe economic conditions in many parts of the world. Moreover, he was an avid reader who kept abreast of current economic trends. It is therefore no wonder that Hoover seemed more at ease in the company of economists and financiers than with politicians.

Carl Parrini's paper that follows explores some of the theoretical premises apparent in Hoover's economic outlook and the programs he did so much to inspire as they developed during the war years and then found expression during the 1920s. Much of this economic thinking was pretty orthodox American economic doctrine shared to varying degrees by political leaders who believed in the efficacy of the gold standard, the protective tariff, the need to expand America's export trade, opposition to state intervention in the private economic sphere except under extraordinary circumstances, and the need to invest surplus capital abroad. What makes Hoover's economic analysis of interest is his keen sense of the intimate relationship between economic health and political stability. He weighed each specific economic action, to use Parrini's words, against the criterion of its relation to the long term expansion or contraction of the world market. He already feared that future international warfare could readily lead to the breakdown of the capitalist order. Hoover recognized the close relationship between government, the national interests, economic policies, and the prevailing social structure. Hence, it followed that government

Carl Parrini is professor of history at Northern Illinois University, De Kalb.

must exercise discretionary powers with great care. Whereas Hoover showed serious concern about the preservation of America's national well being, he was also inclined to connect that well being to the preservation of the capitalist order.

Parrini interprets Hoover as maintaining a remarkable consistency in his economic thought throughout the years 1917–24. By his near obsession with the expanding American export trade while at the same time supporting the need for high tariff schedules, Hoover's position approximated a neo-mercantilist model. Accordingly, emphasis would be placed on the use of economic power abroad in order to further the national interest. Hoover's tendency to define world interests and values within an American idiom often gave rise to certain incongruities as became apparent in the relation between foreign trade and the resolution of the war debts and reparations. Historians interested in the formation of American economic policies during the postwar decade would do well to pursue the various issues considered in this paper. Were Hoover's expectations with reference to the gold standard realistic? Did Hoover appreciate the significance of America's emergence as a creditor nation during the war years? Whether one agrees or disagrees with Hoover's judgments, it seems noteworthy that Hoover exercised a remarkable capacity for relating the various pieces of the large jig-saw of economic arrangements into a broad political picture which he kept constantly in mind. It is this cumulative picture that Parrini's article seeks to describe.

Hoover and International Economics

It is the purpose of this paper to examine some aspects of Herbert Hoover's international economic policies. Although Hoover regarded himself as a pragmatist and as "non-ideological," our modern conception of social theory makes us aware that pragmatism is itself an ideological stance. From Hoover's standpoint it was the duty of statesmen like himself to examine society, determine where it was going as the result of the natural evolution of the marketplace, and pursue policies that would assist that development. But Hoover did not make every decision on the basis of narrow market criteria.

Hoover was a thorough believer in democratic capitalism. His experience in World War I proved to him, that without question, the greatest enemy of such a social system was protracted war among the industrial states. Hoover regarded the World War as the midwife of the Bolshevik revolution and he understood that socialism was the first "real" (rather than "theoretical") threat to democratic capitalism as a system. As a statesman, he took the intellectual stance that he must use his influence against policies which would likely lead to war. To the extent that Hoover understood the interrelatedness between economics and politics and based his decisions on a complex of such variables, he was a political economist.

Since he regarded the United States as part of an international system, his domestic decisions, were in part, directly related to his view of the international imperatives. He was an economic interventionist, but of a particular kind. He wanted the large corporation executives to act in a socially responsible way.[1] If they did so, the need for governmental intervention would be limited to a kind of public utility regulation, confined to industry where absolute monopoly existed. In general, he opposed the kind of intervention in the market that made the state a competitor with private industry. He also opposed state allocation of resources, and through resources, income. Many businessmen in the United States, and even more in Europe, held contrary views. They believed that the economic lesson of World War I was that state intervention in raw material allocation and capital investment decisions contributed to economic efficiency and more equity. Hoover believed that such intervention did not contribute to equity and efficiency, but only appeared to do so under war conditions. The war had induced an outpouring of genuine patriotism as well as economic expansion which blunted questions about relative income shares. He understood that the way in which the war had to be conducted led to a massive shift of income shares to the large corporations.[2] Once the war was over, he felt it would be clear to all that the state as allocator of income was taking sides.

Wilsonian progressives, including Hoover, had already been confronted with the problem on the debates over the Federal Reserve, Federal Trade Commission, and Clayton Anti-Trust Acts of 1913 and 1914. Each competing group had demanded that it be freed of the fear that the antitrust laws would be enforced against it. The large corporations wanted the right to fix prices and divide markets. Small business units wanted the same privileges, but wanted the law enforced against their large competitors and against labor. Farmers wanted the right to establish agricultural cooperatives and state subsidies to finance their production surpluses, as well as the ability to fix prices and allocate markets. On behalf of a labor movement which was expanding considerably, Samuel Gompers demanded that organized labor be granted the right to restrain trade in order to increase the volume of income going to organized workers.[3]

It was in this effort of various economic interests to use the state for their own private purposes that Hoover saw the great danger both to the domestic *and* international political economy. In domestic terms he visualized three possibilities if persons like himself did not succeed in blunting and defeating the efforts of the competing economic interests to use the state's political power for their own ends: (1) the corporations could come to dominate the state and initiate a kind of industrial feudalism which would make of state power a special preserve of large capital; (2) the trade union movement could come to dominate the state, apportioning income in its own favor, oppressing small and large capital alike; or (3) the development of a "syndicalist state on a gigantic scale"[4] could take place with the state acting as a broker among competing economic units, and apportioning state funds in response to the strength of pressure from the respective economic interests at any given time.

The drive of different interests and classes for larger shares of income tended to make foreign trade more necessary, for foreign trade expanded the volume of resources available for distribution without greatly affecting the shares which each group was receiving naturally from the marketplace. Hoover understood that when rapidly growing foreign trade was necessary to the internal social health of a society the pressure of various interests to involve the state would grow enormously. We are, said Hoover, in December of 1920, "at that changing point in our national economics that the British Empire faced in 1860, when no longer could Britain take full value" for commodities which it exported; if it was to continue to expand, "it had to invest the realization of these commodities abroad. We as the states of Europe before the war must take compensation for the labor of our people in . . . assets outside our borders."[5] Surplus capital had to be invested abroad; if it were not, the system would be assaulted from the right and the left.

Hoover accepted enough neoclassical theory to believe that the function of the entrepreneur, as an individual before 1890 and as a corporation subsequent to that date, was to accumulate capital for investment and hence development of resources. Once it was acknowledged that surplus capital existed, as Hoover did, and could only be invested at home with wrenching changes in the social structure, the possibility grew that some group or another would call into question the historical need for private accumulation and private accumulators. To prevent debate about social change it was necessary to invest surplus capital abroad. The alternative was that some form of "statism" would likely emerge as a rival and perhaps replacement for what Hoover called "American individualism."

Yet Hoover understood that the constriction and narrowing of world markets relative to investment capital produced, which had begun in the 1890s, forced the United States, like other developed industrial nations, to seek for new fields to develop, new outlets for goods and capital. In Hoover's view these market contests by themselves were relatively harmless. But the intensity of the conflict and the degree of need for larger and larger shares of a relatively slowly expanding world market which the political leadership of the industrial powers began to assume, tended to involve the diplomatic, political, and military resources of the industrial states in the contest about markets. Hoover agreed with Edward N. Hurley, chairman of the United States Shipping Board, that had governments not "been struggling for commercial conquest there would have been no war" in 1914. Each nation was not simply trying to "get its share of foreign trade, but . . . trying to find out how much it can take away from other nations."[6]

Hoover understood that World War I had not solved the market concerns of the industrial nations.[7] On the contrary, the war destroyed millions of human lives, billions of dollars worth of capital (especially means of transport), while immense quantities of raw materials were unproductively consumed. The war's impact was nearly to destroy the world market—for all powers—victors and vanquished alike.[8] At the same time each industrial nation had organized to administer its economy for purposes of winning the war. Each economy was "nationalized" and in a sense "militarized." Administered economies brought about a degree of merger between state power with finance and the commercial objectives of the private corporations. It seemed to Hoover that the very mechanism which caused the war had become intensified and indeed firmly entrenched among the victorious states of Europe. But at the end of the state-capitalist road Hoover believed was a new world war, which as the Bolshevik revolution demonstrated, could imperil the existence of democratic capitalism (including American "individualism") itself. From approximately 1918 onward, Hoover devoted himself to an intensive effort for the purpose of developing world markets in which private business units would be allowed relatively equal access. He hoped that private success in developing world markets would encourage and in some measure coerce all nation-states to withdraw their political power from the market-place.

Hoover weighed each specific action over which he had some control and which might have an impact on the world economy against the criterion of its relation to the long-term expansion or contraction of the world market.[9] In this connection there is a record of consistency with respect to Hoover's position on the reconstruction of Europe (especially Germany and Russia), control of foreign capital investment, opposition to raw material commodity cartels, forcing victor and vanquished in Europe onto a modified gold standard, and the degree to which the United States would take upon itself the world military police powers which Great Britain had exercised prior to 1914, in face of the fact that America's market and security needs were by no means an exact analogue of those of Great Britain.[10]

In large measure Hoover was part of a consensus of American views toward the world market, a consensus that provided continuity from the Wilson to the Harding administrations. He shared with both a conviction that the reconstruction of Germany lay at the heart of how to obtain an expanding world market in which democratic capitalism could thrive. He agreed that the Allies were setting a reparations bill well beyond Germany's capacity to pay. He supported the tactic initiated by the Wilson administration and continued by the Harding administration of using war debts as a negotiating instrument to force the other victors to ease those burdens on Germany.[11] He also shared with both administrations the assumption that an economically reconstructed Russia would ease German reconstruction, and realized that United States capital must fuel the reconstruction of Germany. He also believed that until the victors as well as Germany returned to a modified gold standard the United States tariff should be kept high in order to protect the American market against European dumping under cover of constantly depreciating currencies.[12]

In several important particulars Hoover dissented from both administrations. Woodrow Wilson and his policy-making supporters generally believed that the United States ought to participate in a

League of Nations from which vantage point the victors, and the vanquished too, when they became like the United States, would police the rest of the world, including the underdeveloped areas.[13] The Harding administration as a whole dissented from the Wilsonian policing conception. It substituted the Washington Arms Limitation Agreements of 1921 and 1922 (combined with an effort to stabilize and expand without excessive inflation in the world economy). The Wilsonians seemed to believe in an almost exact parallel between the United States and Britain; that the markets of Europe were as necessary to America's well being as they were to the British; that the balance of power in Europe was as important for United States security as it was for British security; that America would be obliged to police the underdeveloped areas as Britain had done in order to get their primary commodities and food supplies. Hoover disagreed. Although he supported the Versailles Treaty, he opposed an Article X-based League of Nations which he felt might involve the United States in world-wide policing. He supported a League but with strong reservations, which would, as Wilson well understood, have been a toothless League. Above all, Hoover sought to preserve United States freedom of action.

In strategic terms Hoover did not favor automatic United States participation in a European or Asian war. Nor did he accept the school-boy diplomatic view of the Wilsonians that a pledge to participate would obviate the need to take part in such a war. Since, in Hoover's view, world war, or for that matter any large or protracted war, was the proximate cause of bolshevism, the problem was therefore to avoid war, not qualify the circumstances under which the United States might participate in such war. Neither did American national economic interest demand that the United States somehow take part in a League's policing of the underdeveloped areas. Whereas Europe politically controlled most underdeveloped areas and the European powers used their exports from Asia and Africa in order to balance their unfavorable import trade from the United States, Hoover would leave Asian policing, and also whatever confrontation occurred with Japan, to the European Allies.[14] In Hoover's view the real problem was (and really is now) to pursue policies which would stabilize and expand the world economy without excessive rates of inflation, which Hoover knew would end in an economic crash, which would, in turn, most likely lead, through state capitalism, to world war.

As a private citizen in 1920, Hoover tried to organize a cooperative system controlling and regulating the flow of private

American capital in such a way as to avoid its wasteful, fraudulent, and speculative uses. Hoover wanted to confine American investment to reproductive ventures. Military spending was tabooed. He thought Italy should not receive private American capital, which it would use for military operations against Yugoslavia or Albania. He also opposed loans to the French for financing their plans to use force to extract economically unsustainable reparations from the Ruhr.[15] Hoover vetoed the plans of American bankers to valorize or subsidize the planned restriction of production and artificial rigging of prices of raw materials such as potash, rubber, petroleum, tin, coffee, and jute.[16]

Valorization schemes for raw materials cartels by definition interfered with an extensive as well as intensive development of world markets. If the British and subordinate Europeans controlled petroleum, rubber, and tin prices by means of restricting supply, the potentiality for the mass production, distribution, and sale of automobiles (which was becoming the largest single industry in the United States) would be sharply diminished. A decline in auto production would act as a "reverse multiplier," decreasing the demand of the United States for steel, rubber, glass, tin, cotton-leather (for upholstery), as well as other feeder, semiprocessed, and finished imports. It was indeed this automobile boom which was largely responsible for the expansion of the American economy in the 1920s (and the end of the boom brought on the domestic aspects of the economic crisis of 1929).[17]

While Hoover was secretary of commerce, that department, as well as the State Department and the Tariff Commission together participated in drafting the Fordney-McCumber Tariff Act of 1922. Hoover endorsed the tariff with its high protective schedules and made few criticisms of it. Shortly after its enactment in the late fall of 1922, Hoover defended the tariff against the charge "that the new tariff will so diminish our imports as to strangle the buying power of foreign countries for our exports," explaining that "a critical examination of the actual factors involved" refuted the claim.[18] Two important issues arise out of Hoover's tariff policies: to what extent was Hoover responsible for the high rates in the Fordney-McCumber Act of 1922; and to what degree did the Act inhibit the growth of future European exports?

There is no evidence that he opposed the high rates. Indeed Hoover showed by his actions that he agreed with United States Tariff Commission Vice-Chairman William S. Culbertson that "many of the rates . . . are much too high," but that until British prices were stabilized and Britain returned to the gold standard those high rates were necessary. One of Hoover's central assumptions in the 1920s was that the whole industrial world had to be returned to a gold standard. He planned to use the surplus gold which the United States was acquiring from its positive export balance to aid "in making foreign currencies convertible into gold," and so to "stabilize foreign exchange and improve foreign commerce."[19] The Europeans had hoped, as Walter Leaf, chairman of the board of Westminster's Bank of London, explained, "that the accumulation of gold in America would inevitably bring about some inflation on the other side of the Atlantic."[20] "There seems to be a sort of chortle in Europe," Hoover wrote in June 1923, "over the commercial strategy in shipping gold to us. It is assumed that we will incorporate this gold into our credit system and be put out of action by the price rises resulting from it." If a structure of credit and currency were created upon the whole of this gold it would portend the greatest era of inflation and speculation in United States history. Such action would increase American price levels to a point that would attract foreign goods and curtail exports. It "would thus quickly produce an adverse trade balance and cause this gold to flow abroad with a rush from under our castle of credit and we should have an unparalleled financial crash." In order to avoid an inflationary over-expansion in the domestic economy—that is, the artificial creation of productive capacity for goods and services for which no commercial market existed—Hoover cooperated with the Federal Reserve Board to neutralize the monetary impact of the inflow of gold. Against this background, a high tariff (as well as a conscious policy of gold neutralization) was an absolute necessity, at least until Britain and Germany returned to gold.[21]

Hoover was in favor of investing surplus capital abroad, especially in Europe as part of the reconstruction process, if some measure of security for the capital could be obtained. The losses suffered by investors who had purchased non-gold standard German municipal bonds prior to 1923, tended to make them wary, as their investments had been virtually confiscated by the continuous depreciation of the mark. In the foreign investment of capital a gold standard with a "relatively fixed par of exchange assuring stability of exchange rates with another country is a great advantage." On the other hand, "widely fluctuating exchange [tends to] bring a large element of speculation and risk into a country's export trade and import trade, make the service of its foreign public

debts to a great extent a variant of uncontrollable exchange fluctua-
tion and thereby cause serious interference with the preparation
and balancing of a country's budget."[22]

From Hoover's standpoint, the Dawes negotiations in 1923 and
1924 were in part concerned with conditions affording safety for
the investment of American surplus capital. Superficially, the question at issue was whether or not the new German central bank
would secure its credit on a gold or a sterling basis. A gold basis
would make investments calculable and secure against exchange
fluctuations. In addition, the German central bank would be able
to purchase some of the huge quantities of sterilized gold which the
Federal Reserve System was holding; a gold standard for Germany
would also increase the confidence of American investors in
Germany's attempt to stabilize itself. On the other hand, "if the
German monetary unit under the new [Dawes] plan is based upon
sterling, it will be out of fixed parity in relation with gold and will
therefore result in making dollar exchange a fluctuating exchange." If the mark were placed on a sterling basis (as security for
currency and credit issues) "then there would be a fixed par of exchange between Germany and England on the one side," and a
fluctuating exchange between those two powers and the rest of the
world including the United States on the other.[23] This would encourage theoretical British investment in Germany, and tend to
discourage American investment—a preposterous situation, since
Americans held the surplus capital.

American national interest would suffer if Germany went on a
sterling rather than a gold basis. In addition a sterling basis for
Germany would relieve France, Belgium, and Eastern Europe, as
well as Britain, of any pressure to resume a gold basis for their
respective currencies;[24] and consequently all the capital short areas
would remain unattractive as targets for the investment of
American surplus capital. *Ipso facto* the flow of capital from the
United States, so necessary for Europe's reconstruction, would not
take place. Capital would remain in the hands of American private
investors; the capital investment outlets would be in the hands of
Great Britain. British policy was designed to obtain just such a
deadlock in both long and short term international investment.

As early as April 18, 1922, Ulysses Grant-Smith, American
minister to Hungary, reported "certain impressions which I have
obtained during the past two years and a half relative to the general
attitude . . . throughout Europe to the United States. This attitude
might be stated succinctly as follows: cancel our war debts, loan us

more, keep out of our markets. I recently made this remark to a prominent English person just arrived here by way of Berlin, who smilingly replied that I was not far wrong."[25] In the whole of Eastern Europe, British policy seemed to be to prevent direct American investment of reconstruction and new resource development. On May 5, 1922, Richard Washburn Child, American ambassador to Italy, argued to Secretary of State Charles Evans Hughes, "that all information gleaned here . . . discloses interesting secret British delegation viewpoint and purpose. It is to manage so far as possible the processes and capture the profits and trade on products and influence of investments we may make in Europe leaving us the bare interest rates. . . . The British unquestionably regard us as gullible enough to be anxious to put our gold surplus out through British controlled pipe lines as are owned or may be procured by treaties, concessions or international conferences."[26]

If the British and their European allies succeeded in blocking a resumption of a general gold standard, the United States would be faced with a serious dilemma. With gold reserves of 77% against currency issues,[27] the Federal Reserve would be under severe pressure from various economic interests to make credit available for foreigners to purchase American agricultural and industrial surpluses, thereby stimulating inflation. Meanwhile, Europe would increase its pressure on the United States government to lend its gold to the British and allow them to manage and set the rules for the reconstruction of Germany, Eastern Europe, and ultimately, Bolshevik Russia. The danger here was obvious; British controlled reconstruction would protect old, and lead to new, special concessions. This kind of inefficient utilization of world resources would in turn tend to discourage broad, rapid, low-cost market development, and encourage inflation. British management would also tend to legitimize state-trading and put pressure on the United States to engage in state-trading too. This, in Hoover's view, would constitute a turn in the road toward war in the form of political contests over world markets.

Prior to the arrival of Montagu Norman, governor of the board of the Bank of England at Paris during the Dawes negotiations in April of 1924, the British delegation to the Dawes Plan conferences had unofficially agreed to a gold basis for the projected German central bank of issue. After Norman arrived the British delegation took the position "that the new German currency should if possible be based for the present upon sterling rather than upon the American [gold] dollar."If the British were to succeed, a "sterling

exchange standard," that is to say, a paper standard, "will be adopted in Germany . . . partly because it is more economical," in the
sense that the new German central bank would not have to
purchase any of the Federal Reserve System's surplus of gold. This
in turn would mean that "the reserves of the new bank are likely to
be kept in foreign [paper] currency rather than in gold in
Germany. . . . It is therefore obvious why the British have an immediate interest in the non-adoption of the gold basis. . . . British
banks would in that case probably hold the greater part of the reserves of the German bank, and the tendency to divert to New York
a portion of the commission and profits on financing and exchange
operations would be obviated."[28] The British finally opposed resumption of the gold standard because of their own national interest, as defined by a technical expert, such as central banker Montagu Norman, who obviously had the authority to change financial-
diplomatic policy. A sterling basis for Germany would allow British
banking to retain control of the day-to-day financing of the world's
merchandise trade.

Although a gold standard for the new German bank would be in
the national interest of the United States, and in the interest of
bankers in particular, American bankers as a group did not press
for the gold basis; "when the issue was raised they were consulted
and indicated as a preliminary view that they would not insist as a
condition of participation" on the gold basis in the projected Dawes
loans to Germany. They also "expressed the view that the
American market desires to follow London in this financing."[29]
The Hoover-Harding administration position on the German central bank simply illustrated the point that, because of America's
enormous capital surpluses and relatively steady price level, its interests and the long-term interests of western capitalism as a system
were largely the same.[30]

Once the new German central bank was placed on a gold basis,
then American and British bankers could cooperatively make a 200
million dollar loan, which would provide a gold reserve for
German currency. This gold reserve would in turn allow German
industrialists to purchase raw materials, for example, coal from
Polish Silesia and iron ore from French Alsace, or wheat from the
United States. These raw materials would in turn allow German industry to begin to produce enough to start reparations payments
on the new scaled-down "Dawes" basis. Once a regular flow of reparations payments proceeded, American investors would begin to
buy the bonds of German industry and government units, for

Germany would then give the appearance of a secure investment outlet for surplus capital.

Once again Hoover's instinct about the abnormal nature of the world market after the disaster of the war told him that the surface stability and reality could be vastly different. In order that principal and interest of foreign investors could be made secure, Germany had to earn something beyond the costs of its production, plus a certain amount of (gold based) marks to pay some reparations. In some way German export earnings had slowly but surely to be increased, the foreign exchange costs of reparation had somehow to be minimized, and the budgets of the central, regional, and municipal governments had to be put in relative balance. Altogether, the major portion of foreign investment in Germany had to be productively employed. Hoover did what he could to see to it that these essential requirements were met.

As early as April 14, 1922, Hoover tried to place "restrictions or partial restrictions upon foreign loans in the American market, designed to influence the borrowers (when governments) to bring their national budgets into balance and reduce unproductive expenditures."[31] In general, the private bankers, the Federal Reserve Board and, in the final analysis, the Harding administration as a whole, opposed any formal means of imposing such restrictions. Nonetheless, United States Commerce Department's commercial attachés issued reports to Washington, and Hoover did try to get the German and other borrowing governments to balance their budgets so that they would have a chance, other things being equal, to amortize, over time, their foreign debts. Hoover also made an effort to force German government and industry to see to it that the investments were used productively.[32]

A study, which Hoover ordered from Grosvenor M. Jones, chief of the Finance and Investment Division of the Commerce Department, tried to systematize the department's approach to "German Financing in the United States." Jones reported that "German financing could be divided into four classes: (1) private financing by industries engaged in international trade. These industries make their own exchange and cannot be affected by any action of the [reparations] transfer committee." As an example, he cited the German General Electric. "(2) Private financing for productive purposes but by borrowers who are not engaged directly in international trade." Here he listed farm loan banks or an electric power corporation in an urban area. "(3) German municipal and state financing which is productive." As examples he cited a dock improvement which would allow more production to be marketed at somewhat reduced cost. "(4) German municipal and state financing which is not productive." As an example, Jones used, "beautification of a city." Jones thought that one and two should be permitted on the "assumption that no private interest," unless it "could repay in the currency of the loan," would borrow such sums.[33]

Although Jones thought it desirable to distinguish between productive and unproductive (German) municipal loans (for example three and four), this theoretical basis had to be controlled by the practical consideration that the administration would have to "give public notice of a policy which would hurt all German credit or instances of . . . responsible bankers complying with the policy of the administration and irresponsible bankers ignoring it. A prohibition of all German municipal financing would deprive the American investment public of some of the best foreign loans. England may soon . . . be a competitor."[34] ". . . If it is the policy that there should be a discrimination between (3) and (4) then that discrimination cannot be made in the United States but must be made in Germany where the facts are known." In way of illustration, Jones explained, "a city may borrow ostensibly to build an electric light plant and use its other funds to beautify the town. Without information on and control of the city's budget we would be helpless to decide whether the loan was productive or not. The only practical method is for the establishment of some body in Germany capable of making this discrimination." Jones then outlined the complexities. "Is it," he asked, "our policy to prohibit all German financing? . . . if it is permitted is it to be restricted to (1); to (1) and (2); or to (1), (2) and (3)? . . . if (4) is to be eliminated what machinery is to be set up for determining which is (4) and which is (3)?"[35] Charles E. Herring, the Commerce Department's commercial attaché in Berlin, also reported back to Hoover much the same phenomena as had Jones. Herring saw a series of unstable elements affecting foreign investment in Germany. As foreign capital began to flow into Germany under the Dawes Plan, the money, explained Herring, "artificially stimulates the balance of payments and makes it unnecessary to liquidate the shorter-term investments from actual *national surplus.* Later, however, when the limit of absorption of foreign capital is reached and the period of liquidation begins there must be a notable increase in productivity and export, . . . or foreign earnings of some other sort, if the balance of payments is to cover service on foreign commitments . . . four or five years hence . . . ." Herring believed that there were sharp limits to the "real surplus available during the next few years for service on private foreign debts." Since Germany had few resources (for export) and no colonial empire, Herring could see no capacity for generating any substantial surplus. Germany would not be "able for long to transfer sums in excess of the favorable balance of payments without affecting the stability of the new German currency." Germany's future ability to meet its external payments "depends largely," in Herring's view, "on the extent to which foreign capital enters Germany and the uses to which it is put." Herring's data indicated that there had been "too great a tendency on the part of German credit seekers to seek loans for purposes not strictly productive."[36]

Hoover moved on three fronts at first to diffuse and then solve the combination of problems he was confronting. First, he tried to minimize the amount of foreign exchange which the Germans would have to raise in order to satisfy reparations needs. He tried to encourage (as was envisaged in the original Dawes Plan agreements by Henry M. Robinson) payments of reparations to France by Germany in kind. But as the chief of the Commerce Department's Bureau of Foreign and Domestic Commerce, European Division, S. H. Cross, reported to Hoover, "the issue is clearly drawn . . . between allowing this business to go to Germany through facilitating payments in kind or retaining it for domestic plants." The trend was more and more to frustrate payments in kind in the interests of domestic employment.[37]

A second area in which reparations could be paid without any extensive earnings of foreign exchange was by Germany's participation in the so-called "assisted schemes," that is, the development of the exclusive commercial spheres of the victorious Allies. Henry M. Robinson, one of the architects of the Dawes decisions, and John H. Fahey, as well as other officials of the International Chamber of Commerce (and Hoover) had been hopeful that the Allies would accept, in the areas of their commercial empires, German specialty exports. These would be under complete Allied control as to destination as well as purpose. Instead, Cross reported that it appeared, "more likely that the interested countries would try to borrow in the United States and keep' the resulting orders for their domestic industries."[38]

Hoover also moved within the administration to get a reconsideration of German financing. On December 20, 1924, he sent Hughes information describing questionable German loans. On March 4, 1925, Hoover again wrote Hughes expressing the view

that they ought to consider "the subject of placing some restrictions on the floating of German credits until such time as
there was actual determination of fundamental questions affecting
repayment of such loans, such as the attitude of the reparations organization." He went on to suggest to Hughes that "definite steps
should be taken to determine this matter and that American investors should be advised that such steps are" being taken in order
to stop American citizens from making unsafe and unreproductive
loans.[39]

On February 4, 1925, Hoover obtained a copy of Herring's report on the balance of payments difficulties bound to emerge from
continued unplanned lending to public and private borrowers in
Germany. He sent this copy to Undersecretary of the Treasury
Eliot Wadsworth. He suggested to Wadsworth that it might be desirable to send out a condensed version of the Herring report to the
major American banks dealing in German loans. Although Hoover
felt uncomfortable about projecting the government into business
in this way he explained that American leaders "do have an obligation to protect American investors when the problem involves international relations of which we have knowledge and the public
generally has not." Wadsworth replied that "we are inclined here in
the treasury to believe that it would not be advisable to get out even
an expurgated version [for] it might shake confidence in foreign
loans and would tend to put the government into an advisory
capacity on such loans."[40] The negative attitude of the Treasury
did not stop Hoover from trying to rationalize American banking
investment in Germany. Hoover escalated his warnings. On April
18, 1925, Hoover wrote Secretary of State Frank Kellogg to the
effect that unless the United States could get a statement from
Director General of Reparations S. Parker Gilbert, that foreign exchange would be made available in the future to service present
and future American investment in Germany, the Coolidge administration ought to, "advise the American public in order that
immense loss to American investors may be thus prevented."[41]
Henry M. Robinson and Owen D. Young conferred with Gilbert on
the issue, but he refused to make a commitment on the priority of
private loans over reparations in terms of access to German foreign
exchange in the future.[42] Hoover still could not get the administration to support his attempt to slow the flow of American loans to
Germany as a technique to force the German government and industry to stop unreproductive investment.[43]

The State Department did begin to send out to American
bankers a form asking them to determine whether "the loan pro-

ceeds are being used for productive and self-supporting objects
that will improve directly or indirectly the economic condition of
Germany and tend to aid that country in meeting its financial obligations at home and abroad."[44] In recognition of the fact that the
Weimar Republic could not control the character of foreign investment within its borders, the department explained that the
Republic was opposed to unproductive loans. Beyond this kind of
"informational pressure," the Coolidge administration would take
no measures to direct American investment in Germany based on
such criteria. In effect, reluctance to assert definite criteria left the
question of the productive utilization of American capital in
Germany to the ethical acceptance of "social responsibility" on the
part of United States bankers as they might construe the degree to
which productive outlets for American capital came into being outside Germany.

Hoover understood that growing capital surpluses and diminishing productive outlets for investments tended (and do
tend) to make marginal investments appear to be well secured; only
the most disastrous investment outlets then would appear to be
marginal. Hoover believed that when investment bankers were
confronted with a broad array of relatively productive and secure
investments they would be better able to sort out those which
might be questionable and thereby diminish the percentage which
might then sink into default. Hoover tried to contribute to the
number of attractive investments available by informally attempting to block bad investments in Latin America and by encouraging
loans to Latin American governments (by floating their bonds) for
purposes of developing basic, but low profit margin facilities such
as roads, railroads, dams, and electric plants, in areas in which new
resources, attractive to private capital, might be located. In this way
the production of copper, rubber, tin, and other primary commodities used in exploiting the electrical and auto technologies
would help to open new markets for capital within the industrially
developed countries.[45] In this manner a kind of balanced spe-
cialization would take place.

To the extent that he was able, Hoover tried to press the victor's
empires to open up the investment outlets which they controlled to
free competitive development. For the most part, efforts to open
up such investment sanctuaries as French Morocco, the Belgian
Congo, the Dutch East Indies, or British East Africa were a
failure.[46] The potential of Russia as a new market for capital and to
a lesser extent as a supplier of raw materials seemed to Hoover to

hold the key to the future well-being of non-statist corporate capitalism as a system. He believed that Russia had reached the point, by 1914, where it was on the brink of an enormous economic development. It had successfully been placed on the gold standard in the 1890s under the financial management of Sergei Witte. This in turn had brought about a large influx of French capital, which led to the development of an extensive railroad network, stimulated the creation of a skilled labor force of coal miners, steel workers, and railroad factory labor, and in general laid a wide base for industrialization. Except for the fact that the Bolsheviks held political power in Russia, Hoover believed that all significant indices pointed toward a potential for an enormous, sustained economic expansion comparable to that of the United States after 1860. In Hoover's view, neither India, China, Eastern Europe, nor Latin America offered any comparable potential. [47]

In this connection Hoover supported, and was in part an architect of, the Harding-Coolidge administrations' policy of opposition to the development of special spheres of influence in Russia. He also favored the embargo of American long-term investment to Russia until Lenin returned Western holdings to the original investors or was succeeded by a regime reversing the trend to socialize Russian as well as foreign private property in Russia. [48] Hoover refused to take any action to bring about the economic reconstruction of Russia, until one or the other development occurred.

In part, the policies which he pressed the administration to pursue toward Russia were designed to enable "Americans to undertake the leadership in the reconstruction of Russia when the proper moment arrives." Hoover fully believed that, "the hope of our commerce lies in the establishment of American firms abroad, distributing American goods under American direction and, above all, in the installation of American technology in Russian industries." When Charles Evans Hughes asked whether the United States ought to support German penetration of Russia, perhaps to redirect German competitive energies toward their prewar area of economic expansion, Central and Eastern Europe, Hoover vetoed the idea. "I trust," said Hoover, "the policies initiated by this department will be adhered to." [49]

Hoover expected the momentary transformation or overthrow of the Bolshevik regime. In this he was in consensus with most American observers who regarded the Bolsheviks as visionaries (ideologues) who would prove incapable of managing the Russian economy. This, Hoover believed, would lead to their transformation or displacement.

Superficially it might seem that Hoover's whole analysis of the needs of corporate capitalism in the West might have led him to encourage and even assist private American corporations to invest in the development of Russian resources even while those resources were politically overseen by the Bolsheviks. Hoover rejected that approach for three reasons. He thought that (1) Bolshevik political management would inevitably result in the waste of capital; (2) such a course would in a small but growing measure cause the partial reorganization of the American political economy along state-capitalist lines, destructive of private capitalism;[50] (3) if American capital helped to stabilize the revolution, bolshevism might prove attractive in other less-developed countries and even in some developed states such as Weimar Germany.

Hoover's political economy proved to be a failure, not because he did not understand the social system of Western Europe and North America, but because he expected the elites within the system to act in a socially responsible way, eschewing short-run profit and seeking the long-run stabilization of the system. But as soon as serious economic difficulties infected the system, elites and ruling classes, with a few notable exceptions, such as Hoover, Henry M. Robinson, and Owen D. Young, lost sight of the general interests of the system as a whole and pursued policies of national economic autarchy, concentrating on state-capitalist techniques of isolated national economic and social stabilization.

NOTES

1   Hoover himself can confuse students of his political economy. He warned against certain categories of government intervention in the economy. Leaders must define the "boundary where [that is beyond which] the government steps into tyranny." A proper government abstinence from tyrannical intervention was dependent on "the growth of the sense of trusteeship to the nation in the responsibilities of the corporate management." Yet Hoover knew that some corporate managers did not act as trustees. Indeed, Hoover believed this irresponsibility could go so far that "dominant private property is assembled in the hands of groups who control the state," and thus the "individual begins to feel the state as an oppressor." See Hoover, *The Challenge to Liberty* (New York: Scribner's, 1934), 161–63, and his *American Individualism* (Garden City: Doubleday, 1922), pp. 8, 10–11, 15, 17, 38.

2   This shift began as a result of the expansion of production and profits which World War I induced. From the summer of 1914 forward the large corporations began to obtain upwards of 50% of their investment capital needs from internal

sources. With an expanding war market the corporations were able to use the price system to charge prices which covered their costs of production plus half their need for new capital. Instead of asking small investors to invest, the oligopolistic corporations took investment by what came to be called target pricing. Thus did World War I see one of the most massive property shifts (upward) in American history. On the shift of income and productive property ownership, three sources are most significant: Tom C. Cochran and William Miller, *The Age of Enterprise* (New York: Macmillan, 1961), pp. 302–03, discusses the role of war orders in industrial self-financing, hence an enormous shift of property and income *via* what we now call capital gains; Grosvenor Clarkson in his *Industrial America in the World War* (Boston and New York: Houghton-Mifflin, 1923), pp. 156–57, 170–74, 230, and 313, shows prices were fixed and that this had the impact of "very large profit to low cost producers," although Clarkson wrongly claims that most of this excess profit was recovered by the government by means of the excess profits tax, it was not because excess profits taxes only applied to income left after investment in capacity expansion, which was not taxed. But this yields what we now call capital gains, that is, increases in the productive property ownership of existing owners, further concentrating industry and its real ownership. Hoover understood this because he allowed the same price-fixing-investment policies in food processing; William S. Comanor and Robert H. Smiley, "Monopoly and the Distribution of Wealth," *Quarterly Journal of Economics,* 89 (May 1975), 177–94, explain theoretically how monopoly pricing leads to concentration of wealth. Those who suspended the anti-trust laws did not aim at concentration of wealth; they aimed at maximum production for war, but the one led to the other.

3 Arthur S. Link, "The South and the New Freedom: An Interpretation," *American Scholar,* 20 (1951), 314–24, also Link's *Woodrow Wilson and the Progressive Era,* 1910–1917 (New York: Harper, 1954), *passim,* but especially the account of the Congressional debates on the Federal Trade Commission and Clayton Anti-Trust Acts.

4 Hoover, *American Individualism,* pp. 41–43.

5 Hoover, "Momentous Conference," printed in the *Journal of the American Bankers Association,* 13 (January 1921), 462–63. Hoover indicated here that he understood the relationship between expanding the foreign commerce of the United States and establishing domestic social harmony on a nonstatist basis.

6 Hurley to Attorney General Thomas W. Gregory, May 21, 1918, enclosing Hurley to Bernard Baruch of May 21, 1918, in Department of Justice File No. 60–01–10.

7 Hoover to 1923 Convention, Investment Bankers Association of America, October 29–31, 1923, *Proceedings, Investment Bankers Association,* 11 (Chicago, 1923), 177. He explained to the bankers that he understood that "the loaning of some of our surplus capital abroad is . . . necessary . . . ." But Hoover realized that investment had to be in "rightful proportions." Thus he did not share the neoclassical assumption that investors of capital seeking their own profit would automatically obtain the profit of the social system as a whole.

8 It is difficult to determine which side behaved more aggressively in economic terms and so contributed most to the destruction. If one assumes that the Germans

began the process, one is still left with the fact that the British contributed in full measure.

9   It is true, as Joseph Brandes has pointed out in his *Herbert Hoover and Economic Diplomacy* (Pittsburgh: University of Pittsburgh Press, 1962), pp. 192–95, that Hoover did veto loans by American banks designed to expand the German chemical industry, subsequent to pressure from American chemical interests. Whatever his *real* motivation, Hoover was correct in thinking that such bank loans were designed to finance a European chemical cartel which would raise the real costs of economic growth, constrict the world market, and limit opportunity for capitalism as a social system of nation states.

10   Geography alone meant that the United States had less concern than did Great Britain about who dominated the continent of Europe. In economic terms the United States could survive so long as it "policed" the Western Hemisphere.

11   U.S. World War Foreign Debts Commission, *Combined Annual Reports of the World War Foreign Debts Commission: With Additional Information Regarding Foreign Debts Due the United States* (Washington: GPO, 1927), pp. 69–70, 74, 299–302.

12   William S. Culbertson, vice-chairman United States Tariff Commission, to Charles E. Hughes, July 14, 1922, NA RG 59 611.003/1092; J. R. McKey, chief of the Latin American Division of the Bureau of Foreign and Domestic Commerce in *Commerce Reports* of August 18, 1924, pp. 410–11.

13   In an address before the Union League Club of New York on May 26, 1919, this is substantially what Wilson's son-in-law, William G. McAdoo, secretary of the treasury, argued. See his statement in Woodrow Wilson Manuscripts, Series 4, File 331 (Library of Congress, Washington).

14   Indeed when the first significant confrontation with Japan broke out over Manchuria, Hoover differed sharply with Secretary of State Henry L. Stimson exactly over this kind of policing question. Stimson believed that the United States had to maintain (and even expand) a large fleet in the Pacific in order to police Japan. As a corollary to this, Stimson advocated economic sanctions against Japan over Manchuria. On both matters, Hoover pursued his own non-policing policy: he rejected sanctions against Japan and in 1932 invited Japan and other powers to join the United States in further naval disarmament. See Richard N. Current, *Secretary Stimson* (New Brunswick: Rutgers University Press, 1954), pp. 104–05, 107–08, and chapter 5 generally. In Hoover and Gibson, *The Problems of Lasting Peace* (Garden City: Doubleday, 1943), Hoover subjects the whole Wilsonian peace-keeping war participation nexus to sharp criticism; in a speech entitled, "Our Future Economic Defense," given on September 18, 1940, more than a year before we entered the war, Hoover argues that if we enter the war we will become a "totalitarian dictatorship ourselves," despite the fact that this American non-entry will mean that the "totalitarian domination of Germany and Italy will cover most of the continent of Europe . . . and will also include the dependencies of these former European states." Even though 60% of the world's population and 40% of the world's trade would be so controlled, we still should not enter, because by not entering we can best protect our liberty. In Hoover Presidential Library, Presidential Statements.

15 See E. E. Agger, "The Battle of the Franc," *Journal of the American Bankers Association*, 16 (April 1924), 660–61.

16 Hoover and the Harding and Coolidge administrations were concerned about access to raw materials and blocking valorization or other price maintenance schemes for both long-term and short-term reasons.

17 Roy Harrod, *The Dollar* (New York: Norton, 1963), p. 58. Of course, Harrod is a Keynesian, but even traditional neoclassicals such as Theodore Morgan in his *Introduction to Economics* (Englewood Cliffs: Prentice-Hall, 1956), pp. 551–54, would grant that the decline in automobile investment was a major cause of the downturn, even if they disagree with the Keynesian secular stagnation of the decline in investment.

18 "The Effect of Tariff on Exports," in *Tenth Annual Report of the Secretary of Commerce* (Washington: GPO, 1922), 20.

19 Hoover, "Our Castle of Gold," *Journal of the American Bankers Association*, 15 (June 1923), 813, and William S. Culbertson to Hughes, May 31, 1922, NA RG 59 611.0031/155.

20 American Acceptance Council, "The Return to Gold," *Acceptance Bulletin*, 5 (July 1924), 6.

21 Hoover, "Our Castle of Gold," *Journal of the American Bankers Association*, 15 (June 1923), 813. Indeed, before American entry into World War I, American leaders realized that the war-born expansion could create a serious domestic downturn unless some way were found to neutralize the domestic impact of the constant flow of gold.

22 Edward I. Kemmerer to Charles Evans Hughes, June 24, 1924, NA RG 59 462.00R296/386. On the paper standard as a means of confiscating investments in Germany before the return to gold, see NA RG 151, BFDC, Indexed 640, Germany, February 7, 1925, Confidential Circular No. 97, Finance and Investment Division, "Finances of German States and Municipalities."

23 Kemmerer to Hughes, June 24, 1924, NA RG 59 462.00R296/386.

24 *Ibid.*

25 Ulysses Grant-Smith, in Budapest, to Charles Evans Hughes, in Washington, April 18, 1922, NA RG 59 800.51/324.

26 Richard Washburn Child, in Genoa, to Hughes, in Washington, May 5, 1922, NA RG 59 800.51/325.

27 Hoover, "Our Castle of Gold," *Journal of the American Bankers Association*, 15 (June 1923), 813.

28 Arthur N. Young, State Department Foreign Trade adviser, to Hughes, April 14, 1924, NA RG 59 462.00R296/285 1/2.

29   *Ibid.*

30   Although to some extent the United States received its immediate interest from a return to a gold base for German currency, the impact of the return to gold was also in the general interest of the world industrial capitalist system. I say this despite the fact that I am fully aware of the enormous suffering occasioned in Great Britain by the deflating effects of the return to gold forced on Britain by a German return to gold. No Marshall Plan kind of approach was really possible. Without a return to gold, little American capital would have flowed, on a private basis, to Europe. In this connection the national advisory council to the Federal Reserve Board argued, "in the opinion of the council the sooner Germany can be placed on a gold or gold exchange basis, the sooner can England, and other countries, return to an unrestricted gold basis . . . if the new German central bank is placed on a sterling exchange basis the world must prepare itself to remain on the basis of exchange instability . . . while the adoption of the gold basis would accelerate the return to world wide stability"; in NA RG 59   462.00R296/348, June 29, 1924.

31   The words are Benjamin Strong's paraphrase of Hoover, in NA RG 59 800.51/316, April 14, 1922.

32   "Circular No. 108-Finance and Investment Division," NA RG 151, BFDC, Indexed 640, Germany, March 21, 1925.

33   Grosvenor M. Jones, "German Financing in the United States," October 1925, Hoover Presidential Library, Commerce-Official, Foreign Loans-Germany.

34   *Ibid.*

35   *Ibid.*

36   Herring Memorandum, Transferability of Debt Service, January 2, 1925, Hoover Presidential Library, Commerce-Official, Foreign Loans-Germany. Hoover was of course always under great pressure to pursue unique and immediate American national interest. In general my own examination of the record indicates that when Hoover had a choice between the national interests of the United States and the national interests of another power (nation-state), he sought American interest. But the key test was whether, in Hoover's view, pursuit of an immediate American interest would interfere with the long-run interests of the system to which all the industrial states belonged. In such circumstances he defined American interests in the long run—i.e., he was willing to surrender a short term gain to obtain a long term interest. For example, on October 17, 1921, he commented on a query from Assistant Secretary of State F. M. Dearing as to whether or not it was true that certain special arrangements for French imports from Germany blocked American exports to France. "My own conclusions are," he answered, "such imports would not under present prospects be likely to come from the United States in any event and there is consequently no important displacement of American commerce." But more importantly "the indirect economic gains are far more important. Any payment of the indemnity in this fashion will directly absorb German industry and thus relieve the pressure of German exports in competition with our products in other markets. It will transform money payments of reparations into commodity payments and thus relieve to some extent the present damaging pressure upon world currency. Of even greater importance, these arrangements will secure to France larger re-

sults in reparations, creating a direct mutuality and causing interpendence of the countries involved, and will thus tend to stabilize the entire political situation. In fact, this is the most hopeful event of the entire reparations dispute." In NA RG 151, BFDC, Indexed 046.21, October 17, 1921.

37 S. H. Cross to Hoover, January 14, 1926, in Hoover Presidential Library, Commerce-Official, Foreign Loans-Germany.

38 *Ibid.,* plus attachment BFDC attaché in Paris, Chester Lloyd-Jones to Lewis K. Morse, dated December 28, 1925. Jones pointed out that in addition to French resistance to deliveries of payments in kind, the fall in the value of the French franc had made such payments difficult.

39 Hoover to Hughes, December 20, 1924, and Hoover to Hughes, March 4, 1925. Hoover Presidential Library, Commerce-Official, Foreign Loans-Germany. In this connection Jones wrote Herring in Berlin on August 31, 1925 that "a great deal of publicity is being given to the liquidation of the Stinnes concern, all of which is rather unfavorable advertising for German loans. The collapse of the Stinnes scheme will doubtless have an adverse affect on American bank credits to other German industrial enterprises. There seems to be little that we can do to discourage unwise loans to Germany. Confidentially I might tell you that the State Department was agreeable to our passing on to the American bankers in a quiet manner the gist of your admirable report on the dangers involved in loans to Germany, in view of the reparations situation. Mr. Hoover, I believe, was anxious to use a more direct method, but the Treasury frowned upon this." NA RG 151, BFDC, Indexed 640, Germany, August 31, 1925.

40 Hoover to Wadsworth, February 4, 1925, and Wadsworth to Hoover, February 14, 1925, Hoover Presidential Library, Commerce-Official, Foreign Loans-Germany.

41 Hoover to Frank B. Kellogg, April 18, 1925, Hoover Presidential Library, Commerce-Official, Foreign Loans-Germany.

42 Hoover to Robinson, October 12, 1925, and Robinson to Hoover, October 16, 1925, Hoover to Robinson, October 23, 1925, and Hoover to Andrew Mellon, November 6, 1925, Hoover Presidential Library, Commerce-Official and Commerce-Personal.

43 Finance and Investment Division Circular No. 108, NA RG 151, BFDC, Indexed 640, Germany.

44 Assistant Secretary of State Leland Harrison to Guaranty Trust Co. of New York, October 24, 1925, printed in U.S. Senate Committee on Finance, 72nd Cong., 1st Sess., 1932, *Sale of Foreign Bonds or Securities in the United States, Hearings on Senate Resolution* No. 19, 953–54.

45 See Robert Neal Seidel, *Progressive Pan Americanism: Development and United States Policy toward South America, 1906–1931,* published in the Cornell University Latin American Studies Program Series, complete but especially pp. 187–202, 218–19, 269–77, and 290–312. In addition to showing the key role played by developing means of transport in Hoover's Latin American program, Seidel also shows

that Hoover encouraged private bank loans to stabilize (or harden in our terminology) Latin American currencies, which in turn tended to make the government obligations of such countries "safe" and hence attractive.

46   H. W. V. Temperley, *A History of the Peace Conference of Paris* (London: Frowde, 1921), 5:66–70.

47   Hoover was struck by the parallels between the United States and Russian economics as geographical entities. See Hoover to Hughes, December 1, 1921, and Hughes to Hoover of the same date, in NA RG 59 661.6215/1a.

48   See my *Heir to Empire* (Pittsburgh: University of Pittsburgh Press, 1969), chapter 6, "The Lion and the Eagle."

49   Hughes to Hoover and Hoover to Hughes, December 21, 1921, NA RG 59 661.6215/1a.

50   Herbert Hoover, *The Memoirs of Herbert Hoover,* 3 vols. (New York: Macmillan, 1952), 2:27. Here Hoover comes very close to equating "state capitalism" with fascism as when he explained that "a new mixture later known under the name of fascism . . . was a mere continuation of war time economic controls."

ROBERT F. HIMMELBERG

Hoover's Public Image, 1919–20:
The Emergence of a Public Figure
and a Sign of the Times

EDITOR'S INTRODUCTORY NOTE

John Maynard Keynes is the reputed source for the often quoted testimonial: "Mr. Hoover was the only man who emerged from the ordeal of Paris [the Peace Conference of 1919] with an enhanced reputation."[1] This assessment written in 1919 is a commentary on the public image of Hoover's activities during the war and the Peace Conference. Whatever the reasons, Hoover did not become tarnished in the American public mind through his association with the Wilsonian cause at the Paris Peace Conference.

Robert Himmelberg's paper places its emphasis on the critical months following Hoover's return to the United States during the summer of 1919. The emerging components of the creative engineer, humanitarian, and moderate liberal political views all contributed to the favorable image of Hoover as some American knight in shining armor. According to Himmelberg, more articles appeared in the media projecting Hoover than for any other American leader excepting Woodrow Wilson and Warren Harding. Moreover, the Hoover craze was overwhelmingly enthusiastic with only pockets of dissent limited largely to the agricultural press.

The favorable, popular image of Hoover was essentially a product of his wartime experience. First, as director of the Commission for Belgian Relief and later as American food administrator, Hoover had been disposed toward a strong public relations program. In the process of calling attention throughout the United States to the needs of European relief and to compliance with a food conservation program, Hoover became personally identified in the public mind with these virtuous causes. Whatever chances these programs had for success depended on the effectiveness of

Robert F. Himmelberg is professor of history at Fordham University, New York, N.Y.

those campaigns launched through the mass media. As Craig Lloyd reveals in his incisive study, *Aggressive Introvert: A Study of Herbert Hoover and Public Relations Management 1912–1932* (Columbus: 1972), Hoover "turned instinctively to his friends in the mass media, men upon whom he could depend in his efforts to solicit the needed funds and apply the 'wide propaganda of newspaper publicity.'" Individuals like Edgar Rickard, Millard Shaler, and Ben S. Allen, while in the process of explaining the need for various public programs, also were constructing an appealing image of Herbert Hoover. It is possible to comprehend the impact of this public relations campaign by noting the increasing number of articles relating to Hoover and Food Relief listed in the *Readers Guide to Periodical Literature* and the *New York Times Index* beginning in 1916.

Whether there actually existed a deliberate campaign to create a positive image of Herbert Hoover by late 1919 and 1920 is not terribly important. Hoover had already achieved sufficient notoriety that the reporters and their newspapers were eagerly seeking copy about his actions, his ideas, and his plans for the future. About Hoover's image in the media, there existed a paradox. At one and the same time, Hoover projected a leader who was politically and economically orthodox while the image also projected Hoover to be a progressive liberal. In his paper, Himmelberg insists that the progressive liberal image was dominant during these years of war and postwar reconstruction. If indeed Hoover saw himself clearly as a progressive, he declined to join forces with Democrats because the party appeared to be torn asunder. Probably more important, Hoover during these years symbolized an administrative management which eschewed politics as such, preferring instead to offer efficient leadership, working through the parties but essentially outside of them.

1   J. M. Keynes, *The Economic Consequences of the Peace* (New York: Harcourt, Brace and Howe, 1920), p. 274n. Keynes's complete comment reads as follows: "This complex personality [Hoover], with his habitual air of weary Titan (or, as others might put it, of exhausted prize-fighter), his eyes steadily fixed on the true and essential facts of the European situation, imported into the Councils of Paris, when he took part in them, precisely that atmosphere of reality, knowledge, magnanimity, and disinterestedness which, if they had been found in other quarters also, would have given us the Good Peace."

Hoover's Public Image, 1919–20:
The Emergence of a Public Figure and a Sign of the Times

Great public interest and acclaim focused on Herbert Hoover during the months following his triumphal return to the United States in September 1919. He was, between September 1919 and June 1920, probably more often biographized, his views more often presented in national magazines, and probably more often the subject of newspaper editorial comment than any other public figure of the period. In volume, intensity, and content, this outpouring was quite remarkable and deserves analysis because it has significance for understanding Hoover and the times.

Hoover's reputation, the favorable image so many Americans had of him, rather than his strength among the politicians, was the key factor in his successes during the 1920s and in his nomination and election as president in 1928. Recent evaluations of the 1928 image of Hoover have stressed that it embodied both modern and traditional elements. As the "Great Engineer" Hoover epitomized modern life, according to Kent Schofield. But the machine-like nature of this projection was softened by the "Great Humanitarian" qualifier and by Hoover's orphaned farm-boy origins and his romantic fulfillment of the rags to riches myth. In an interesting analysis of the reasons for the collapse of Hoover's reputation during the Depression, Craig Lloyd has argued that the publicists of the 1920s stressed too much the "social engineer" theme. They obscured the most important element in what was traditional about Hoover, his attachment to the concepts of individualism and limited government. Loyalty to these ideals prevented him after 1929 from economic experimentation which, it appears, many Americans were led by the "engineer" image to expect, and this accounts for the profound disillusionment with Hoover which reached such enormous proportions. The purpose here is to assess Hoover's image at the time he emerged from his war work as a major national figure. The subject is interesting in its own right, and it may suggest further desiderata for the study of the crucial question of the nature of Hoover's reputation later and the cause of its collapse.[1]

This reconstruction-era Hoover image is interesting too because of the sheer volume of its presentation. Why was Hoover singled out or, at least, given so much attention? We commonly assume that such figures somehow speak to their times, that there is a sym-

pathetic relation between the figure and his admirers, that he sym-
bolizes their hopes, reinforces their values, or, perhaps, reassures
them against their fears. In what way did Hoover speak to the
postwar era, a troubled and unsettled time of inflation with widespread labor unrest, fear of radicalism, race riots, mutual recrimination between the economic groups, sterile political battles
over the League Covenant—all at a time when the president lay
crippled, unable to give even a semblance of effective leadership,
either to the government or to the people. Following interpreters
such as Stanley Coben and Paul Murphy, we expect the leading
figures of the era to be expressive of insecurities and fears and to be
symbolic gratifications of the yearning of the middle class for the
reestablishment of normalcy. In short, we commonly think of the
reconstruction era in terms of social and political unrest, with the
most popular policies and public figures being those which expressed the exhausted idealism, the fear of change, the conservative mood of, at least, the dominant segment of the nation's
feeling.[2]

Was Hoover perceived and projected during the reconstruction
era, by opinion-makers, in a manner appropriate to such a mood?
Was his image molded according to the lineaments of anti-
radicalism, hyper-Americanism, and social-economic conservatism? It was not. In the middle-class, general-circulation
periodicals, in a high proportion of newspaper editorializing, in
several branches of the press devoted to particular economic and
social interests, Hoover was conceived of and celebrated as a
positive figure. The most widely conceived figure was that of the
great administrator who had accomplished great things and
brought much glory to himself and the American people. This
figure, moreover, became merely the basis for the Hoover conception developed by the many image-makers who discussed him in
the context of the politics of 1919–20, speculating upon his role or
supporting him for the presidential nomination. In this context
Hoover's image became not merely heroic but salvific, the image of
the one just man, the one man capable of resolving the great issues
of the day in a forward looking and universally acceptable manner.

If this is true, and if it is true that Hoover actually was discussed
and applauded pervasively in the type of literature indicated, there
would be grounds for wondering whether we have not misunderstood somewhat the mood of the era. But there are prior
speculations and questions. What precisely was the content of these
positive, heroic, and savioristic images of Hoover? Did they arise

spontaneously or were they in some sense manufactured? If they were not universally accepted, what segments of the press and periodical literature, representing what social interests, tended to reject them?

The sources available for the writers who interpreted Hoover during the year following his return to America were of two kinds. First, there was the record of Hoover's accomplishment as mining engineer and, from 1914, as Belgian relief administrator, director of the Food Administration and head of the American and Allied relief program. Second, there was the contemporary Hoover himself, very much on the scene and part of it, making news consistently through his activities and a steady stream of speeches and press statements on current problems. The main features of Hoover's career before and during the war are well known. His role during 1919–20 and the image he projected of himself through his actions and statements during the period can be briefly summarized. The welcoming banquet given for Hoover by the American Institute of Mining and Metallurgical Engineers on September 16, 1919, three days after his return aboard the *Aquitania,* and the major address he delivered before it, received wide attention. During October and November, his speeches, given in California and in the East, on the League, on the European situation, and on home problems, were often noted in the press. In December Wilson appointed Hoover as a member of the second Industrial Conference, but this generated relatively little publicity for him.[3]

Early in January, the occasional public proposals heard during the previous months to make Hoover a presidential candidate became a boom. Julius Barnes, head of the Grain Corporation and a chief Hoover lieutenant during the war, publicly proclaimed Hoover a "progressive" and a Republican, but many Democrats named him as a plausible candidate too. On January 21, Frank Cobb's New York *World,* a leading journalistic prop of the Wilson administration, startled politicians by projecting Hoover, and asserting willingness to support him as a candidate of either party or as a third-party nominee. Hoover ignored these political maneuvers and apparently had little or nothing to do with them or with the amateurish state committees booming his nomination which sprang up across the country.

Hoover's installation as president of the American Institute of Mining Engineers on February 17, 1920, was the occasion for another major address, one in which he provided a national program. In early March in a statement to the "Make Hoover President Club" of California, Hoover declined to run, though he acknowledged willingness to serve if the call were spontaneous and overwhelming. Unfriendly commentators much ridiculed his refusal to state a party preference (though he admitted to "progressive" Republican allegiance before the war). Likewise did they criticize Hoover's insistence that he could not endorse a party until it had stated its position on the issues. A few weeks later, however, in what he interpreted as a move to give California voters an opportunity to reject Hiram Johnson's anti-League campaign, Hoover agreed to let California Republican backers put his name in the primary, announcing that this was his party, the only one whose nomination he would accept. The Michigan primary a few days later, in which Hoover ran well among the Republicans and topped all the Democrats (he had been entered on both sides, his permission not being necessary in that state), brought to a peak expectation that popular support might force the politicians to treat Hoover as a serious candidate. Still, however, Hoover refused to campaign, maintaining the role of a receptive but not active candidate. His two-to-one defeat in the California primary on May 4 eliminated, in the view of most observers, his status as a serious contender, though a dark horse nomination remained a remote possibility.[4]

Hoover's speeches and writings during the winter of 1919–20, which were numerous and often commented upon, were addressed mainly to current economic and social problems and their solutions. The pose was Americanistic and anti-radical, as befitted the times, but in a relatively moderate style. His first major address, delivered at the A.I.M.E. dinner in September, sounded all the themes which appeared in the following months. In a class-divided, enervated, and war-torn Europe, socialism was "bankrupting itself" as a valid means of social progress. The strength and vitality of America forbade "us to allow the use of this community for experiment in social diseases [i.e., socialism]." Nor could America "abandon the moral leadership we have undertaken of restoring order in the world." Amelioration of unrest required renewal of the instincts of self-interest in a setting which allowed personal and class progress. This required a more just division of the national product, through "liquidation into the hands of the many of the larger industrial accumulations in the hands of the few," and in addition some "voice in the administration of production to all sections of the community concerned in the specific problem." "Moral leadership" in achieving the best solution of European problems meant League membership.[5]

Subsequent statements on restoring balance and stability at home made due reference to the immediate economic problems (railroads, shipping, institution of the budget system, and so on). But Hoover continued to propose major reforms for the renewal of the American system of equal opportunity and expanding wealth. The September suggestions on the labor problem became a firm recommendation for government encouragement of collective bargaining on a shop basis, with provision for conciliation services. Hoover continued to discuss heavier taxation of inherited wealth. A series of proposals to improve and stabilize farm income and maintain balance between agriculture and industry were broadcast widely during the winter. On the League question Hoover never faltered in demanding American participation. But he quickly took the position that revision of the Covenant so hotly debated between Wilson and the Republicans was actually of little consequence and that compromise could readily be achieved if each side would be more flexible.[6]

Throughout these months, Hoover's stance was aggressively Americanistic. Repeatedly, the restoration of order, the defeat of bolshevism, and the protection of American interests were cited as the essential reasons for entering the League. Millions applauded his December 1919 advice to Europe to "get back to work" rather than ask for undeserved American aid. On the situation at home the stance was reformist and optimistic, but the specter of "social disease" which "every wind that blows carries to our shores" was alluded to frequently.[7]

In sum, Hoover projected himself during 1919–20 as an apostle of the theory of American uniqueness, explaining how America could avoid European decadence through social reform and defend its interests in the world through League participation. He was a man with creative solutions to unprecedented problems that beset the American system of equal opportunity and competition, which it was his fundamental aim to preserve.

Turning to the central question of this study, how widely was Hoover approvingly discussed and how was he portrayed in the periodicals and newspapers of the postwar era? The answer is summarized in Tables I and II. Table I lists the periodicals which could be expected to give attention to a figure of central concern to the public. It lists, in other words, general circulation magazines of the type which to some extent consistently devoted some coverage to

American political and public affairs of general concern. The list was constructed from the magazines of this type which were indexed by *Reader's Guide* in 1919–20. To it were added any other magazines of this type listed by *Ayer and Sons American Newspaper Annual and Directory* for 1920.

Of the thirty-six periodicals listed, only seven failed to carry a piece on or by Hoover, and many carried several, as the first column of Table I shows. It is interesting that, of the four periodicals of large circulation which ignored Hoover, two, *Hearst's Magazine* and *Metropolitan Magazine*, had more or less obvious political reasons for the omission. The latter journal styled itself the carrier of the Roosevelt tradition, and Leonard Wood was billed as the inheritor of Roosevelt's mantle. Wood was in fact a regular contributor to its pages.

The unusually large number of references exceed by a substantial margin references made about any other major public figures of the day except Wilson and Harding (most of the latter's references dating from his nomination).

No relative index is available to compare the frequency of editorial reference to Hoover and other public figures occuring in the nineteen newspapers of Table II. Column one of this table gives the number of separate editorials on Hoover for each newspaper. The total number of editorials is 157 for the period September to June 1919–20. Although no count of the relative frequency of editorials on Hoover and on other public figures was performed during the count and examination of the Hoover editorials, a thorough scanning of these editorial pages leaves the strong impression that the number of Hoover references far surpass references to any other figure except perhaps the president. Impressions do not pass as evidence perhaps, but Table II clearly establishes the very great frequency of editorial notice of Hoover and this is what needs to be shown, not necessarily that Hoover was so noticed more than any other figure.

The newspapers of Table II represent the nation's big city press, for the most part, and several of the nation's regions. Their announced political affiliation varies. The New York City press is over-represented because it was so influential and widely read. The *World* and the *Tribune* were regarded as the leading Democratic and Republican papers, respectively; the *Times* was usually cited as the nation's single most influential newspaper and the *Evening Post* as the leading independent. To a degree, newspapers elsewhere took their cue from the New York papers, at least took their news reporting and editorial ideas into account. The three major business newspapers, all published in New York, are included.[8]

The almost universally accepted and celebrated image of Hoover in the sources which provide the data for Tables I and II may be dubbed the "heroic administrator." Column one of Section One of both tables lists the references which contributed to a substantial degree to the frequency of exposure of this image, although many of these develop the picture only partially. The portrayal is of an administrator of unique stature. Several distinguishable elements compose the image. The scope of Hoover's accomplishment, for example, often was seen as unparalleled. "Probably no man has ever at one time held positions involving affairs of such administrative magnitude," as did Hoover when director of relief for the Supreme Economic Council. His was "the greatest work performed by any single private citizen during the war." During the war he had compiled a record of accomplishment which "staggered statesmen by its difficulty," a "record" which had made "a peculiar appeal to the American imagination."[9]

The most emphasized motif however was Hoover's profound problem-solving skill, his ability to execute his purposes. Intertwined here was the element of the freshness and clarity of his conception together with the breathtaking scope of his solutions. Hoover always wanted "to do new things in a new way." A plan of his invariably "scares little men to death by its comprehensiveness, and . . . delights big men by its imaginative appeal and its sound constructive vision." Hoover was "a Big Man . . . , perhaps the biggest man in sight," and "the rare combination of thinker and doer" who "cerebrates clearly and sincerely and . . . acts with energy and decision." His projected solutions for contemporary problems were "remarkable for their common sense, for their profound understanding of economic conditions and principles . . . . He stands with few rivals as a leader of thought in the most trying and puzzling period of American, if not of world, history." His was the "constructive-engineer type of mind," eminently fitted for "rebuilding the world," because this was "a job of construction, a business job."[10]

Other, complementary attributes filled out the image of the "heroic administrator." Hoover even looked the part with his "fighting chin and firm mouth," his "face of a strong executive" as a leading woman's magazine sketched him. He was "physically tough-minded" and "comes at one with a kind of caught-from-under determination and drive that is quite upsetting." Yet he was "diffident" and sincere, the only one of the men suggested for the nation's highest office, an interviewer claimed, who "seemed to regard the Presidency as a position which it would tax all his powers to fill." He had returned home quietly, many remarked significantly, like Cincinnatus, without trumpeting his achievements. When others panicked, Hoover kept cool. "Hysteria offends him." His foresight was almost preternatural, as often cited anecdotes of his ability "to 'get the jump' on the situation" went on to show.[11]

But what made this man of profound analysis and decisive execution tick? Hoover himself, as we have seen, posed as the tough-minded realist, almost as though consciously bent upon revising the "humanitarian" label which had sometimes been attached to him. Column two of Section One of the tables shows how relatively infrequently Hoover was so labeled during these reconstruction months. Certain of his admirers did insist upon saccharine exploitation of the title. Hoover must have winced, for example, at a friendly newspaper's effusion, "Herbert Hoover just can't help being a big brother to someone," when he announced his intention of working for higher pay for professors. Hoover had explained his move as a tactic in the war against the spread of radical ideas! Vernon Kellogg, a Hoover aide in Europe during the previous year, probably jangled the same nerve with his lengthy serialized biography in *Everybody's* during the spring of 1920. The whole, especially the opening essay, pictured Hoover as brought frequently to tears, both by suffering or by its relief. Kellogg's wife tried, in *Woman's Home Companion,* to stir the same emotions in a portrayal of Hoover's earlier work in Belgium. But most commentators avoided the "great humanitarian" concept.[12]

Hoover himself during 1919–20, as we have seen, stressed the preservation and welfare of the American system of political economy as the great goal of his efforts and recommendations, and this was rather faithfully incorporated by commentators into the image of the "heroic administrator." Policy goals are not the same as personal motives, of course, but there simply was little interest exhibited in inquiring into these, almost as though it was accepted that the drive to achieve was simply the natural concomitant of Hoover's enormous executive abilities. Interpreters did frequently voice satisfaction with Hoover's exemplary Americanism, however, as is indicated by Column three, Section One, of the tables. Newspaper editorialists often commented approvingly on Hoover's forthright denunciations of radical revolution, on how he had used food supplies earlier during 1919 to stem it in Europe practically single-handedly, and praised his current stand that "worthy nations struggling upward . . . not be left to be engulfed in the chaos of Bolshevism." Newspapers applauded Hoover's strong attacks on radicalism at home and his pleas that "the great cause for which we fought" would not be won until, through Americanization of the immigrant, "life and liberty are purified and safeguarded." They also praised his loyalty to orthodox economic principles and his opposition to the "undigested economic panaceas" of "Academic idealists."[13]

Wide recognition greeted Hoover's defense of American interests against the Allies as well as the Bolsheviks. The Chicago *Tribune* at one point regarded Hoover as an ally in its war against the "Anglophiles," who in the *Tribune's* reckoning, dominated the Wilson administration. Release to the press in March 1920 of a memorandum Hoover had written for Wilson in April 1919, advising against participation in commissions administering the Treaty and warning of entrapment by the Allies, won the former presidential adviser many congratulations on his "far-visioned Americanism." Hoover's insistence on strict limitation of economic aid to Europe was warmly commended. If England and France "could shift the burden [of solving the European economic crisis] to Uncle Sam they would be able to grab the economic opportunities coming with the peace while we were occupied with dispensing charity. This is the condition Mr. Hoover exposes. He warns us not to be caught in a trap." In general, it was accepted by all, except political opponents looking for an angle of attack, that Hoover, despite his unique experience with and knowledge of Europeans, was thoroughly Americanistic. His own impeccable credentials as a "real American by generations of ancestry," and by reason of his farm background and his rise to success through self-help, often were stressed. As for foreigners, Hoover "heartily detests the lot," so far as their institutions and political-social traditions were concerned. His belief in the "incomparable superiority of America over other lands" nearly reached the proportions of "monomania," as one admirer explained it.[14]

The most frequently encountered image of Hoover in the literature of 1919–20 is that of the "heroic administrator," often embellished with vivid Americanistic coloration. Hoover, in his own utterances and writings during 1919–20, had provided the basis for this latter emphasis but had tended to stress not his achievements but his ideas, his analysis of and plans for overcoming the current economic and social crisis. These ideals were by no means ignored, but neither did they play the essential role even in the second widely heralded image of Hoover which was popularized, the image of the "indispensable man," the appearances of which are summarized in Column one of Section Two of the tables. The image is essentially a more exalted form of the "heroic administrator," which is seen now not simply in terms of achievement and ability but specifically in the context of the nation's urgent need for valid leadership.

TABLE I

		SECTION ONE		Americanism		SECTION TWO			
Periodical	Number of References	The Heroic Administrator I	The Great Humanitarian II	Anti-Bolshevist, Anti-Radical III	America First	The Indispensable Man I	The Progressive II	The League Liberal III	Derogatory of Hoover IV
Circulation 500,000+									
Colliers	2	Ja24..Ap3'20		Ap3'20					
Ladies' Home Journal	1	Au'20							
Literary Digest	7	D27'19:Mr13'20			S13'19; Ja24'20	Ja31..Ap10.Mr6'20			
McClure's	1	Jy'20							
Saturday Evening Post	10	D27'19;Ja3,17,31, Mr27..Ap10,24'20		Ap10'20		Ja3,17,31,F21,Ap17. My29'20	D27'19; Ja31..Ap 10'20		
Woman's Home Companion	2	Mr,Ja'20	Ja'20	Mr'20					
Pictorial Rev.	0								
Circulation 100,000 to 500,000									
Everybody's	6	F..Mr..Ap(2),My. Jn'20	F'20	My..Jn'20		My1'20			
Hearst's Mag.	0								
Leslie's Illustrated Mag.	1	My1'20							
Metropolitan	0								
Munsey's	0								
Delineator	1	Mr'20							
Outlook	3	Ap7'20	Ap7'20	Ap14'20	Ap7,14'20		F18, Ap7'20	Ap14'20	

Publication	No.	1	2	3	4	5	6	7	8
Review of Reviews	2	O'19;Mr'20							
Sunset	9	Ja,My,Jn,Jy,Ag,S'20					F'20	N'19	
System	1	Jy'20					Jy'20		
World's Work	4	N'19;Mr,Ap'20	Ap'20	N'19;F'20			Ap'20	Ap'20	
Bellman	1	Ja11'19							
Annals Am. Academy	1	Ja'20		Ja'20	Ja'20				
Atlantic Mly.	0								
Current Opin.	3	Mr,My(2)'20				Mr,Mr'20	My'20		
Current Hist.	0								
Forum	2	F'19		F,D'19			F'19		
Industrial Management	2	F,My'20				F,My'20	F,My'20		
Independent	6	S27,D13'19;My29'20	D25'20			D13'19;F7,My29'20		S6,D19'19	
Century	1	Jn'21							
Harper's	0								
Nation	6	S20'19;Ja31,F28,Jn5'20	S20'19		Ag30'19	Jn5'20	F28,Jn5'20	Ja31'20	
New Republic	7	Ja14,21'20			S3'19;F11'20	Ja14,21,F18,Ap14'20	F4'20	F11'20	
Overland	1	Mr'20							
Scribner's	0								
Touchstone	1	My'20							
Yale Review	1	Ap'20							
World Outlook	1	Jn'20		Jn'20				Jn'20	
The Review	3	Ja31,My29'20			My22'20	Ja31'20	Jn'20		
TOTALS	86	58	6	17	15	23	15	7	0

TABLE II

Newspaper	Number of References	SECTION ONE				SECTION TWO			
		I The Heroic Administrator	II The Great Humanitarian	III Americanism: Anti-Bolshevist, Anti-Radical	America First	I The Indispensable Man	II The Progressive	III The League Liberal	IV Derogatory of Hoover
Chicago Daily News	2	S18,26'19		S18,26'19					Ag23'19; Ap3,7 '20
Chicago Tribune	7	Ja8,Ap1'20	Mr3'20	Ja8'20		Ap1'20(L)			
Cincinnati Enquirer	4	F18'20		F8,My6'20					
Cleveland Plain Dealer	15	S18,O7'19;Ja14, 30,My10,26'20	O7'19	Ja23,F10 '20		Ja27,F10,Mr23,Ap7, 8'20		Ap1'20	
Des Moines Register	14	O2,N13,30'19; Ja22,F10,14,24, Mr11,Ap4,My4'20		F10'20		F4,10,23,Mr11, Ap4'20	F23,Ja 26,Ap4 '20	Ja22,31, My4'20	
Los Angeles Times	3	O12,18,N2'19		N2'19		O18'19			
Milwaukee Journal	15	O8,N28'19;Ja29, F1,18,My11,Jn6 '20		S26'19	Mr19'20	Ja29,30,F1,6,9,18, 23,Mr7,9,My10, Jn6'20	F1,18, Jn6'20	O8'19; Jn6'20	
Minneapolis Journal	7	Ja23,24,Mr31'20			Mr18'20	F1'20(L)	Mr31, Ap9'20		
New York Commercial	6	S17,O29'19;Ja8, F19,Jn15'20		O29'19; Ja8'20		My12'20		My12'20	

Newspaper									
New York Evening Post	10	S25,D11'19;F6,Mr 31,Ap29,30,My10 '20				F6,Mr31,Ap29,My10, 22'20	F6,My 10'20	F6,Ap 29,My10 '20	F9,21. Mr10'20
New York Journal of Commerce	11	S18,O4,31,D19'19; F19,Ap3'20		S18,D19'19; F10'20		Mr11,Ap3,12,My29 '20	Ap12'20		
New York Times	7	S16,D30'19;Ja8, 16,F19,Ap3'20		S16,D30'19		Ap3'20		Ap3'20	Ap30'20
New York Tribune	9	Mr26,Ap1'20					Ja16, Ap1'20	Ja16, Ap1'20	Ja22, F10,19, 29,Mr11, 26'20
New York World	21	Ja4,21,F19,20'20		Ja8'20	S24'19	Ja21,24,26,27,28, 29,F1,27,Mr9,11, Ap7,My6'20	Ja21, F19'20	S18'19; Mr31'20	
Pittsburgh Gazette-Times	7	D25'19;Ja13'20		Ja8'20	Ja13,My10 '20				Mr9,19, Ap1'20
Topeka Daily Capital	9	S21'19;F10,Ap16, 30,Jn5'20		Ap30'20	S21'19; Ap30'20	F10,Ap30'20(L)	Ap30, Jn5'20	Ap16'20	
Wall Street Journal	3								Mr13,Ap 7,My27 '20
Washington Evening Star	4	D25'19;Ja25'20					Mr31'20		Mr19 '20
Washington Post	3	S15',D20'19		D20'19	S15'19				Ap1'20
TOTALS	157	75	2	21	8	49	18	16	21

The need was desperate because, according to a frequently re-iterated interpretation of the condition of the country, the economy was in a chaotic state and political parties and politicians were in the last stages of decadence. The parties existed for partisan reasons only; they had ceased to define "wide divergences in political and national feeling"; they were merely "ornate signboards on empty houses." The voters were "weary of the everlasting jargon of politics," and in "revolt against politics and leadership which places partisan and personal advantage above their country's interests." The party system had become "artificial, is perhaps obsolete," and a "new alignment upon the essentials of the day perhaps impends." The stalemate over the Treaty, administration and congressional ineptitude in dealing with postwar problems, had bred impatience, it appears, with the prevailing political structure. All during the fall of 1919 the contention that existing political leadership and party programs were irrelevant had been cropping up. In January two powerful organs, the *Saturday Evening Post* and the New York *World* focused national attention upon a critique which pictured Hoover as the most promising hope for the correction of "political disintegration." Millions were "weary of the Penroses, Bryans and Hearsts," the *World* proclaimed, enough "to elect the next President."[15]

It was not so much Hoover's specific ideas and policy proposals which made him the indispensable man, although, as we shall see, substantial approval of these was registered. It was rather that the economic and social crisis seemed amenable to solution through sound administration of the government by "trained common-sense business executives" such as Hoover and the sort of men he would select to assist him if he were president. The situation re-quired not a man on horseback but "a man on foot; a man sturdily and steadily walking down the middle of the road . . . . Forward looking, his mind unencumbered with theory and his thought un-clouded with a mushy utopianism or an alien radicalism." Hoover, it was thought, was "the one man whose achievements and character mark him out as signally qualified to meet" the nation's critical problems. He would be "a candidate who can be depended upon as a man of straightforward accomplishments . . . . A practical man who will do the business of the nation."[16]

The most frequently urged elements of Hoover's indispensability were—in addition to his "remarkable executive and administrative successes" and abilities—that he was "forward-looking," attuned to the new issues "emphasized by the war," and an "industrial engineer," who could act as a mediator between clashing interest blocs. Especially popular was the claim that Hoover was "a man who directly faces the new day and the new needs," that the reason he appealed to so many people was "because of his possession in a conspicuous and almost unique degree . . . [of] the very qualities needed in dealing with modern . . . problems."[17]

Hoover thus was envisioned in this figure of the "indispensable man" as a progressive, for these were the essential notes of the progressive definition in the prewar sense—the man who can mobilize the good men of the community against partisan and self-seeking economic interests, the man who can find new ways to make the traditional machinery work properly. The terms "progressive" or "liberal" were used interchangeably. Always the terms appeared in discussions of Hoover's specific economic and social proposals for increasing workers' share of the national product, tax reform, improvement of farm income, and so on. Always these were understood in the spirit Hoover intended, "of social and industrial reforms being taken 'from the radical world to the liberal world of moderate men working upon the safe foundation of experience.'" His labor proposals were seen as advocacy of "fair play" in industry, and as stressing "the human side of industrial problems." He was, the New York *Tribune* ultimately admitted after Hoover declared his party, a "Progressive Republican of the kind Roosevelt loved and dreams of social justice." But for the *Tribune,* this meant the progressivism of equal opportunity, the touchstone of Hoover's liberalism. His own career showed that "the Republic still means opportunity," and he was "much interested in praising America as a land of free opportunity and social justice." The liberal journals understood this equally. The liberal *Nation* did not view Hoover as "the man of the hour" because his proposals fell so far short of its own more advanced liberalism. The *New Republic,* however, continued to support Hoover through the spring of 1920, not because it had illusions that his philosophy was "collectivist," but rather because he was a "realist," who would administer even a conservative program (by the *New Republic*'s standards) in a "decent and liberal spirit."[18]

Hoover's liberalism was understood then as having the aim of ameliorating the faults while strengthening the structure of market capitalism. Similarly, his support for the League rarely was misunderstood as implying some failure to heed American interests. By early 1920 Hoover had spoken against the recalcitrance both of Wilson and Lodge and urged reasonable compromise of the

League question. The seeming practicability of this middle-ground solution and Hoover's frequent appeals for prompt settlement of the issue provided one more element of the "indispensable man" image, that of a liberal on the League question. Here, too, his standing and forthrightness seemed, to many commentators, to make him the most effective proponent of reasonable solution of the League issue. References of this kind are given in Column three, Section Two, of the tables.[19]

The Hoover of the "indispensable man" portrayal was then not merely a great and Americanistic executive, but the instrument of national salvation. He was capable of mobilizing the right-thinking and the righteous. He was "the man toward whom intelligent voters in every party, men and women alike, are looking as a possible Presidential candidate." He had "evoked a response from voters everywhere so swift and spontaneous that it suggests the sweep of a prairie fire." His nomination would cause "such a demolition of strict party lines in November as Americans have seldom seen." In fact, "old-line partyism . . . [had] been shattered by the spontaneity of the Hoover movement." The imagery was contagious. Even party-faithful commentators who rejected the notion of disintegrating party structure sometimes felt compelled to admit that Hoover's candidacy was necessary since it would "compel a more vigorous consideration of actual problems."[20]

But the appearance of this representation of Hoover owed something to the propaganda needs of the commentators who created it. While the image undoubtedly had enormous validity in terms of popular demand for and willingness to accept it, it also had something less than an entirely spontaneous origin.

In the case of the newspapers, it seems clear that political manipulation was the inspiration and purpose in some cases. The New York *World's* case is the most evident of this type. The *World* was the originator, among newspapers, of the Hoover boom, offering to support Hoover no matter what party nominated him. The New York *Tribune* treated this sardonically, opining that the *World's* real purpose was to initiate a popular boom for Hoover; when he was rejected by the Republicans, who would meet first in Chicago, he would be taken by the Democrats at San Francisco, who otherwise would have no candidate with any chance of winning. The fact that the *World,* once Hoover declared his Republican status in late March, soon grew disillusioned and cold toward its candidate, argues the *Tribune's* cynicism was not entirely unjustified.[21]

For any newspaper, however, of relatively liberal persuasion, the "indispensable man" image was useful. It offered a chance to unite the electorate around a forward-looking, progressive candidate. The newspapers which endorsed or at least explored the "indispensable man" symbol generally were the less conservative of the fifteen papers upon whose editorials Table II is based. The Washington *Post* and *Evening Star*, the Chicago *Tribune*, the Cincinnati *Enquirer*, and Pittsburgh *Gazette-Times*, the papers which largely ignored Hoover in the context of national politics, proceeded upon the assumption that the existing party structure was quite durable, tended to favor the more conservative candidates (Wood in the case of the Republican papers) and took an extraordinarily hard line in relation to radicalism, strikes, and so forth. A similar logic applies to the leading organ of liberalism. As we have seen, the *New Republic* as much as admitted at one point that there simply was no other candidate remotely capable of moving politics in a more liberal direction. As with the *World*, enthusiasm diminished here too when Hoover closed the door to anything other than a Republican nomination.[22]

The most obvious case in which Hoover as symbol was used to serve the interests of a particular group was the case of the engineers. These had, not political, but status needs which Hoover could answer. During the war and postwar years there was, in the professional journals, much discussion of the engineer's role in industry and society, mostly to the effect that his independence and scope of influence were unjustly and demeaningly limited and by right should be immediately expanded. Hoover, during the war and during 1919–20, became the focus of their expectations. As a leading professional journal said, "Engineers have long been insistent that the members of their profession were capable of performing great things if given the opportunity. Mr. Hoover's recent work is remarkable and striking proof of the soundness of the claim." There were many reports, for example, of the speech given by the toastmaster at the welcoming dinner of the A.I.M.E. in September, which proclaimed that Hoover as a leader in public affairs had established "a precedent for engineers, and for us this is one of his greatest acts." Thus "engineers for Hoover" groups were organized in several states.

While the Engineers' Hoover Committees no doubt had negligible political consequences, the contribution the profession made to the quality and volume of Hoover's exposure in the press was considerable. The A.I.M.E. provided the occasions for Hoover's two most impressive and widely reported speeches of 1919–20, the first at the welcoming banquet in September, shortly after his return, the second in February, when he was installed as the organization's new president.[23]

The exalted representations of Hoover, as is evident, had to some degree been created by the special needs of particular groups. The currency of these representations in the general circulation magazines and in the daily press was far too broad and strong, however, to permit the supposition that they were presented mainly by interested parties for purposes of manipulation. The validity of the "heroic" and "indispensable" images in terms of popular acceptance is supported, too, by their substantial appearance in at least some segments of the class (special group) press. A sample of publications selected for each of the three great functional interest groups, workers, farmers, and businessmen, revealed a mixed pattern. A survey of twelve labor publications for the September to June 1919–20 period produced only two instances of the "heroic" Hoover. These publications had for the most part a relatively low circulation and a narrow focus, rarely departing from union affairs and the latest pronouncements of Samuel Gompers and other labor leaders. The survey would seem to prove perhaps that Hoover was not regarded by labor leaders and labor editors and, presumably, by workers, as a figure of transcendent importance.[24]

A review of several farm periodicals reveals an active hostility toward Hoover in some quarters, adulation in others. Both the *Non-Partisan Leader*, the organ of Townleyism and the discontented Dakota wheat growers, and *Wallace's Farmer*, generally regarded as an authoritative voice of the corn belt, acidly reviewed Hoover's record as food administrator, bitterly denigrated the heroic image so widely circulated elsewhere, and ridiculed the theory of the spontaneous, grass-roots character of the Hoover for president movement. As food administrator, so they charged, Hoover had overruled the FTC's attempt to limit the packers' profits while cheating hog raisers through "bare-faced juggling" of the data which formed the basis for reckoning the fairness of prices. Hoover was "more responsible than any other [man] for starting the dissatisfaction which exists among the farmers." Even Hoover's relief work during 1919–20 was challenged. "As usual, Hoover assumes the role of savior of his country," the *Leader* noted sarcastically. But both journals wondered whether Hoover's various pronouncements on European food needs and the financing of them were not designed to manipulate prices and strengthen the position of speculators and of Julius Barnes's Grain Corporation concerning whose operations "there are very nasty rumors afloat." Hoover was, as Henry Wallace, his soon-to-be cabinet colleague, ultimately concluded, "a typical autocrat of big business—able, shrewd, resourceful and ready to adopt almost any means to accomplish his end."[25]

Farm publications of large circulation, whose audience lay in the East and the old Middle West, as well as in the states further west, seem however to have treated Hoover much as did the general circulation magazines and the newspapers. In one of the three farm magazines of this type reviewed, *Country Gentleman,* Hoover was praised and boomed for president as emphatically as in any general circulation journal. Another, *Farm and Home,* opened its pages in January 1920 to let Hoover reach farmers directly with his proposals for raising farm income. *American Agriculturalist* published several appreciative references to Hoover during 1919–20, ignoring other public figures. *Farm Journal* and *Farm and Fireside,* the largest of the magazines in the sample, published no articles on Hoover. *Farm Journal* did, however, print without comment the interesting results of the straw vote of its readers on the Republican convention hopefuls, showing Hoover and Wood virtually tied for first place.[26]

The sample drawn from the business press yielded the most interesting results from the class publications, however. A day-by-day survey of the editorials of the three main business newspapers, the New York *Commercial,* the New York *Journal of Commerce,* and the *Wall Street Journal,* revealed that the treatment the first two gave Hoover closely paralleled that of those papers in the general circulation newspaper sample which stressed the "heroic" and "indispensable" image emphatically. Hoover was the "one man" who stood out in terms of experience, ability, and nonpartisanship. The political structure was excoriated as dominated by party hacks and as frustrating, by its machine rule, the ability of the middle ground of voters to "register the general will." The *Commercial* never went so far as to call the validity of the Republican party into question, but Hoover was the only one of the prominent Republicans praised in the paper's editorial column during the months before the convention for his "practical statesmanship" during a time of troubles. The *Wall Street Journal,* however, reproved the "indispensable man" conception as a Democratic invention designed to split the Republicans. It stressed fiscal conservatism and backed the conservative Lowden, and wrote Hoover off as one who would "need to scrap some ideas about price fixing and permanent commission meddling before he becomes 'Wall Street's candidate.' "[27]

There is a rather striking contrast between Hoover's public image in 1920 and in 1928. Relying upon the studies which have observed the image of 1928, Hoover was regarded then almost entirely in terms of what has here been called the "heroic administrator" of 1920. The image was more complex at the earlier stage, since it was embellished by a tough and outspoken Americanism. The Hoover of 1928 was also much reduced in stature compared to 1920. At the earlier point he had been widely perceived as typifying the most important virtues of the public man with a Progressive philosophy. He signified the just and competent leader at a time of political decay and social confusion, the antithesis of narrow partisanship, both in terms of politics and group conflict. He reflected the widely accepted belief that the traditional system of political economy could be made to be productive and just. If it is true, as it appears to be, that by 1928 Hoover was portrayed almost entirely as a pragmatic problem-solver, this probably was because of changed values on the observer's part.

It is hazardous of course to place too much weight upon the results of the study of a single popular symbol in judging the temper of a period. Yet the fact is that Hoover was presented as a symbol of hope that the chaos of 1919–20 could be overcome through expert administration, rectification of injustice, and conciliation, rather than through repression, and that this symbol was extraordinarily popular. Historians have come to see in the politics and economic proposals and programs of the 1920s much that resembles more closely the tradition of the Progressive era than the conservatism which previously had been seen as dominating the period. Perhaps the reconstruction era, the prelude to the twenties, needs to be reexamined in this same light.

NOTES

1   Kent Schofield, "The Public Image of Herbert Hoover in the 1928 Campaign," *Mid-America,* 51 (October 1969), 278–93. Craig Lloyd, *Aggressive Introvert: A Study of Herbert Hoover and Public Relations Management, 1912–1932* (Columbus: Ohio State University Press, 1972), pp. 161–63.

2   Stanley A. Coben, "A Study in Nativism: The American Red Scare of 1919–1920," *Political Science Quarterly,* 79 (March 1964), 52–75; Paul L. Murphy,

"Sources and Nature of Intolerance in the 1920's," *Journal of American History,* 51 (June 1964), 60–76.

3 New York *Times,* September 14, 17; October 3, 8; November 13, 16, 27; December 10, 12, 18, 24, 30, 1919.

4 Craig Lloyd, in his recent book tracing Hoover's use of the press as an instrument in his policies, has found no evidence in the Hoover Papers to indicate Hoover was directing or encouraging the presidential boom. See, *Aggressive Introvert,* pp. 81–83.

New York *Times,* January 9, 15, 23; February 18, 19, 24, 26; March 10, 11, 16, 17, 19, 31; April 4, 29; May 4, 14, 15, 1920. New York *World,* January 21, 24, 27, 28, 29, 31, 1920.

5 "Herbert Hoover's Address at the A.I.M.E. Reception in His Honor," *Engineering and Mining Journal,* 108 (September 27, 1919), 547–50.

6 "Report of the [February 7, 1920, A.I.M.E.] Banquet," *Engineering and Mining Journal,* 109 (February 21, 1920), 497–500, for text of Hoover's speech; Hoover, "Some Notes on Industrial Readjustment," *Saturday Evening Post,* 122 (December 27, 1919), 3–4, 145–46; Hoover, "Some Notes on Agricultural Adjustment and the High Cost of Living," *ibid.,* 41 (April 10, 1920), 3–4; for Hoover's statements on the League question, see *Outlook* for February 18 and March 30, 1920, pp. 266 and 638, respectively; also, New York *Times,* February 19, 24, 29, 1920.

7 For a full statement of the reasons for League participation, see Hoover, "Our Responsibility," *Sunset,* 44 (November 1919), 14–16. For statements on avoiding unwanted responsibilities in Europe, Hoover, "The Economic Situation in Europe," *World's Work,* 39 (November 1919), 98–101; Hoover, "Memorandum on the Economic Situation," *Annals of the American Academy of Political and Social Science,* 87 (January 1920), 106–11; "Hoover Tells Europe to go to Work," *Literary Digest,* 64 . (January 24, 1920), 11–13.

For statements advocating Americanization and anti-radical steps at home, see Hoover, "Unto the least of These: Child Welfare as the Foundation of Democracy— Right Feeding Corrects Wrong Thinking," *Sunset,* 24 (February 1920), 24, 110; New York *Times* reports of speeches, November 13, December 30, 1919.

8 A word about the methodology employed is in order. The search of each paper for relevant editorials was systematic. Moreover, the method of classifying the information met in a rough way at least the standard guidelines for content analysis; each item was searched for the presence of explicitly defined categories which were exhaustive (that is, provided a category for all statements about Hoover) and were mutually exclusive. The sample of newspapers, however, can be criticized. It is not a true random sample but a selection of papers chosen to include differing regional and party backgrounds. I think it is clear that the number and variety of papers is sufficient to have obtained a representative sample of ideas most Americans were reading about in editorials, but I do not make exaggerated claims about the scientific validity of the sample. The omission of southern newspapers from the sample unquestionably lessens somewhat the claim of Table 11 to reflect national editorial opinion.

Two newspapers included in Table II were examined, because of availability problems, for September through December 1919 only. These were the Chicago *Daily News* and the Los Angeles *Times.*

The total of the columns in Sections One and Two of each table, of course, exceeds the number of articles (Table I) and editorials (Table II), shown by the initial column of each table. Articles or editorials often developed more than one aspect of Hoover and would accordingly be cited more than once in the columns of Sections One and Two.

Most of the articles Hoover himself published are included in Table I. Not that Hoover purposively portrayed himself as "heroic." But his discussions of current problems and their solutions, and his allusions to his war work, though not self-glorifying, presented him inevitably as a problem-solver of great experience, the essence of the "heroic administrator."

9   The purpose of the quotations here and in the following pages is to illustrate the variations and elements of the stated themes. The tables provide the measure of the frequency of statement of each theme. Alonzo E. Taylor, "Hoover's Fifth Year: Driving the Six-Horse Chariot of International Relief," *Sunset*, 44 (January 1920), 28–30; Los Angeles *Times*, November 2, 1919; Milwaukee *Journal*, June 6, 1920; New York *Evening Post*, March 31, 1920; Minneapolis *Journal*, January 24, 1920; Des Moines *Register*, October 2, 1919.

10   French Strother, "Herbert Hoover: His Qualifications for the Presidency," *World's Work*, 39 (April 1920), 579–80; Clinton Gilbert, "What Kind of President Would Hoover Make?" *Leslie's Illustrated Weekly Newspaper,* 130 (May 1, 1920), 574; Chicago *Tribune*, April 1, 1920; Topeka *Daily Capital*, April 30, 1920; "Business is Business" (ed.), *Saturday Evening Post*, 192 (January 7, 1920), 26.

11   "American Romances—II: Herbert Clark Hoover," *Delineator*, 96 (March 1920), 8; Donald L. Wilhelm, "If He Were President: Herbert Hoover, the Man Who Fed Twenty-One Nations," *Independent,* 100 (December 13, 1919), 170–71; Bruce Bliven, "Hoover—And the Rest," *ibid.,* 102 (May 29, 1920), 275–76; Washington *Post,* September 15, 1919; New York *Times*, January 8, 1920; (ed.), *Nation,* 109 (September 20, 1919), 387; Taylor, "Hoover's Fifth Year," 29.

12   Cleveland *Plain Dealer*, October 7, 1919; Vernon Kellogg, "The Story of Hoover, I, Children," *Everybody's,* 42 (February 1920), 18–22; Charlotte Kellogg, "What the Belgian Women Think of Mr. Hoover," *Woman's Home Companion,* 47 (January 1920), 19.

13   Washington *Post,* December 20, 1919; Cincinnati *Enquirer,* February 18, 1920; New York *Times*, September 18, December 30, 1919; Los Angeles *Times*, November 2, 1919; New York *Evening Post*, September 25, 1919; Cleveland *Plain Dealer*, February 10, 1920; Milwaukee *Journal*, October 18, 1919.

14   Chicago *Tribune,* January 8, 1920; Minneapolis *Journal,* March 18, 1920; Pittsburgh *Gazette-Times,* January 13, 1920; New York *Journal of Commerce*, February 10, 1920; Strother, "Herbert Hoover: His Qualifications," 585.

15   Samuel G. Blythe, "Have Populi a Vox?" *Saturday Evening Post,* 192 (January 3, 1920), 3–4; Milwaukee *Journal,* January 29, 30, 1920; Minneapolis *Journal,* February 1, 1920; New York *World,* January 21, February 27, 1920.

16   "Seize the Government" (ed.), *Saturday Evening Post,* 192 (January 31, 1920), 28; (ed.), *ibid.,* 192 (April 17, 1920), 30; "Hoover," *The Review,* 2 (January 31, 1920), 98–99; Los Angeles *Times*, October 18, 1919.

17   Des Moines *Register*, November 13, 1919; Minneapolis *Journal*, March 31, 1920; Cleveland *Plain Dealer*, February 19, 1920; New York *Times*, February 19, 1920; New York *World*, January 21, 1920; New York *Evening Post*, March 31, 1920; Topeka *Daily Capital*, February 10, 1920.

18   Topeka *Daily Capital*, September 21, 1919, June 5, 1920; Milwaukee *Journal*, February 18, June 6, 1920; New York *Tribune*, January 16, April 1, 1920; "An Independent Progressive," *Nation*, 110 (March 20, 1920), 355; "Hoover and the Issues," *New Republic*, 21 (February 4, 1920), 282–83; "Hoover's Chances," *ibid.*, 31 (April 14, 1920), 196–98. Though editorially disappointed with Hoover, *Nation's* last major statement on him before the Republican convention (Robert Herrick, "For Hoover," 110 (June 5, 1920), 751), echoed the *New Republic's* stand.

19   New York *Tribune*, January 16, 1920; New York *Times*, April 3, 1920.

20   "Herbert C. Hoover on Collective Bargaining," *Industrial Management*, 59 (February 1920), 96; Milwaukee *Journal*, January 30, 1920; Cleveland *Plain Dealer*, February 10, 1920; New York *World*, January 27, 1920; Chicago *Tribune*, April 1, 1920. References of the type mentioned last in the paragraph above are included in Column one, Section 2, but the limited character of portrayal is indicated by the letter L.

21   New York *Tribune*, February 29, 1920; New York *World*, April 13, May 6, 1920.

22   "The Politics of the Hoover Boom," *New Republic*, 31 (April 21, 1920), 238–39.

23   For discussion of the need for improved status, and Hoover's relation to that need, "By the Way," *Engineering and Mining Journal*, 103 (June 30, 1917), 1169; Howard C. Parmalee, "Civic Duties and Opportunities of the Engineer," *ibid.*, 108 (August 23, 1919), 318–20; "Applied Psychology at Carnegie Hall" [Hoover's reception of Civic Forum Medal], *ibid.*, 109 (February 28, 1920), 545; "Engineers Honor Herbert Hoover," *ibid.*, 107 (January 4, 1919), 1–2; W. L. Saunders, "A Precedent for Engineers," *ibid.*, 108 (September 27, 1919), 544–46; "Herbert Hoover to Head Mining and Metallurgical Engineers," *Mechanical Engineering*, 42 (December 1919), 968; "Hoover—On Engineers' Interest in Public Questions," *Engineering News-Record*, 84 (February 26, 1920), 418–19; "Herbert C. Hoover—American Citizen," *Chemical and Metallurgical Engineering*, 21 (October 1, 1919), 414–15.
   For comment upon engineers and Hoover's candidacy, see "Hoover," *Engineering and Mining Journal*, 107 (September 27, 1919), 530; "Herbert C. Hoover Receives Washington Award," *Engineering News-Record*, 84 (March 4, 1920), 491; "Hoover for President," *ibid.*, 12 (March 18, 1920), 522; "California Engineers Favor Hoover for President," *ibid.*, 595; C. H. Snyder letter, *Chemical and Metallurgical Engineering*, 22 (February 11, 1920), 245; "Hoover on Industrial Relations," *Industrial Management*, 59 (May 1920), 345–47; "Now You Can Aid in Securing Nomination of Herbert Hoover," *Engineering and Contracting*, 53 (May 12, 1920), 353. See Edwin T. Layton, Jr., *The Revolt of the Engineers* (Cleveland: Case Western Reserve Press, 1971), chap. 8, for further background.

24   Edwin T. Slosson, "Hoover to the Rescue," *The Painter and Decorator*, 33 (September 1919), 390–91; "Hoover Predicts Failure of Kansas Peon Court," *The Boilermakers' and Iron Shipbuilders' Journal*, 32 (June 1920), 363. The other labor periodicals scanned were *American Federationist; The Garment Worker: Official Journal of the United Garment Workers of America; Shoe Workers Journal; The Carpenter; The Plasterer: Official Journal of the Operative Plasterers and Cement Finishers International As-*

sociation; Cigar Makers Official Journal; Bricklayer, Mason and Plasterer; International Molders Journal; The Advance: Weekly of American Clothing Workers Union; Labor; The Coopers International Journal.

25 "Holding Up the Hands of the Profiteer," *Non-Partisan Leader,* 9 (October 20, 1919), 5; "Senate is Investigating," *ibid.,* 10 (March 1, 1920), 5; (ed.), *Wallace's Farmer* (January 9, 1920), 78; "What's the Matter With the Farmer," *ibid.* (February 13, 1920), 519; "Farm Affairs at Washington," *ibid.,* 523; (ed.), *ibid.* (February 27, 1920), 691; "A Mistaken Daily," *ibid.* (March 5, 1920), 762–63; "Mr. Hoover and the Farmer," *ibid.* (March 19, 1920), 908; "Copyright Notice," *ibid.* (April 23, 1920), 1206.

26 "Hoover and the Farmer," (ed.), *Country Gentleman,* 85 (January 31, 1920), 16; "Facts," (ed.), *ibid.,* 17 (April 24, 1920), 16; E. Davenport, "Hoover and the Farmer," *ibid.,* 21 (May 22, 1920), 12, 42; "Hoover's Warning Against Gluts," *American Agriculturalist,* 104 (September 13, 1919), 5; "Saving the World," *ibid.,* 105 (January 24, 1920), 14; *Farm Journal,* 44 (June 1920), 64. Wood received 21%, Hoover 20% of the straw vote, Lowden only 9%, and Johnson 12%.

27 New York *Journal of Commerce,* September 18, October 4, 1919; February 10, 19, March 11, April 3, 12, May 29, 1920. New York *Commercial,* September 17, October 28, 29, 1919; January 8, February 19, March 24, May 12, June 15, 1920; *Wall Street Journal,* March 13, 24, April 7, May 27, 1920.

INDEX